History from the Sources
General Editor: John Morris
ARTHURIAN PERIOD SOURCES
VOL .4

ARTHURIAN SOURCES

Vol. 4
Places and Peoples, and Saxon Archaeology

ARTHURIAN PERIOD SOURCES

1. **Arthurian Sources, Vol. 1**, by John Morris
    Introduction, Notes and Index
    How to use *Arthurian Sources*; Introduction and Notes;
    Index to *The Age of Arthur*

2. **Arthurian Sources, Vol. 2**, by John Morris
    *Annals (**A**) and Charters (**C**)*

3. **Arthurian Sources, Vol. 3**, by John Morris
    Persons
    Ecclesiastics (**E**) (alphabetically listed)
    Laypeople (**L**) (alphabetically listed)

4. **Arthurian Sources, Vol. 4**, by John Morris
    *Places and Peoples (**P**), and Saxon Archaeology (**S**)*
    Places and Peoples (alphabetically listed)
    Saxon Archaeology:
        The Chronology of Early Anglo-Saxon Archaeology;
        Anglo-Saxon Surrey; The Anglo-Saxons in Bedfordshire

5. **Arthurian Sources, Vol. 5**, by John Morris
    *Genealogies (**G**) and Texts (**T**)*
    Genealogies
        Editions by Egerton Phillimore (1856-1937): *The Annales Cambriae* and Old-Welsh Genealogies from B.L. MS. Harley 3859; Pedigrees from Jesus College (Oxford) MS. 20; Bonedd y Saint from N.L.W. MS. Peniarth 12
    Texts discussed
        Gospel-books; Honorius's Letter; Laws; Martyrologies; Muirchú's Life of St. Patrick; *Notitia Dignitatum*; *Periplus*; Ptolemy; The 'Tribal Hidage'; Welsh Poems

6. **Arthurian Sources, Vol. 6**, by John Morris
    Studies in Dark-Age History
    Celtic Saints—a Note; Pelagian Literature; Dark Age Dates; The Dates of the Celtic Saints; The Date of Saint Alban; Christianity in Britain, 300-700—the Literary Evidence; Studies in the Early British Church—a Review; Gildas

7. **Gildas**, edited and translated by Michael Winterbottom
    The Ruin of Britain; Fragments of Lost Letters; Penitential or Monastic Rule

8. **Nennius**, edited and translated by John Morris
    'Select Documents on British History'; The Welsh Annals

9. **St. Patrick**, edited and translated by A.B.E. Hood
    Declaration; Letter to Coroticus; Sayings; Muirchú's Life of St. Patrick

ARTHURIAN SOURCES

Vol. 4
Places and Peoples,
and
Saxon Archaeology

JOHN MORRIS

PHILLIMORE

1995

Published by
PHILLIMORE & CO. LTD.
Shopwyke Manor Barn, Chichester, Sussex

© Mrs. Susan Morris, 1995

ISBN 0 85033 761 5

Printed and bound in Great Britain by
HARTNOLLS LTD.
Bodmin, Cornwall

CONTENTS

	page
PLACES AND PEOPLES (**P**)	1

SAXON ARCHAEOLOGY (**S**)
The Chronology of Early Anglo-Saxon Archaeology .. 73
Anglo-Saxon Surrey 81
The Anglo-Saxons in Bedfordshire 109

PLACES AND PEOPLES

General abbreviations

Abb.	Abbildung(en)
fl.	floruit
OE	Old English
s.a.	sub anno
s.n.	sub nomine
s.v.	sub verbo
Taf.	Tafel(n)

ABINGDON, Berkshire (*SU 4997*)
Ekwall (DEPN) gives:

Abbandun	*c.*730
Abbanduna	811
Abbanduna	850
Abbandun	931
Abbendone	1086

Domesday meaning 'Abba's *dun*'. Abba is a feminine personal name.
The site of a famous Saxon cemetery.
See Leeds, E.T., and Harden, D.B., *Anglo-Saxon Cemetery at Abingdon, Berks*, 1936; Harden, D.B. (ed.), *Dark-Age Britain*, 1956; Stenton, Sir Frank, *Anglo-Saxon England*, Oxford, third edn., 1971. R.B.W.

ALBA. A Gaelic name for Britain. First recorded *c.*525 B.C. in a sailor's description speaking of Ireland as being 'alongside the island of the Albiones'. Ptolemy gives Άλουιων; here v is used instead of β to render the bilabial [b], the reverse of the more usual confusion of Ptolemy's Κοϱναβιο, for Cornovii. The use of the term *Fir Alban* (the men of Alba) for the Irish colony of Dal Riada led to a narrowing of the meaning of the name, which from the end of the ninth century was localised in Scotland. This has led to some confusion.
The name contains the stem *albho- 'white' (*cf.* Latin *albus*). The Romans took this as a reference to the white cliffs of Dover.
See also: Byrne, F.J., *Irish Kings and High Kings*, London, 1973, 77-79; Bannerman, J., *Studies in the History of Dalriada*, Edinburgh, 1974, 118-119; Anderson, M.O., *Kings and Kingship in Early Scotland*, Edinburgh, 1973, 81-84; *The Oxford Classical Dictionary*, second edn., ed. Hammond and Scullard, Oxford, 1970. R.B.W.

ALCLUD, the kingdom of the Clyde, royal residence Dumbarton (*NS 3975*), Arecluta, see *Gildas*, ed. and trans. M. Winterbottom in Arthurian Period Sources, Vol. 7, Clydeside, the earliest form. Alclut, CT 7, 21, Clyde Rock, etc., in Welsh. Petra Cloithe, Adomnán, v. *Columbae* 1, 15, Latin and Irish, Aloo, Muirchú, pref., Irish. Alo Cluaithi, etc., eighth-century entries in the *Annals*, Irish. The form Strathclyde common in modern usage does not appear before the ninth century and fits a very different context.

ANGLES. Tacitus, *Germania* 40, names the Langobardi, Reudigni, Aviones, Angli, Varni, Eudoses, Nuithones, Suarini last of his north German peoples, after the Semnones, and says that he names them in proper order. The fixed points are the

Langobardi, much better documented than most peoples, and placed about the lower Elbe above Hamburg by Velleius (2,106) and Strabo (7, p. 290) in the first century, by Tacitus (especially *Annals* 11, 17) and Ptolemy (2, 11, 9 & 17) in the second, and the surviving names. Angeln (*Widsith*, Ongel, 8, 35 Engle, its people, 44, 61; O[n]ghgyl, Nennius 37; Angulus, Bede, *HE* 1,15) is still the name of the extreme north-east of Schleswig, against the modern Danish border. The Jutes named and dwelt in Jutland, and are neither Geats, Goths nor giants (R.W. Chambers, *Beowulf*, ed. 3, Cambridge, 1959, especially 261; Chadwick, OEN 97, etc.). The Angles wore cruciform brooches and cremated their dead, in Angeln and in the Anglian districts of England; and in Jutland and among the earliest English of Kent, cruciform brooches were also worn, but the dead were inhumed. These locations are clear enough to attach the names Angli and Varni to Tischler's *Anglische Gruppe*, the name of Jute to at least the greater part of his *Nordseegruppe*, Genrich's *Nord-Mittel-und-Ost-Jetische Gruppe*, and his *Oberjersdaler Kreis* and *Ursaechsisches Gebiet*. In the Offa saga, Anglian fourth-century territory included Schleswig in the north, and was bounded in the south by the Eider, the border against the Myrgingas, until Offa's victory extended their rule. The saga envisaged a considerable fourth-century expansion in Europe, which is matched by the extension of Anglian burial grounds through Mecklenburg into Pomerania.

In England, the term Anglian is used somewhat more widely in later usage than was valid in the fifth century. In Kent, Hengest was a Dane whom chance had made leader of Jutes who had settled in Frisia. Bede calls his people Jutes, as the majority so regarded themselves, but how many of them came direct from Jutland, and how many from the Jutes in Frisia, is not known. The first Bernician settlement 'about Guaul' was said to have been by Hengest's personal relatives. He was a Dane, but the place-name evidence suggests that it included Frisians. The Northumbrians in general were later regarded as Angles. The Deirans were. What proportion of Angles participated in the original Bernician settlement is not known.

The East Angles, Middle Angles and men of Lincoln were also unequivocally Anglian in name, though a high proportion of the Lincolnshire settlers brought pottery from Frisia, and were therefore Jutish or Saxon or Frisian rather than Anglian. On the Icknield Way sites, the ornament and burial rite was from the beginning a thorough mixture of what is elsewhere either characteristic of areas named Anglian, or of areas named Saxon. There is no evidence to show how the large mass migration of the later fifth century was composed, nor how it distributed itself among the regions of earlier settlement in England, save that on both sides of the Thames estuary it included some strongly Scandinavian influences that were neither Jutish, Anglian nor Saxon.

The dynasties, however, apart from the Kentish, were predominantly Anglian, for the Angles had kings and the Saxons had not. In the later sixth century, while grave goods are still available, a large part of the Mercians used Anglian ornaments; but many also used ornaments deriving from the Saxon areas of the middle Thames and of the Saxon settlement south-west of Cambridge. The dynasty of Penda claimed a purely Anglian origin. The Hwicce of Worcestershire and its borders were Angles, pushing southward down the Avon, because their first recorded king is probably Penda. Their native rulers known from the names in Os-, characteristic of the Bernician dynasty, were of originally Danish origin, and were possibly an offshoot of that dynasty. They also used Aethel- names, characteristic both of the Kentish and of the Bernician dynasty, adopted by the Mercian royal house also from the late sixth century. The names of the Essex kings derive, however, from the Deiran house. It is evident that all peoples were mixed in some degree, the names they used denoting the dominant element. Those who are unequivocally Anglian are the East and Middle Angles and the Deirans.

In the seventh century the term Angli hardened. All the English-speaking newcomers, whether Angle, Jute, Frisian, Dane or Saxon, became in a general sense '*Angli*' in Latin, '*Englisc*' in English, but its regional use was more precise. The Bernicians and Deirans did not call themselves the *Nordangli* but Northumbrians. The Mercian kings called their southern subjects, including the West and East Saxons, the *Suthangli*. Regional use was restricted to the East Angles; the short-lived term 'Middle Angles' for the eastern Mercians; and the rare use by Aethelward of West Angles for West Saxons. But the Mercian kings claimed sovereignty over all the Angles, and traced their descent from Offa. Their dynasty was known, however, as the Iclingas, after Offa's grandson Icel, who will have lived about the 460s and 470s. But in the late fifth century, there was not yet a Mercia; it is Icel's great-grandson Cri(o)da who is said to have been the first king in Mercia, a century later. The dynasty must at first have ruled elsewhere. Various indications point to Norfolk. It was the strongest early Anglian concentration. Lincolnshire tradition knew Crioda as Critta Vingning, probably of Venta (Icenorum). Places named from Icel (Icklingham, Ickleton, Ickleford) line the Icknield Way as it leaves Norfolk, and the name of his son, Cnebba, survives at Knebworth in Hertfordshire, two miles from the earliest settlement in the county (Broadwater Crescent, Stevenage: MA 8, 1964, 234), with pottery of the late fifth or early sixth century, a few hundred yards from the Broadwater, the centre and presumably meeting place of the largest hundred in the area. These names indicate expansion from Norfolk. Crioda's Mercian kingdom might imply that the dynasty moved, or that he was a cadet of a royal house whose records in Norfolk have not survived. The later dynasty of the East Angles had its principal seats in Suffolk. It claims descent from an unknown Hrothmund, too early for identity with the Hrothmund of *Beowulf*. The first king named is Uuffa, a variant of Offa, in the late sixth century, and the name, whether acquired through a princess of the dynasty or not, indicates an attachment to the main dynasty. It is possible that the Suffolk East Anglian dynasty began with the Gippingas in the early sixth century, and acquired Norfolk either by conquest or marriage with an heiress, who named her child Uuffa. In the 530s a powerful Anglian king had a brother and a sister, and he or another, ruling a people, lost two children, apparently his only children, in the 540s. Both probably ruled Norfolk, perhaps all Angles south of the Humber. The dynasties of Northumbria, Essex and Kent were made in Britain. It is possible, even probable, that in the late fifth century all Angles in Britain acknowledged the authority of the dynasty, but that the defeat of Badon, in which the men of Norfolk appear to have taken no part, impaired its authority, while the subsequent settlement restricted it to Norfolk.

ANGLO-SAXON. The term is first used by Paul the Deacon, about 790. Egbert was then in exile at the court of Charlemagne. Asser uses it to describe Alfred, though in his laws Alfred himself used the title *West Seaxna cyning*. Ine used the same title, but both he and Alfred legislated for 'Englishmen', never for 'Saxons'. By contrast, Aethelward, a Wessex prince descended from Alfred's brother, consistently called the West Saxons 'western Angles'. Abroad, Anglia and Angli prevailed, Engeleland and Englisc at home. After the conquest, Florence of Worcester writes of 'Anglo-Saxons'; Simeon of Durham and Henry of Huntingdon do not. Throughout, Angle and Saxon are used in regional context, usually with north-, south-, east-, or west- before them. When a general term for the whole people is required, it is very occasionally *Angli vel Saxones*, but almost always *Angli*, from Bede onward, when Mercian kings called themselves kings of all the *Suth Engle*, and did not thereby renounce suzerainty over Wessex, but included the West Saxons among the south English. The hybrid form was a short-lived attempt by ninth-century Wessex patriots to assert their separate and sovereign identity. Its wide use by modern historians since the Reformation is a modern convention, unfortunate because it arbitrarily and mistakenly sunders the modern English from their ancestors. It is valid for pagan Saxon archaeological usage; otherwise the linguistic term Old English is preferable.

ARGOED LLWYFEIN, where Fflamddwyn (probably Aethelric) was beaten by Urien and Owain after demanding hostages from Reged (CT 6), *c.*590.

The name means the forested tract, or the habitable borders thereof, of or by a river named Leven or the like. There are many rivers and lakes so called, and there were doubtless many more, whose names are now English or Scandinavian. The district was, however, probably in Reged; Fflamddwyn demanded hostages before battle was joined, and is therefore likely to have been the invader, already in his enemy's territory.

Leven survives as the name of two rivers in Reged. One joins Windermere to Cartmel Bay (*SD 3778*). The name may earlier have included the lake itself, whose modern name is Scandinavian, its British name unknown. The surviving forest is Grizdale; the term *Argoed* might extend to the cultivatable lands between the hills and the sea, including Furness. The other river is the Lyne; that joins the Esk (*NY 2263*) north of Carlisle, two miles from Arthuret, the site of the battle of Afderydd.

The Lyne lies closer to the route by which an invading Bernician army is likely to have approached Reged, but is less suggestive of an *Argoed*. It rises, however, in Kershope Forest, and *Argoed* might perhaps be used of the broken country about the Roman fort of Bewcastle (*NY 5674*).

ARTHURET (Arfderydd).

A Cm s.a. 573 *Bellum Armterid*.

(B text) '*Inter filios Elifer et Gwendoleu filium Keidiau, in quo bello Gvendoleu cecidit. Merlinus insanus effectus est*'.

'The battle of *Armterid*' (this form shows that the form with the medial -f- is original [TYP 208]).

'Between the sons of *Elifer* and *Gwendoleu*, son of *Keidiau* in which battle *Gwendoleu* died. *Merlinus* became mad.'

Skene's identification (FAB 1, 65-6) of Arfderydd with Arthuret (about 10 miles north of Carlisle near the Roman station of Netherby, probably the *Castra Exploratorum* of the Antonine Itinerary) has been followed by Morris (*Age* 218, also Bromwich TYP 208) in spite of the difficulties such an etymology presents. The forms are

*c.*1190	Arturet
1202	Arturede
1209	Arcturet
1609	Artereth

which perhaps comes from something like *Arthur's head* (as suggested in Clarke, 1973, 161). Influenced by the enormous popularity of Geoffrey's Arthur (*Ar[c]turus*) legends rather than Welsh *Arfderydd*, Triad 84 may preserve a clue:

Yr eil a vu y Gweith Arderydd, a wnaethpvyt o achaus nyth yr Ychedydd. 'The second (futile battle) was the battle of *Arderydd*, which was brought about by the cause of the lark's nest' (TYP, 206).

Nora Chadwick (*The British Heroic Age*, Cardiff 1976, 100; also Clarke, VM, p. 160) pointed out that Caerlaverock at the mouth of the River Nith on the north bank of the Solway translates as 'larks-fort' (*cf.* Laverton, the tun frequented by larks). *Laverstock* is the Scottish variation from ME *laverok* – OE *laferce*. Caerlaverock is in an important strategic position where the Solway begins to narrow and, e.g., the castle fell to Edward I in a (rather over-) celebrated siege in 1300.

The precise site is perhaps not as important as the setting, for both Arthuret and Caerlaverock lie between the walls, the territory of Rheged and God(d)au, and the battle of Arfderydd was fought between Britons, perhaps the descendants of Coel Hen quarrelling over territory. R.B.W.

ATECOTTI. Hieronymus, *Ep.* 69, 2: '*sed Scottorum et Atticotorum ritu ac de Republica Platonis, promiscuas uxores, communes liberos habeant*'; Adversus Iovinianum 2, 7: 'Ipse adolescentulus in Gallia viderim Atticotos, gentem Britannicam, humanis vesci carnibus... Scotorum natio uxores proprias non habet'. In asserting that the favourite food of the *Attacotti* was the teats of the wives and children of shepherds and swineherds, Jerome doubtless reports what he heard rather than what he saw.
Ammianus, 26, 4, '*Picti, Saxonesque et Scotti, et Atacotti Britannos... excavere*' (A.D. 346); 27, 8 '*Picti, in duas gentes divisi, Dicalidonas et Verturiones, itidemque Attacotti bellicosa hominum nation, et Scotti, per diversa vagantes multa populabantur*' (A.D. 367).

Not. Dig. Or. 9, 29; Oc. 5, 197, 200, 218 = 7, 74, 24, 78; *Atecotti; Atecotti Honoriani seniores and iuniores; Atecotti iuniores Gallicani*, four *auxilia palatina* stationed in Italy, Gaul and eastern Illyricum. The two units named Honoriani cannot have been so called before the victory of the emperor Theodosius, but might possibly have formed part of Magnus Maximus' army. They therefore did not exist when Jerome was a youth in Gaul; but the other two units might have been raised by count Theodosius in 368, from vagantes captured by the Roman army. Jerome, here as elsewhere, carefully distinguishes Scotti from Britanni. He calls the Atecotti *gens Britannica*, not *Scottica*.

The spelling in the official text of the *Notitia* is *Atecotti*. As MacNeill suggested (*Phases* 148, following Whitley Stokes) the word could mean the 'very old people' (*cottos*, old, Cornish *coth*, Breton *koz*), the 'aborigines'. Since *cottos* does not occur in Irish, they were probably so called either in British or Pictish, and therefore lived in Britain rather than Ireland. No such people are mentioned in the extensive literature of Ireland. Irish silence as well as the name, and Jerome's express statement (*cf.* Ant. 25, 1951, 126), say that they did not live in Ireland, but lived in Britain. They were, however, a formidable people named between the Picts and the Irish by Ammian.

Northern and western Scotland beyond the Great Glen and the firths near to Inverness has hardly any of the place-names or archaeological sites or objects common among the PICTS (*q.v.*), and no text includes this region in Pictish territory, apart from the insertion of 'Cat' of Caithness in the late Pictish king lists. It is likely that these unlocated people lived in the part of Britain whose inhabitants are not named, north and west of the Great Glen.

Unlike the rest of Scotland, the place-names of the north-west are almost universally Irish. Norse names predominate in Caithness, and occur occasionally in the islands; there are a few English names, and half a dozen that are or might be

Pictish. Otherwise every hill, loch, river, island or inhabited place bears an Irish name. There is little record of Irish migration to the north and west in historical times. The exclusive preponderance of Irish names therefore suggests Irish-speaking settlement long before the end of the fifth century. Irish tradition has many stories about such migrations, and distinguishes three main phases: the wars of Labraid Loingsech several centuries before Christ; the migration of Cairbre Riata, ancestor of the Dal Riada, placed about the second or third century A.D., and reported also by Bede *HE* 1,1 (*Britannia . . . Scottorum nationem in Pictorum parte recepit; qui duce Reuda de Hibernia progressi . . . sedes . . . vindicarunt; a quo . . . usque hodie Dal Reudini vocantur, nam lingua eorum daal partem significat*); and a third major movement by the three Collas early in the fourth century. Either the 'Aborigines' were themselves descendants of the Irishmen who had lived there for many centuries, or they were the native population among whom the Irish settled in numbers that eventually overwhelmed them.

The north-west, and the islands that dominate its coast, have little Pictish archaeology, but plenty of their own. The west coast shares with central and southern Scotland the so-called 'vitrified' forts, defended sites similar to those described by Caesar in Gaul in the first century B.C., whose timber lacing has been burnt; but unlike the rest of Scotland, the 10 west coast burnt forts beyond the Great Glen outnumber the unburnt forts. It seems likely that their builders failed to maintain them. The northern and western fortifications are of two kinds, termed 'brochs' and 'duns'. The broch is a peculiar local development, a tall round tower tapering a few feet above its base, its habitable rooms within the thickness of the walls. Over 400 of them are known, three-quarters of them in the Orkneys, the Shetlands and Caithness with extensions down the east coast and its valleys to the frontier of the Inverness region of Dornoch; and in Strathnaver, with outliers protecting most of the natural harbours of the north and north-west coasts down to Ullapool. A number of them are dated, usually by Roman sherds, to the first two or three centuries A.D.

The duns are the fortifications of Skye and the south-western islands and headlands. The word tends to be used of a variety of structures, but it is only in Skye that both brochs and duns of any kind are found close together in numbers, though in parts of the Hebrides there are broch areas and dun areas. Present evidence suggests that the people of the duns were earlier than the broch people in the west. At Clockhimin in Shetland a preliminary report suggests that a fort, analogous to the 'dun' of Irish literature, was replaced by a broch in the first century A.D., but that by the middle of the second century the broch was dismantled by its owners, and turned to a more commodious, but less formidably defended, 'wheel-house' (IANB 111 ff.). Recent excavation on Tiree and Skye (Ant. 39, 1965, 266 ff.) suggests that a galleried dun, built on Skye during the first century B.C., with pottery that has some similarity with the pre-broch dun of Clickhimin, was violently destroyed about the end of the first century A.D., though unfortified domestic occupation continued. A broch on Tiree was built not much earlier, but was peacefully demolished during the second century A.D. Some Hebridean sites also suggest a violent end for duns and peaceful demolition for brochs, and imply that the later phases of duns were more or less contemporary with the earlier phases of brochs.

Present evidence rests on limited excavation, and few dated sites. But the implications of what is reported are clear when set against the map of all known sites (printed IANB, folding map). The people of the duns settled the south-west, Skye and the Hebrides about the first century B.C., their sites most dense in Dal Riada and Tiree, their furthest ventures to the north coast and northern islands. The distribution of their homes suggests that they came from Ireland. About the first century A.D. the broch peoples mastered the Shetlands, the Orkneys and the Caithness area. Later they mastered Skye, where 25 brochs are known, and established their supremacy securely enough to end the need to live in their uncomfortable castles.

The few outliers of both kinds of fortification suggest detached migrations at particular periods. Four brochs among the southern Picts about the Tay estuary, a couple more in Manau Gododdin south of Stirling, a few in the Lothians and Galloway, are either settlements of invaders who failed to multiply, or else of northerners who fought with the Picts. One, built on the site of the first-century Roman fort at Newstead (*NT 5 3*), near Melrose, covered by the mid-second-century fort, looks like the castle of an Orkneyman allied with the Picts. Two isolated groups of duns suggest a similar context. One, placed on the south side of the Pass of Killiecrankie, commands the only road or route that leads direct from Perth to Inverness, and may well have been built by men of the west coast enlisted by one of the Pictish kingdoms to protect it against the other. A second smaller cluster, south of Stirling in the territory that preserves the name of the Maeatae, with a couple of brochs in the same district, suggests fighting men imported to oppose the Roman garrison of the Antonine Wall, or else the British kingdom of the Lothians, ruled from Traprain Law.

Since so few sites have yet been excavated and dated, further investigation may in the future suggest a different interpretation. But the only inference that may now be drawn must be restricted to the evidence we have. These inferences outline a situation. They suggest that for a period a single power controlled both Orkney and Skye. In later and better recorded times, the Norse were to demonstrate the power of a people who controlled these islands, the natural fortresses that command northern and western Scotland. How long the power of the broch people in these islands lasted is not known. By Columba's time, the Orkney kings were clients of king Bridei of Inverness, and may have been subdued long since. A few Pictish symbol stones in the broch territory show that Pictish notables were at some time there, sufficiently free and independent for their followers to bury them.

It is not yet possible to give names to these peoples with confidence. The relatively late appearance of the broch power does not suggest that they would be termed the 'very old people', if that be the meaning of Atecotti. But the sudden short prominence of the Atecotti in the later fourth century suggests that they had emerged from subjection and obscurity not long before. It may be that they rebelled and broke the power of the Orkney and Skye kings earlier in the fourth century. They might have been the Irish of the south-western duns; or else descendants of still earlier people, possibly those who spoke the language of the *Geonae cohortis primarius* of Skye, and the people who carved the unintelligible inscriptions of Pictland.

BADON

1 GILDAS 26, 1

Ex eo tempore nunc cives, nunc hostes, vincebant ... usque ad annum obsessionis Badonici montis, * novissimaeque ferme de furciferis non minimae stragis, quique quadragesimus quartus,* ut novi, oritur* annus, mense iam uno emenso, qui et meae nativitatis est.

MS. Variants. 'Ex eo tempore... Badonici montis', reproduced word for word, Bede *HE* 1,16, eighth century. 'Badonici montis, qui prope Sabrinum hostium habetur', MS. X, 13th century. quartus omitted MS. A, 12th century. oritur, MS. X.

'From then on victory went now to our countrymen, now to their enemies... This lasted right up to the year of the siege of Badon Hill, pretty well the last defeat of the villains, and certainly not the least. That was the year of my birth; as I know, one month of the 44th year since then has already passed.'

(Translation, M. Winterbottom)

2 GILDAS 2
... pauca de ... vastatione ... de victoria ... de saeviore multo primis hoste, de urbium subversione, de reliquiis, de postrema patriae victoria, quae temporibus nostris Dei nutu donata est, dicere conamur.

'... I shall try to say a little about ... devastation ... about victory, about ... an enemy much more savage than the first, about the destruction of cities; about those who survived and about the final victory of our country that has been granted to our times by the will of God.' (Translation, M. Winterbottom)

3 NENNIUS 56
Tunc Arthur pugnabat ... dux erat bellorum ... Duodecimum fuit bellum in monte Badonis, in quo corruerunt in uno die DCCCCLX* viri de uno impetu Arthur. MS. Variants DCCCLX, DCCCCCXL.

'Then Arthur fought ... He was the leader (of the British) in battle ... The twelfth battle was on Badon Hill, and in it 960* men fell in one day, from a single charge of Arthur's.'
Variants 860, 940. *[DCCCXL, nongenti sexaginta]

4 NENNIUS 67
De Mirabilibus Britanniae ...
Tertium miraculum stagnum calidum *in quo balnea sunt Badonis*, quod est in regione Huich,* et muro ambitur ex latere et lapido facto, et in eo vadunt homines per omne tempus ad lavandum et unicuique, sicut placuerit illi, lavacrum sic fiat sibi secundum voluntatem suam; si voluerit, lavacrum frigidum erit, si calidum, calidum erit.
MS. Variant. Huiccorum, Huictorum.

'The Wonders of Britain ...
The third wonder is the Hot Lake *where the Baths of Badon are*, in the country of the Hwicce.* It is surrounded by a wall, made of brick and stone, and men may go there to bathe at any time, and every man can have the kind of bath he likes. If he wants, it will be a cold bath; if he wants a hot bath, it will be hot.'
*The country of the Hwicce approximately corresponds to Gloucestershire and Worcestershire and their borders.

5 CAPITVLA NENNII
LXVIII De stagno calido, in quo balnea sunt Badonis secundum uniuscuiusque voti desiderium.

68 (for 67) 'Of the Hot Lake, in which are the Baths of Badon, agreeable to the desire of each man's wish.'

6 ANNALES CAMBRIAE
Annus 56 Episcopus Ebur pausat in Christo anno CCCL aetatis suae (**A** 499).
Annus 72 Bellum Badonis, in quo Arthur portauit crucem Domini nostri Iesu Christi tribus diebus et tribus noctibus in humeros suos et Brittones victores fuerunt.
Annus 77 Sanctus Columcille nascitur. Quies sanctae Brigidae.

'Year 56 Bishop Ibar died in the 350th year of his age.
Year 72 The Battle of Badon in which Arthur carried the Cross of Our Lord Jesus Christ on his shield* for three days and three nights, and the British were victorious.
Year 77 Saint Columba was born. Death of Saint Brigit.'
*The Latin of the Welsh author evidently confused the Welsh words *ysgwyd*, shield, and *ysgwydd*, shoulder, *humerus* in Latin. The same error occurs in Nennius 56 (**3** above), where at the eighth battle Arthur is said to have carried a representation of the Virgin *super humeros suos*, '... on his shoulders'.

7 ANNALES CAMBRIAE
Annus 221 Primum Pasca* apud Saxones celebratur. Bellum Badonis secundo. Morcant moritur.
'Easter was first* celebrated among the Saxons. The second battle of Badon. Morcant died.'
*In 665, the first Easter after the Synod of Whitby; see **E** Wilfred.

8 SAXON CHRONICLE (MS. E)
Anno DLXXVII Her Cvðwine and Ceawlin gefuhton wið Bryttas and hi iii ciningas ofslogon, Coinmagil and Candidan and Farinmagil, in ðaere stowe ðe is gecweden Deorham, and genamon iii ceastra, Gleawcestre and Cirenceaster and Baðan ceaster.
'A.D. 557 In this year Cuthwine and Ceawlin fought with the British and slew three kings, Conmagil and Candidan and Farinmagil, at the place which is called Dyrham, and took three chesters, Gloucester, and Cirencester and Bath chester.'

9 SAXON CHRONICLE (MS. A)
A.D. 477 (= *c*.456) Her cuom Aelle on Breten lond.

'In this year Aelle (of the South Saxons) came to Britain.'

10 BEDE HE 2,5
Aedilbert rex Cantuariorum ... tertius ... in regibus gentis Anglorum cunctis australibus eorum prouinciis ... imperauit ...
Nam primus imperium huiusmodi Aelli rex Australium Saxonum ... obtinuit.

'Aethelbert king of Kent ... was the third ... among the kings of the English nation to hold empire over all the southern territories ... For the first who held such empire was Aelle, king of the South Saxons.'

11 SAXON CHRONICLE (MS. A)
A.D. 449 (= c.428) Hengest and Horsa ... gesohton Bretene.
 'Hengest and Horsa ... came to Britain.'
A.D. 455 (= c.434) Feng to rice Hengest and Aesc his sunu.
 'Hengest took the kingdom, and Aesc his son.'
A.D. 488 (= c.467) Her Aesc feng to rice and was xxiiii* wintra Cantwara cyning.
*Variant. xxxiiii MS. E.
 'In this year Aesc took the kingdom, and was king of the Kentishmen for 24 years' (to c.493).

12 NENNIUS 38
Et dixit Hencgistus ad Guorthigirnum ... 'Invitabo filium meum cum fratrueli suo ... ut dimicent contra Scottos, et da illis regiones quae sunt in aquilone iuxta murum qui vocatur Guaul' ... et invitavit Octha et Ebissa ... At ipsi ... venerunt, et occupaverunt regiones plurimas ... usque ad confinium Pictorum.

'Hengest said to Vortigern ... 'I will invite my son and his cousin ... to fight against the Irish; give them lands in the north, about the Wall known as Guaul' ... and he invited Octha and Ebissa ... they came, and occupied several districts ... as far as the border of the Picts.'

13 NENNIUS 58
Hengist genuit Octha, genuit Ossa, genuit Eormoric, genuit Ealdbert.
'Hengest begot Octha, who begot Ossa, who begot Eormanric, who begot Athelbert.'

14 BEDE HE 2,5
Aedilbert filius Irminrici, cuius pater Octa, cuius pater Oeric cognomento Oisc, a quo reges Cantuariorum solent Oiscingas cognominare; cuius pater Hengist, qui cum filio suo Oisc ... Brittaniam primus intravit.

'Aethelbert son of Eormenric, whose father was Ochta, whose father was Oeric, named Oesc, from whom the kings of the Kentishmen are commonly called Oescingas; whose father was Hengest, who, with his son Oesc ... was the first to enter Britain.'

15 NENNIUS 56
Mortuo autem Hengisto, Octha, filius eius, transivit de sinistrali parte Brittaniae ad regnum Cantorum, et de ipso orti sunt reges Cantorum.

'On Hengest's death his son Octha came down from the north of Britain to the kingdom of the Kentishmen, and from him are sprung the kings of the Kentishmen.'

16 BONEDD Y SAINT (MS. H) 70-71
Oswallt ap Oswydd Aelwyn ap Ydeldred Vrenin ap Eda Glyn vawr ap Gwybei Drahawg ap Mwg Mawr Drefydd ap Ossa Kylleluawr Vrenin Lloegyr, y gwr a ymladdodd ag Arthur yNgwaith Vaddon.

'Oswald [brother] of Oswy, [the father] of Aelfwin, son of king Aethelferth, son of Adda of the Great Glen,* son of Gwybie the Arrogant (Ida?), son of Great Smoke of the Homesteads (Eoppa?), son of Ossa Big Knife king of the English, the man

who fought against Arthur at the Battle of Badon.'
*Or possibly 'Big Knee'.

For Ossa Kyllelluawr, *see also* the Mabinogion, The Dream of Rhonabwy (ed. Melville Richards 8, 20 ff.) 'Caradauc Vreichvras . . . marvelled at the vast host . . . who had promised to be . . . at the Battle of Badon, to fight with Osla Gyllellfawr . . . 'We will go together', said Arthur . . . They came to middle ford of the Severn . . . Arthur and his army of mighty men dismounted below Caer Badon'; Kulhwch and Olwen 'Osla Gylellfawr who carried a short broad dagger'; and the Book of Taliesin 75,15 'Cyllellaur', *cf.* 75,13 'heb Eppa'. The genealogy places Ossa Kyllellfawr in the same generation as Ossa son of Hengest and Ossa son of Aethelbruth (?Hengest).

17 SAXON CHRONICLE Parker Preface (MS. A)
Thy geare the waes agan fram Cristes acennesse cccc wintra and xciiii wintra tha Cerdic and Cynric his sunu cuom up aet Cerdices oran . . . Ond thaes ymb vi gear thaes the hie up cuomon geodon West Seaxna rice . . . and he haefde thaet rice xvi gear and tha he gefor tha feng his sunu Cynric to tham rice.

'In the year of Christ's nativity 494 (= *c*.473) Cerdric and Cynric his son came to Cerdicessora . . . and six years after they came (500 = *c*.479) they conquered the kingdom of the West Saxons . . . and he had that kingdom for 16 years (to 516 = *c*.495) and when he died his son Cynric took the kingdom.'

The text of the Chronicle enters two differing series of discordant dates for these events.

In the discussions which follow, the figures (1) to (17) refer to the texts cited above.

The Date
Gildas wrote about 540, or a little before (*cf. Gildas*, ed. and trans. M. Winterbottom, APS, Vol. 7, and *Age*, 35 ff.). The battle was fought 44 years and one month before he wrote, in the year of his birth (1), therefore in the early or mid-490s. This contemporary statement, written when many who fought in the battle were still alive, takes precedence over later calculations of the date, made when the event had passed from living memory.

Bede (*HE* 1,16) fortuitously appears to give the same date. He, or the version of Gildas which he used, altered 'the 44th year' to read XL^{mo} circiter et IIII° anno adventus eorum (Anglorum) in Brittaniam. The 44th year from the arrival of the English is during the reign of Marcian (and Valentinian III) who 'ruled for seven years', beginning with 448 (by error for 450), giving 449×456, for 450×457 for the English arrival, 493×501 for Badon; the Saxon Chronicle and many later writers simplified Bede's date bracket to its first year, giving 449 for the English arrival, and therefore 493 for Badon. But the fifth-century dates in our texts of the Saxon Chronicle, like Bede's 449 from which they derive, are about 20 or 21 years too late, and are additions made by editors, which misrepresented the dating intended by its first authors, who did not use A.D. dating. If the date was valid, it should denote a year about 472. But since Bede misread Gildas's use of the 44th year, and was also misled in his dating of the English arrival by Gildas's mistaken dating of the letter to Aetius (*see Age*, 40), the double error deprives Bede's statement of any value as evidence; the fact that it happens to coincide with Gildas's date is purely accidental.

MS. A of the Cambrian Annals (6) is written in columns, in which each line begins with the word *an[nus]*, year. Every tenth year is noted as *an. x., an. xx*, etc. The great majority of the early years are blank, and the first 150 years contain only 21 entries. Fifteen of them are selected transcripts from the Irish Annals; one is of continental origin, perhaps derived through Ireland. Five British entries are inserted into this epitome of the Irish Annals, the battles of Badon, Camlann and Arfderydd, and the deaths of Gurci and Peredur of York and of Daniel of Bangor. Badon is inserted between the death of Bishop Ibar (499 in the Irish Annals) and the birth of Columba of Iona (521 in the Irish Annals), which are spaced 21 years apart. The *an[nus]* entries err slightly, since the death of Brigid is placed in the same year as Columba's birth, though all extant Irish Annals place three or four years between. All other years between 56 (499) and 77 (521) are blank. Badon is inserted at year 72, five years before Columba's birth, implying 516. The last entry in the MS. is placed in the year 510 (A.D. 954), the last blank *an[nus]* is at 533 (A.D. 977), and the original manuscript was probably written in the late tenth century. The reason that prompted its author to insert Badon at the place he chose can only be guessed. The most probable of several explanations is that he was familiar with the dating system of the Saxon Chronicle, since 516 is the year given in the Parker Preface (17) for Cerdic's death, and corresponds to 495 in the intended dates of the original.

The date of Badon therefore rests upon the evidence of Gildas, at approximately 490×495, perhaps nearer to 495 than to 490.

The Place

The Cambrian Annals report a second battle of Badon in 665 (7). Whether or not the following note of the death of Morcant (of Glywysing, or Glamorgan) is part of the same entry, implying his death in the battle, the Annals clearly report a battle in which the Welsh were engaged. At that date, no Welsh army is likely to have penetrated far to the east of the Severn. The general location is confirmed by a gloss, added to an earlier manuscript of Gildas, and incorporated in the thirteenth-century MS. X, 'Badon Hill, near the Severn estuary' (1).

Nennius's 'Wonders of Britain' include Bath, in the territory of the Hwicce, about the lower Severn, and the Contents Table, preserved only in a thirteenth-century MS., with an internal ninth-century date, calls the place Badon (4). The statement is a plain assertion that in the ninth century Badon was the British name for Bath. It is wholly independent of any traditional association with Arthur or his battle; had the author been conscious of the connection, he could not have refrained from adding *ubi corruit Arturus*, 'where Arthur fell', or some similar phrase.

The name Badon is certainly of British (Welsh) origin, since it was used by Gildas (1). Its connotation has not been satisfactorily explained, but its use in place names is not uncommon in the South and Midlands. British *Din Badon* gives English *Baddanbyrig* (K.H. Jackson, JCS 2, 1950, 153), an explanation to be preferred to Ekwall's 'Badda . . . a legendary hero who was associated with ancient camps'. Places so named include Badbury, in Dorset, in Wiltshire, and in Berkshire. Badby in Northamptonshire, Baðumber in Lincolnshire, and possibly Bampton in Devon (*cf.* EPNS 530).

Baðan is also the name used of Bath by the English before they settled in the town. In the MS. E Saxon Chronicle entry for 577 (8) the personal names 'have the look of contemporary records' (K.H. Jackson, LHEB 677, *cf.* 464, 465, 680), and the two other places, Gloucester and Cirencester, are given in the anglicised forms of their British pronunciation. *Baðan ceaster* cannot therefore be an exception; it is the name by which the English knew Bath in or not long after 577. No English settlement is recorded, by archaeological or written evidence, in or near Bath until at least half a century later.

The earliest English reference to Bath is in the foundation charter of its abbey (BCS 43), dated to 676 *civitati quae vocatur aet Baðum*, the city called Hot Baths, given in the plural form. The full name occurs again, in the locative dative form *aet Hatum Baðum*, at the Hot Baths, in BCS 509 and 1257 (A.D. 864 and 970), but the normal form in charters until the mid-tenth century omits the adjective, and gives *Baðum* (with or without *aet*), in locative dative plural, frequently used as a nominative (e.g., BCS 241, 277, 278, 670, 973). From the mid-tenth century the elegant Latinised form *Bathonia* and the antiquarian *Acemannes ceaster*, *Aquamania* (e.g., BCS 1287), perhaps derived from the Latin *Aquae Sulis*, tend to prevail.

The forms *Baðan* or *Baðor* appear as weak dative plurals in late Old English, but could not be so used before the tenth century. *Baðan* occurs, however, in the Saxon Chronicle's account of Edgar's coronation, at 973, in verse, in MS. A,

on ðaere ealden byrig Acemannes ceastre
eac hi igbuend oðre worde beornas
Baðan nemna.

'In that old borough Acemannes Chester
That the island's people otherwise also call Baðan.'

The word is here in the accusative, and could not form any part of the declension of the Old English word *baeth*, 'bath'. It is a poetic reminiscence of the old British or Welsh name, used in the earliest version of the Chronicle, here preserved in MS. E (8) and by Nennius (3, 4 and 5), in the Cambrian Annals (6 and 7) and by Gildas (1).

The identification has sometimes been swept aside without examination of the evidence, chiefly because the superficial similarity between British Badon and English Bath seems an improbable coincidence. But the specific testimony of Nennius (5), of the Saxon Chronicle at 577 (8) and 973, and the sharp difference and the sharp contrast between British (Welsh) *Baðan*, elsewhere regularly transliterated in *Baddanbyrig* and similar forms, and the dative plural Old English forms *Baðum*, regularly used as an English description of the Roman baths, sufficiently demonstrate the identification.

'Badon Hill' is not the city of Bath, but a hill near Bath. The probable conditions of the campaign (*see* below and *Age*, 96 ff., 112 ff.) suggest a small isolated hill. Soulsbury Hill, by Batheaston, *ST 77 67*, seems best fitted to these conditions.

The Campaign

There is little direct contemporary evidence for the nature of Arthur's wars against the English; but there is much strong circumstantial evidence (*Age*, 96 ff.). Procopius, a contemporary but distant writer, explicitly asserts that the English were wholly unacquainted with cavalry, and the evidence of their graves confirms his statement. On the Roman side, the only contemporary evidence of determined late fifth-century military resistance to Germanic settlement in the western empire, the short-lived campaign of Ecidicus in Gaul, describes the attacks of a wholly cavalry Roman force upon a wholly infantry Germanic army. The only extant Old Welsh poem that concerns Arthur's wars, the 'Elegy for Geraint' (*Age*, 104-105), which may be a translation of a contemporary original, also describes an engagement between Arthur's cavalry and English infantry. The numerous contemporary or near-contemporary accounts of the British armies of the north Pennines also describe cavalry formations, though the kingdom of York may have maintained an infantry force as well, and infantry appear to have been normal in much of Wales; and in Brittany, cavalry were the decisive and predominant force. Late Welsh tradition (16) regards Arthur's forces at Badon as 'mighty' mounted men.

There is, therefore, no reasonable doubt that the armies of the English consisted of foot soldiers alone, and it is more than probable that Arthur's striking force consisted exclusively of cavalry, with no infantry outside their homelands of the west country.

The homeland of the British lay in and west of Salisbury Plain and the Cotswolds, the homeland of the English in East Anglia and Kent (*Age*, map 5, p. 101), with the main area of fighting in between. The same localisation is emphasised by the distribution of late Roman hoards of metal work (*Britannia* 3, 1972, maps pp. 227 and 248, where, however, the suggestion [p.249] that the hoards are 'votive deposits' does not explain their distribution, wholly different from that of early Roman and pre-Roman votive hoards, or their absence from areas outside the fifth-century War Zone) and also of late Theodosian coin hoards.

The situation of Bath, deep in the heartlands of the British, argues a massive attempt by the English to destroy the bases of their enemies. Nennius (3) and later Welsh tradition (16) name Arthur as the British commander at Badon, and no evidence gainsays them. The composition of the English armies, however, can only be inferred, since early English tradition rarely recorded defeats. Circumstantial evidence suggests the main force was involved. A tradition, already old by the eighth century (9 and 10), regarded Aelle, king of the South Saxons in the late fifth century, as the first supreme commander of the southern English. Later kings who were credited with the same wide authority over all the English south of the Humber, Ceawlin, Aethelbert, Redwald, Edwin, and others, all won their authority by fighting and conquering other English kings. It is not possible that the tiny kingdom of the South Saxons could have fought and conquered the rest of southern England at any time, least of all in the course of the wars against the British. Aelle's supreme authority can only have been conferred by consent, in a grave emergency; though his kingdom was small and recent, he was the oldest of the kings of the late fifth century, the most experienced in warfare against the British. The tradition implies that he was chosen as the commander of an allied army. No date is given for his death: if his reign was regarded as of the same length as that assigned to Hengest, 39 years, two score less one, his death would have fallen in or about 495.

The evidence that concerns the king of Kent is more striking. Tradition is uncertain whether the king named Aesc, Osc, Oisc, Ossa or Osla was son or grandson of Hengest. But two separate documents in Nennius's collection and the independent Welsh tradition of the English genealogies agree that an English force was established north of Hadrian's Wall in Hengest's time, and that its leader returned to Kent and fought at Badon at the end of the century (11-16). The dating would better fit a grandson than a son of Hengest, but the relation is unimportant, since it may well be contrived; the later dynasty of Kent, the Oescingas, took their name from Oesc (14, Bede), whose name must therefore be substituted for Octha in Nennius's explanation of the dynasty's foundation (15). The Saxon Chronicle names Aesc frequently, but only once calls him Hengest's son (11), in a passage that reads like an added explanatory gloss. It was the normal tradition of English and Welsh genealogists to treat a king's successor as his son, whether or not he was related to him (*see* **G** introduction), and to turn a man with two names into two people, as the list of Roman emperors gives 'Octavian son of Augustus Caesar',

'Philippus son of Gordian son of Maxim(in)', etc. The clear tradition is that Aesc was Hengest's successor in Kent; that Hengest's successor in Kent came from Northern Britain; and that Ossa Big Knife, whose descendants ruled Bernicia, fought against Arthur at Badon. Aesc's death is placed at about 493.

No tradition directly links Cerdic of Wessex (17) with Badon, though the English of his territory are represented as Arthur's enemies in an earlier battle (*Age*, 104); but the Parker preface (17) puts his death also at about 495.

The location of the battle argues a full-scale invasion of the British heartlands by the united forces of the southern English. The coincidence that two of the three southern English kings of the late fifth century are said to have died at about the time of the battle, 493×495, and that the third was chosen supreme commander of their armies, forcibly suggests that the invading army comprehended the full mobile fighting strength of the three kingdoms, under Aelle's command. The necessary objective of such a large infantry force was to destroy the bases where the British bred and trained their horses, and to overrun South Cadbury and other fortified centres of the British heartland.

Gildas (1) calls the battle a siege, and was near enough in time to know the facts. Nennius (3) says the engagement lasted for three days and three nights, a statement also consistent with a siege. No source says who besieged whom, but the circumstances imply that the large infantry army invested the smaller cavalry force. Though cavalry might excel in raids and field battles, it was ill-adapted to siege operations without considerable trained infantry support. The numbers of Arthur's cavalry are not known but, since the success of Ecidicus's campaign in Gaul against some thousands of Goths was achieved initially by 18 mounted men, and subsequently by a few score, the British cavalry is unlikely to have exceeded 1,000 men, if so many. Nennius's account (3) implies that after three days the British horse were able to break out of their encirclement in a single decisive charge, and records the number of English said to have been slain in that charge, a little short of one thousand. The combined English army is unlikely to have been larger than a few thousand, since the logistics of feeding and maintaining a large force deep in enemy territory clearly presented formidable difficulties.

The Consequences

Badon was the decisive battle of the war, nearly, but not quite, the last engagement (1, Gildas). The East Anglian armies may or may not have been engaged; they and the middle English, with the English of Lincolnshire and the East Riding, may have been reduced to submission before the campaign (*Age*, 111 ff.). The remaining fighting is likely to have involved the reduction of a few remaining pockets of active resistance. But, though Badon prevented an English victory, a cavalry force was unable to storm a large number of stockaded villages defended by men whose families lived within them. The campaign ended with the 'final victory of our country', but victory was unable to exterminate or expel the English. Britain was partitioned (*Age*, 134 ff., and map 8, p.135), the English were suffered to remain in a number of separate eastern districts, the lands between them were either cleared, or subjected to a British authority that forbade the English the use of their national burial rites. British supremacy was to last for some three generations.

BEANDUN. Possibly Beanwood, but almost any Benton, Benworth or the like would fit. A textual corruption of a B(e)ean Down is not excluded, but the search is profitless. At that date the British enemies of West Saxon kings will have been the Dumnonians or whatever was left of the men of Gloucester, the encounter most probably in the Cotswold or Mendip regions.

614 'In this year Cynegils and Cwichelm fought at *Beandun* and killed 2,045 (A and E, 2,065; G, 2,046) Britons.'

Beandun is usually identified as Bindon on the Devon-Somerset border near Axminster.
R.B.W.

BERNICIA, Beornice OE, Brennych OW, and similar forms. The territory of the north-eastern Angles, from the mid-fifth century. Its chief centre from the mid-sixth century was Bamburgh (*NU 1834*). The cemetery of Howick, and most of the archaeological sites that might be early, and the concentration of *botl* place-names about Bamburgh lie north of the Aln, as does the later royal vill at Yeavering. It is doubtful whether the territory reached southward to the Tyne until the late sixth-century conquests. Thereafter, it is uncertain whether the border between Deira and Bernicia, within united English Northumbria, lay on the Tyne or the Tees; the doubt is explained by the twelfth-century life of Oswald (SD 1, 339, cited Plummer *Bede* 2,120) by the theory that Durham, between Tyne and Tees, was deserted.

The name is not connected with the Brigantes, and may mean the 'land of mountain passes', if the Old Irish *bern*, gap or pass, also existed in British (Jackson LHEB 701 ff.).

BINDON. *See* BEANDUN.

BOHEMIA. The inhabited area, containing more than 90 per cent of all known Germanic sites, is confined to a strip of territory, about 75 miles from east to west, averaging 10 to 20 miles from north to south, containing the valleys of the major rivers that meet between Prague and the Elbe, with Prague on its southern extremity; *cf.* the maps in K. Motykova Sneidrova, *Pocatky Doby Rimske v Cechach* (The Early Roman Period in Bohemia), *Fontes Archaeological Pragenses*, Prague, 1963, and H.J. Eggers, *Der römische Import im Freien Germanien*, Hamburg, 1951, etc. These 200 odd sites lie a hundred miles north of the Danube, with little known habitation of the Roman or migration periods between them and the Danube. Even earlier, when the valley of the Moldau was blocked against Roman advance by a series of immense Celtic *oppida*, there is comparatively little evidence of settlement outside the immediate neighbourhood of the *oppida*. A similar expanse of empty upland separated Bohemia (the Marcomanni) from the Quadi, of Moravia and south-western Slovakia, about the March (Morava) Gran and other rivers that drain to the Danube below Vienna and Bratislava.

The archaeological evidence for the migration period has been collected by B. Svoboda, *Cechy v Dobe Narodu* (Bohemia in the Migration Period), Prague, 1965. Urns and ornaments from the lower Elbe occur with increasing frequency from the later second century, and become the majority in the fourth, with a lesser influence from central Germany. Svoboda's inference that the principal users of these urns were Langobards carries conviction: the sites contrast with the proto-Bavarian vessels of Prestovice (in south-west Bohemia), whose character has little connection with the main concentration, though these also have some lower Elbe echoes. Of nearly 200 sites all except Prestovice and Pilsen lie within Marcomannic territory.

This long-continuing, evolving population was sharply replaced by a people using exclusively Frankish grave goods, virtually identical with those buried in Rhineland graves in the first half of the sixth century, but no later. Svoboda's archaeological dates match the written evidence. Langobardi are reported to have entered Marcomannic territory for the first time in or about 165. The Franks overcame the south-eastern Germans on Clovis's defeat of the Alamanni at Tolbiac in the autumn of 496, and were overwhelmed on the Elbe by the Avars about 567 (Paulus Diaconus 2,10; Greg. Tur. *HF* 4,23; 4,29; see SLAVS, below). The Lower Elbe-Langobardi population therefore probably yielded to Frankish conquerors about 500.

Before their removal, a few of the Bohemian grave goods are categorically Anglian or Saxon (e.g., the pedestal *Buckelurn* from Besno, Svoboda Tafel 37,6, and the late fifth-century cruciform brooches of Åberg Group 11 [B/C], Svoboda Tafel 80,9), while many others are very similar. More numerous are unskilled copies of particular Anglo-Saxon vessels (e.g., Svoboda Tafel 17,1 and 5, copying *Buckelurnen*), presumably the work of Anglo-Saxon immigrants who lacked a professional potter. The impression given by Svoboda's illustrations is that Anglian and Jutish vessels outnumber Saxon; and that the majority of the professionally-made vessels are late fourth- or very early fifth-century, the majority of the copies fifth-century. The inference is that the Marcomanni accepted a considerable immigration, predominantly Langobard in the second and third centuries, including Anglo-Saxons in the late fourth and early fifth, with some from the Vandal-Burgundian areas to the north, but that the immigrants blended into a single political community, whose principal element was Langobard. Svoboda was not acquainted with the English material, and a few of his dates therefore need revision, but these revisions scarcely change his overall picture.

BREFI. The church of Llanddewibrefi is in Dyfed at (*SN 6655*), close to the Roman auxiliary fort BREMIA (*SN 6456*).

BREMIA, a river name, corresponding to modern Welsh *bref* ('roaring' – a river name) will regularly give Welsh *bref* (for the difficulties raised by the suffix 'i' in this and other cases *see* LHEB 351-353).

There is an important group of early Christian inscriptions at Llanddewibrefi; they are

(i) (D)ALLVS/DVMELVS = Dallus Dumelus (lies here).
(ii) Sixth-century (broken and built into the church wall) (HI)C IACET (I)DNERT FILIUS IA(/QVI) OCCISV(S F) VIT PROPTER PR(AEDIVM [?]/ ... SANCTI) = Here lies Idnert, son of Ia ... who was killed near the farm of the holy ...
(iii) Sixth-century pillar-stone with confidently executed cross, *c.* eighth-century.
(iv) Sixth-century pillar-stone with a Latin cross having bifid scrolled foot and trifid arm terminals, *c.* eighth-century.
(v) Sixth-century pillar stone with roughly pocked cross, *c.* eighth-century.
(vi) Pillar-stone with incised cross inscription below reading CENLISINI BT (? = *benedicat*) DS (Deus) meaning 'The Cross of Cenlisnin. God bless him'. Half-uncial letters indicate an eighth- or ninth-century date.

The synod held at Llanddewibrefi (apparently) to debate the Pelagian heresy is described in the *Vita Sancti Cadoci* and the *Vita Sancti David* (VSBG 55, 164). The scene is set in the *Vita Cadoci*: 'Cadocus quidem peregrinatus est, David uero post eius discessionem magnum sinodum in Civitate Breevi congregauit' (para. 13). (= 'Cadog went on his travels, and David after he had gone, assembled a great synod in *Civitas Breevi*').

Subsequent events are described in the *Vita Sancti David*, paras. 49-56, and Cadog's reaction on his return in the *Vita Sancti Cadoci*, para. 17.   R.B.W.

BRITAIN. The earliest record is that of Pytheas (c.300 B.C.), who gives Pretannikoi, cognate with Irish *Cruithin* (= Picts = painted people?). The Romans called the province *Britannia*, modern Welsh *Prydein*. The difference (if any) between Alba and Britannia is not clear.

BRIXWORTH, Northampton (*SP 7470*).
Ekwall (DEPN) records:

Brickleworde	1086	Domesday
Brihteswrde	1198	
Brikelesworth	1223	

meaning '*Beorhtel's homestead*', a personal name. Brixworth has a fine early church.

BROCKWEIR. Ryt Tindyrn, Vadum Tindirn (Ford of Tintern) LL 141. Pwll Brockvail, LL 141, glossed Brockewere, p.340 (*SO 5301*).

CADBURY/CAMELOT. 'At the very south ende of the church of South-Cadbyri standith Camallate . . . the people . . . have hard say that Arture much resortid to Camalat', John Leland, 1542.

Domesday Book gives *Sud cadeberie*.

Excavations by Leslie Alcock, 1966-70, revealed a sequence of occupations from the Neolithic (c.3000 B.C.) through to the reign of King John in the early thirteenth century A.D., including a post-Roman Arthurian period's defensive rampart and gateway. Internal buildings of this period included a timber hall. Finds included sherds of imported Mediterranean pottery of the fifth and sixth centuries A.D.; *see* Alcock, L., *By South Cadbury is that Camelot*, 1972.

CALCHFYNYDD.
Poems. BT 38, 11-12; 39, 11; FAB 1, 363, 364; 2, 162, 163.

Kychwedul am dodyw o Galchuynyd,
Guarth yn deheubarth . . .
Kychwedyl am dodyw
O leutired deheu.

'A whisper has come from Calchvynydd, a reproach in the south . . .
A whisper has come from the fair (?) south country.'

The poem concerns the wars of Owen, son of Urien. The allusion is vague, but no more so than the rest of the allusions in the poem, save that some of the other places named, Alclud, Reged, etc., are well known.

CALEDONII. Placed by Ptolemy (c. A.D. 150) along the east of the Great Glen, the *drumos Caledonios* on the west of the Glen, *drumos* translating *saltus*, in this sense a large uncultivated region, usually forested. Ptolemy called the northern ocean *Duecaledonius*.

Ptolemy places the Vacomagi in the Grampians, the Taezali in Aberdeenshire, the Venicones in Strathmore, and knows no other peoples between the Damnonii of the Clyde and Votadini of the Forth and the Great Glen. Beyond the Glen, he has Epidii in Kintyre and Argyle, Creones Carnonacae and Caereni on the west coast, Cornovii in Caithness, Lugi and Decantae south of them on the east coast to Inverness, Smertae in the interior about Larg.

Tacitus (*Agricola* 10; 11; 25; 27; 31) applies the name Caledonia to the whole of the northern territory he penetrated in the 80s. Statius and other late first-century writers use Caledonii as a generic term for the northern barbarians.

Cassius Dio (75, 6, 4) divides the northerners (*c.* A.D. 200) into the Maeatae (MIATHI, *q.v.*) nearest to the Roman frontier, and the Caledonii beyond, adding that almost all the other peoples had been absorbed into these two.

The language of Tacitus implies that the Caledonii had absorbed their neighbours by A.D. 80. Ptolemy's detail of northern Scotland probably rests on knowledge acquired during Agricola's campaign. Agricola was at pains to discover the geography, sending his fleet to circumnavigate Britain by way of the Orkneys. About A.D. 84 an eminent scholar, Demetrius of Tarsus, visited the Western Isles (Plutarch, *Moralia*) presumably with the fleet. Tacitus's language expressed a political situation; Ptolemy was concerned with geographical detail.

Eumenius (*Panegyrici Latini*, 1, 103f.) knew of '*Dicaledonum aliorumque Pictorum silvas et paludes*' in the 290s. Ammianus 27,8 '*eo tempore* (368) *Picti in duas gentes divisi, Dicalidonas et Verturiones* (FORTRENN, *q.v.*) *itidemque Attacotti . . . et Scotti*' (were plundering the Roman province).

The name appears on a third-century inscription of Colchester. RIB 191 '*Donum Lossio Veda de suo posuit nepos Vepogeni Caledo*', implying that Lossio would have used a Latin plural Caledones. The name survives in Dunkeld (*NO 0242*), Perthshire (Dun Caillen AU 873; *cf.* Book of Deer), blocking the pass whence the Tay and the main route from Inverness debouch from the hills; at Rohallion nearby; and at Schiehallion mountain (*NN 7154*), further into the highlands, between Lochs Rannoch and Tummel. These names indicate the border districts and will have been bestowed by the neighbours of the Caledonii. The name is probably distinct from Coit Calidon, Nennius 56. The first-century Latin pronunciation was Caledo (Ptolemy; Statius, *Silvae* 5, 2, 142, etc.).

CANTERBURY, Kent
Ekwall (DEPN) records:

Cantawaraburg	734	SC
Cantwaraburg	851	SC
Cantwaraburg	*c.*890	Old English Bede
Canterburie	1086	

meaning 'the *burg* (fort) of the people of Kent'.
The British name of Canterbury appears as:

Darovernon	*c.*150	Ptolemy
Duroverno	fourth-century	'Antonine Itinerary'
Doruvernis	*c.*730	Bede

K.H. Jackson (cited Rivet, *Britannia*, 1, 1970, p. 73) translates this as British *duro* (walled town with gateways) with a second element *verno* (alder-swamp), hence 'The Walled Town by the Alder-Swamp', an important Roman city.

Bede's account of the conversion of the people of Kent (*HE* 25,26) speaks of the old church '*built in honour of St Martin during the Roman occupation of Britain*' (*HE* 1, 26). *See* Chadwick, O., 'The Evidence of Dedications in the Early History of the Welsh Church', p. 181, in SEBH; Frend, W.H., 'The Christianization of Roman Britain', in ed. M.W. Barley and R.P.C. Hanson, *Christianity in Britain*, Leicester, 1968, 37-49; Frere, S., *Roman Canterbury, the City of Durovernum*, third edition, Canterbury, 1962. R.B.W.

CAPUT REGIONIS. Columba met a ship of Gaul when he went '*ad Caput Regionis*', Adomnán, 1, 28. Adomnán commonly latinised place-names, and the words are evidence of his attempt to translate *Cenn* (Head), *Tír* (Country, regio)

(Kintyre) see ed. William Reeves, Dublin, 1857, p. 57, followed by Watson CPNS 92. Anderson's contrary assertion (Adomnán's *Life of Columba*, 264) that *Caput Regionis* means the 'capital of the district', Dunadd, is improbable. This is not Adomnán's usage. Though he might have employed it for the chief centre of a distant country unknown to him, he knew the name of the royal residence of his own state. Moreover, to Adomnán, such sites were not 'capitals' but (correctly) *'regis Brudei munitio'*, a royal fortress. Had he wished to name Dunadd or any other site, he would have named it as he named Alclud, *Petra Cloithe*. In any case, a Kintyre harbour, possibly Campbeltown, as Watson, is a reasonable port of call for a Gallic ship on its way to or from north-eastern Ireland; a diversion to Dunadd up the sound of Jura is a hazardous undertaking for a foreign shipmaster ignorant of its waters.

CATRAETH, Catterick, perhaps Cath Ratha in Druad, **A** 598 (Tigernach, Ulster, Inisfallen).

'Gwyr a aeth gatreath oed fraeth eu llu' (The *Gododdin*, VIII). 'Men went to Catraeth, swift was their host.'

The site of the battle celebrated in the *Gododdin* of Aneirin, identified with some certainty as Catterick on the River Swale in Yorkshire. We have the name in Ptolemy, the Antonine Itinerary and Bede as well as other sources. A summary of the forms is as follows:

Katouraktonion (Ptolemy), second century
Cataractonivm (Antonine Itinerary), third century (ablative Cataractone [Antonine Itinerary], third century)
Cataracta (Bede), c.730 (ablative Cataractone [Bede], c.730)
Cetrecht (Old English Bede), c.890
Catraeth (The *Gododdin*), ninth century
Catrice (Domesday), 1086.

The Welsh is slightly surprising in that we might have expected Cataractonium to give Welsh *Cadraeth*, so e.g., *latro*, 'thief, freebooter' gives Welsh *lleidr*, but we do have *petrual* (that is four-sided) in the White Book *Mabinogion* version of *Branwen* (Ifor Williams, *Pedeir Keinc y Mabinogi*, Cardiff, 1930, 45 and n.) which seems to be from *petruso*, *cf.* Gaulish *Petru-corii*, 'the four hosts', Latin *quadr-* 'square'.

On the face of it the name means 'battle-strand' (i.e., *cad* 'battle' + *traeth* 'shore'), but we also have Latin *Cataracta* 'waterfall', and there are waterfalls in the River Swale at Catterick. So the river name may have been 'the waterfall river'; *cf.* the modern name Swale, which Ekwall (DEPN 434) says is identical with *Schwalh, Schwale*, 'whirling, rushing', and the Roman station then took the river name, as they often did (on this *see* Margaret Gelling, *Signposts to the Past*, Chichester, 1988, Chap. 2, *passim*). In any event the name is ambiguous and apt in both meanings, and this ambiguity may have appealed to the poet Aneirin. Returning to the one line out of about 1,480 of the *Gododdin* with which we began

Gwyr a aeth gatraeth oed fraeth eu llu

it may not be as straightforward as it first seems, for the rhyming words have many shades of meaning.

Latin *cataracta* can be rendered *fraeth* in Welsh, and *fraeth* can be rendered *schwale*. Swale is the river at Catterick and thus the words swirl in the mind with images and connections, not at all intended by Aneirin. This underlines the difficulty in using poetry such as this as an historical source: a task made almost impossible if the original language cannot be understood, and translations have to be relied on. See Ifor Williams, *Canu Aneirin*, Cardiff, 1938 (in Welsh); Kenneth Jackson, *Language and History in Early Britain*, Edinburgh, 1953, 409; Jackson, *The Gododdin*, Edinburgh, 1969, 83 ff. R.B.W.

CELIDON. This name derives from, or is related to, the CALEDONII (*q.v.*) of Ptolemy. This is the *Coit Celidon* of Nennius, *Coed Celyddon* in the Welsh Myrddin poems, *Calidon* in the Latin *Life of Merlin* and *Caledonius Saltus* of Ptolemy. The forest of Celidon was real enough to the Romans, for Tacitus makes the barbarian Calgacus highlight the difficulties of terrain encountered by Agricola before the battle of Mons Graupius thus: '... *corpora ista ac manus silvis ac paludibus eminiendis inter verbera ac contumelias conteruntur* ...' (*Agricola* 31) '... our bodies and hands are ground down in clearing (a way through) woods and marshes, all under blows and insults ...'.

But by the time the forest of Celidon reappears in the early Welsh tradition it has become much more vague, even mysterious – a sort of otherworld forest somewhere up north, not unlike the Mirkwood of Tolkien's *Lord of the Rings*. It is to this magic place that the storyteller sends the aged yet ageless Merlin in his tale. The fugitive British wild man of the woods is pictured as having sought refuge in the forest after a battle, perhaps the battle of *Arfderydd* of *c*.573 (*see* ARTHURET). Medieval Scottish tradition supported by the odd place-name places the forest of Celidon from Stirling north and west through Perthshire as far as the Grampians (Bellenden, 1536). *See* J. Bellenden, *The Hystory and Croniklis of Scotland*, Edinburgh, 1536; Basil Clarke, 'Calidon and the Caledonian Forest', BBCS, 23 (1968-70), 191-201, and references cited; Clarke, *Life of Merlin*, Cardiff, 1973, 170 ff. R.B.W.

CHANNEL. *See* ICHT.

CIRCINN. Last-named of the seven provinces of the Picts in the king-lists, CPS 4, 25, 323, 396. Cirig or Circin is named as the first ruler; Angus and the Mearns, in *de Situ Albaniae* (CPS 136) and later lists, form the northern portion of Strathmore, probably earlier denoting all Strathmore.

Circinn and the Mearns have been wrongly identified by Skene with Magh Dergind, followed by Watson CPNS, 108-109, on the basis of an inferior MS. variant Gergindi. In many instances given in translation by Skene as Girgin and the like, the text he prints reads Circin (e.g., CPS 319).

A 599 *Circinn* for Adomnán's MIATHI (*q.v.*).

COMBROGI. The word means 'fellow-countrymen', literally 'people within the same border'. The form *Combrogi is not anywhere attested but has been back-constructed by philologists from Welsh *Cymry*; but *cf.* the place-name *Cumbraland* (SC *sub anno* 945) *Cumberland*. The earliest use of the name is perhaps that in the poem in praise of the Welsh king Cadwallon (*fl.* early seventh century, *ob. c*.630), which we have only in an eighteenth-century copy, but the manuscript tradition is at least as old as the twelfth century (Idris Foster, 'The Emergence of Wales' in ed. I.Ll. Foster and G. Daniel, *Prehistoric and Early Wales*, London, 1965, 230 citing Ifor Williams, BBCS, 7 [1933-5], 23-25, 29-32). The poem 'evokes the language, formulaic patterns and the ethos of Taliesin and Aneirin' (Foster, *op. cit.*) and if genuine must have been composed in the first quarter of the seventh century. The name is not tribal, but rather seeks to differentiate those inhabitants of *Britannia* who are *Brython* (*Brittones*) from *Saeson* (Saxons). Thus the name dates in all likelihood from the time of the major 'Saxon' advances of the turn of the seventh century. The *Gododdin* by way of contrast speaks only of *Brython*.

CORNOVIA, 'The land of the Cornovii'.
British *Cornovia* gives Welsh *Cernyw*, Breton *Kerneo*, Cornish *Kernow*, 'Cornwall', that is promontory dwellers. Ptolemy records Cornovii in the west Midlands and northern Scotland. The north Anglesey name Llanfair yng Nghornwy also has the name, being *Cornwyllys* and *Cornwyllan* in the fourteenth century. The Ravenna Cosmography gives a place name *PUROCORONAVIS*, an error for *DUROCORONAVIS*, the *DUROCORNOVIO* of the Antonine Itinerary, and usually identified with the Roman station near Wanborough, Wiltshire. (*DURO = 'walled town'.)

See Rivet, A.L.F., 'The British Section of the Antonine Itinerary', *Britannia*, 1 (1970), 58, 73; Jackson, K.H., LHEB, 377; Webster, G., *The Cornovii*, 1975, 18 (the west Midland *Cornivii*); Watson, W.J., *The Celtic Place-Names of Scotland*, Edinburgh, 1926, 16.
R.B.W.

CYMENES ORA, SC 477, landing place of Aelle and the south Saxons; *cf.* BCS 64 (Ceadwalla's grant of Selsey to Wilfrid). The bounds of the Selsey peninsula begin *ab introitu portus qui appelatur anglice Wynderynge* (on Pagham harbour EPNS Sx 96). *Post retractum mare* is probably Pagham harbour itself. *Ora* means 'river-bank', 'sea-shore' or 'edge of a hill', 'slope' (EPNS 2,55). The obvious place in Pagham harbour to acquire such a name in the early years of conquest is the earthwork, of Iron Age origin, with Roman material on the water's edge at Church Norton (*SZ 8695*), wherein Wilfrid built his church, whose cross shaft, and some of whose stonework, remains. Norton in Selsey contrasts with Sutton, the old name of modern Selsey (EPNS 83). The suggestion in EPNS that Cymenes Ora was the sandbanks off the south-west coast of the peninsula by modern Selsey and Medmerry called the Owers does not seem probable. The Owers probably means *ora*, and the erosion of the peninsula recorded in the last three centuries has been so rapid that the Owers might have originated as 'the old ora' after they had ceased to be the coastline. But nothing connects this *ora* with Cymen. The place described in Ceadwalla's charter is a particular place, neither a sandbank out to sea, nor a stretch of coast. The rest of the boundaries named in the circuit are villages, rivers or estuaries.

DAL RIADA. A small territory on the north-easternmost tip of Ireland (its limits defined, Hogan 325, with references), its mainland capital at Muirbolc.
Its king, Fergus, transferred his residence to Argyle about 500. It is unlikely that he did so before a considerable number of his subjects had already migrated. Nor are they likely to have been the first Irish in southern and western Scotland. Irish legend has many tales of migration in both directions, and the narrow distance between the Irish and Scottish coasts makes migration probable. From Neolithic times onwards, several archaeological cultures are common to both sides of the Irish sea. The evidence of place-names suggests that it was prolonged and heavy, and some archaeological pointers make the first century B.C. a likely date for some of it (*cf.* Atecotti). Irish tradition knew three main migrations, placed in distant centuries B.C., in the second century and the early fourth. The second-century migration, assigned to Cairbre Riada, whence the name Dal Riada, was known to Bede, who understood that Riada's settlement was in territory then Pictish. In his day it was therefore believed that Dal Riada had ceased to be Pictish, and become Irish, several centuries before Fergus's time.

The migration of the dynasty occurred at about the same time as the Irish invasions of north and of south Wales and of Cornwall (*cf.* **L** Theodoric, **E** Fingar). But it is unlikely that Fergus's movement was a hostile invasion. His men occupied Kintyre, controlling the estuary of the Clyde, and had they been strongly opposed by the British of the Clyde, it is probable that some echo of such conflict would have survived in the traditions of one or both peoples. What hints survive from that tradition suggest the contrary. The then king of Alclud married his son to an Irish princess; the bridegroom was named Tutwal, itself probably an Irish name adopted into British. Alliance rather than enmity seems to underly the tradition. Alliance had a purpose, because the Irish kingdom of Kintyre, and northward to Loch Lynnhe, provided a buffer between the British and the northern Picts of Inverness and the Great Glen, while the establishment of a dynasty in Kintyre did not threaten the occupation of Alclud territory. Irish ships, if they were hostile, might raid and interfere with navigation, but from Kintyre to Dumbarton is more than 100 miles by land, and settlement in Dumbarton territory could not easily be protected from Kintyre. The Irish dynasty therefore helped rather than hindered the interest of the British, so long as peaceful relations avoided coastal raids.

The growth and extent of Dal Riada settlement in the future Scotland, after Fergus's migration of 500, is principally evidenced by place-names. The earliest settlement was in Kintyre (*Caput Regionis*), its royal fortress at Dunadd (*NR 8393*) in Knapdale, north of Loughgilphead, at its northern extremity, the territory of the Cenel Gabrain. Northward the Cenel Loairn extended to the neighbourhood of Loch Lynnhe, the southern end of the Great Glen; they may have crossed with Fergus, or some time afterwards. The Cenel Aengusa, in Islay and the islands, descended in the main tradition from a brother of Fergus, in some variant tales (cited Hogan 216) from an Aengus made son of Niall of the Nine Hostages, who lived a century earlier.

The first expansion is dated to the reign of Comgall, died 541, who named Cowall, the peninsula north of Bute, between Loch Fyne and the Firth of Clyde. It is reckoned as a separate *cenél* in a genealogical tract of *c.* 700, but comprehended within the Cenel Gabrain in the *Senchus* of *c.* 650. There are indications that his successor, Gabran, 541-60, extended his colonisation much further. A poem, of the tenth century or possibly earlier, cited from MS. Rawlinson B 502, 86 a 47 (not in CGH) by Watson CPNS 53, through ZCP 2, 134, makes Gabran, and Aedan after him, rulers of *Foirthe*, the upper Forth, Fortrenn, between Loch Lomond and Perth (the verses hardly bear Watson's interpretation that Foirthe was 'beyond [Gabran's] own bounds'). Place-names carry Gabran further. Gowrie, north of Perth, centred about Blairgowrie (*NO 1745*), bears his name, and Brechin, at the northern end of Strathmore (*NO 5960*), has the name of an Irish Breccan. An Irish tradition of the late tenth century (CPS 315, in some MSS. of the pedigree of Malcolm mac Cinaeda attached to *Genelach Albanensium*) makes the sons of Domnall Brecc (died 643), Conaid (Conall) Cerr (died 531) and Fergus Gall sire new branches, Conaid in Fife, Fergus's named the Gabranaig. Their date is probably too late; Domnall's death was followed by the subjection of the Dal Riada themselves, and it is unlikely that Irish settlements recently founded by his sons could have endured deep in Pictish territory to give them their permanent names. Moreover, the district names *Gafran* and *Brecheiniawc* occur in one of the Gwallauc poems (CT 11, 42); that is probably seventh century, and may be as early as the time of Domnall Brecc. It is therefore more probable that the first expansion into Circinn (Strathmore) belongs to Gabran's time.

Gabran did not keep his conquests. He was defeated and killed by Bridei of the Picts in 560, whose centre lay in Inverness. It is likely that Gabran's conquest had overrun southern Pictland, and that he was himself destroyed by a king who was compelled to rule from the north.

His successors retained at least Aberfoyle, commanding the only route from Dal

Riada to southern Pictish territory which does not pass though British territory; for Aedan was able to establish the monk Berachus in its fort.

Columba landed in Iona three years after Gabran's defeat. Thereafter Dal Riada remained in firm alliance with the northern Pictish king Bridei for 30 years. In his last years, southern Pictland rebelled against Bridei. Aedan won a battle in *Manann*, probably Manau Gododdin, in 583, presumably against the southern Picts, and in alliance with Bridei. Bridei died in 584, and in 599 Aedan won a costly victory in Circinn, Strathmore, presumably regaining his father's conquests. His son Eochu is described as 'king of the Picts' in the Book of Cuanu, according to AU 628. But when Eochu's son Domnall Brecc was killed by the British in 643, after a series of disastrous campaigns in Ireland and about the Forth, the contemporary abbot of Iona lamented that Dal Riadan Scots had passed under the dominion of foreigners, evidently including the Irish whom Gabran and Aedan and their successors had established in southern Pict territory in Strathmore and Fife.

The Cenel Gabrain dynasty was for a time eclipsed; and at the end of the century the Cenel Loairn on their north asserted the kingship of Dunadd and Dal Riada. But for nearly 200 years Dal Riada was hard pressed by the southern Picts, re-established in Fortrenn. The Picts, however, increasingly chose Irishmen as kings, and from the later eighth century elected Dal Riada kings as their own rulers, the kings installing their sons or brothers as kings in Dal Riada, until Kenneth mac Alpin permanently established a dual monarchy under one king in 844.

See also Bannerman, J., *Studies in the History of Dalriada*, Edinburgh, 1974.

DECANGI (Deceangli). A Romano-British tribe in what is now Clwyd (Flintshire and Denbighshire) in north-east Wales. The name is not in Ptolemy's Geography, but two lead pigs from near Chester have moulded inscriptions:

IMP. VESP [V.T.I]MP.III.COS
   DECEANGL

Imp(eratore) Vesp(asiano) [V, T(ito) I]mp(eratore) III co(n)s(ulibus): (plumbum) Decaengl(icum)

= '(Made) in the fifth consulship of the Emperor Vespasian, and the third of the Emperor Titus: Deceanglian (lead)'.

This is A.D. 74.
Likewise

IMP. VESP. AUG. V. T. IMP. III[CO]S
   DECEANGL

also A.D. 74.

The district between the Clwyd and the Dee, rich in lead, is called *Tegeingl*, which preserves the name. It has been suggested that the name *Degannwy* (now a town on the east bank of the River Conwy) is also from Deceangli, but ACm has *Arx Decantorum* (s.a. 812) which would give British *Decantovion*, suggesting a tribal name something like *Decantii*.

Ptolemy lists *Decantae* in Scotland.

See Jackson, K.H., LHEB, 39; Wright, R.B. and Richmond, I.A., *The Roman Inscribed and Sculptured Stones in the Grosvenor Museum, Chester*, Chester, 1955, Nos. 196 and 197; Jarrett, M.G. and Mann, J.C., 'The Tribes of Wales', *Welsh History Review*, 4 (1968/9), 161.

DEIRA. Southern Northumbria, between the Humber and the Tyne (SD 1, 339) or Tees (cf. Plummer, *Bede*, 2, 120), after the late sixth-century English conquest. Previously English settlement in Deira was virtually confined to the East Riding. The name, *Deor, Deur, Deura*, in early Welsh texts from the late sixth century onwards, in subsequent centuries *Deifr*, sometimes denoting all the English (*cf.* GPC, 1, 921, s.n. *Deifr*), is almost certainly of British (not English) origin, from an equivalent of *Dewr*, 'brave', not *Dwfr*, 'water', LHEB 419 ff. It will therefore originally have denoted the British inhabitants of the East Riding, among whom the English settlers lived. *Deor* is not uncommon in place and district names in other parts of England. EPNS treats it as always identical with English *deor*, a (wild) beast (German *Tier*), specifically = a deer, and in names like Deerhurst, Deerfold, it plainly is. But the *Deoringas* who named a Kentish land (BCS 449) are an unconvincing 'beast folk' and the Roman roads called Deer Street (*Deorstrete*) are unlikely to have been reserved for deer or any other wild animals. *Deorham* (Dyrham) in Gloucestershire is named in the SC annal of 577, whose other spellings are very nearly contemporary; the *deor* who inhabited and named it at that time were not English deer, but British people. It is therefore likely the word was a generic term applied to themselves by some of the British analogous to *Combrogi*, fellow countrymen. *Dewr* means 'brave' or 'strong'. The term is appropriate to a military force. The East Riding had been the base area of the *Superventores* of Malton, protected by the Yorkshire signal stations, and is probably the area whence the British ruler of York recruited his army, the home of *viri fortes*. The term, found in different parts of Britain, probably means no more than it says, but it might possibly be inspired by a translation of the name of the late Roman army units called *Fortenses*, one of which had garrisoned Othona in Essex. The word is not found in the poets, who are concerned with the cavalry *teulu* of northern and western heroes, and did not survive among medieval Welsh institutions. Its probable general connotation would therefore be static infantry defence, heirs of the garrisons who manned the walls and bastions of Roman towns, who are equally unremembered in the much fuller record of the Roman provinces. Foot forces, brave or otherwise, must have defended not only Dyrham, but Cadbury and the numerous other strong points and regions on which late fifth-century British armies were based.

DENT. [the following text is from the footnote in *Age*, 124.4 – *Ed.*]
regio Dunotinga is one of the districts of north-western Yorkshire overrun by the English in or before the 670s, Eddius 17. The passage is overlooked in EPNS WRY 6, 252, where the early spellings Denet(h) are rightly related to a British *Dinned* or the like, and Ekwall's derivation from a non-existent British equivalent of the Old Irish *find*, hill, is properly dismissed. EPNS does not observe that Dent was, and still is, the name of a considerable region, and that the village is still locally known as Dent Town, in contrast with the surrounding district of Dent. *Regio Dunotinga* plainly takes its name from a person named Dunawt, Latin *Donatus*, as does the district of Dunoding in Merioneth, named from another Dunawt, son of Cunedda.

[Bede (*HE* 2, 2) records the abbot of Bangor on Dee as *Dinoot*, which Jackson (LHEB, 41,295) argues is from an early written account of the battle of Chester. This would suggest Primitive Welsh *Dunod* from British Latin *Donatus* which reinforces the suggested etymology for *Dunotinga*, not from Old Welsh *Dunawt* (above), but from the earlier *Dunod* R.B.W.]

DERGIND. *Cairpre Cruithnechain a quo Eoganacht Maigi Dergind i nAlbae .i. dia rabi Oengus ri Alban'* CGH 196, R 148 a 31.
A MS. variant, Gerrgind (Lec., BB.), has caused confusion. A derivative and

interpolated version printed by Skene, *Celtic Scotland*, 3,475, makes Cairpre Cruithnechan and Cairpre Luachra into different persons, and gives him an additional brother, '*Maine Leamna a quo Leamnuigh a nAlban*'. Also it makes Mongfind's father a Cruithne 'of Alba', ancestor of the Cruithne Eamain. For *Maigi Dergind* it reads *Muighe Gearraih*, which Skene translated as 'The Mearns'; wrongly, for the Mearns have a later and quite different origin (Watson CPNS 110). Watson (108-109) turns *Gergind* to *Chirchind*. From at least the thirteenth century, Irish and Scottish genealogists naturally understood Leamna and Leamnuigh as Leven and Lennox, and gave the earls of Lennox an Eoganachta with 'Leamhain' origin personified as the 'wife' of Corc so convincing that one of them named a child Corc (Watson, 220 ff.). Such identifications were natural and inevitable once the meaning of the word Alba was restricted to Scotland. But in traditions concerned with the late fourth and early fifth centuries, it is used for the whole of Britain as far as the Channel.

There is no instance cited of a spelling *Cercing*, let alone *Gercind* for Chircind (CIRCINN, *q.v.*). Dergind is not Irish, but is the British Deruenid, Derwent, Dart, Leamna, of the Leven-Lyne group of river names (LHEB 488, 490, 672; Ekwall, ERN, s.v.) which is extremely common throughout the British Isles, and includes the Lemon (Lymen, tenth century; Leman Water, sixteenth) (EPNS Devon 8), which runs parallel to the Dart, from four to eight miles to the north, to join the Teign at Newton Abbot. The addition of Maine Leamna might of course have been invented *ab ovo* for the benefit of the Lennox clan, but it belongs to the earlier tradition, and is equally apt for Devonshire.

There is no reason, other than the variant spelling of *Dergind*, to suppose Munster (or Leinster) settlement in any part of Scotland, let alone on the east coast. The whole of the earlier tradition adheres to geographical probability, linking Scotland with northern Ireland, Leinster with all Wales, Munster with south Wales and Dumnonia. The most decisive evidence is the distribution of Irish inscriptions: 80 per cent of all ogam inscriptions in Ireland (about 300 in all) came from Munster; Wales has 25 or 26, Scotland one, England six, apart from Pictish ogams. The one Scottish inscription is from Argyll, and Scotland has no Latin inscriptions that could refer to Irishmen (except possibly CIIC 511, Peebles). Two of the six ogams in England, and five of the eight persons with Irish names, are concentrated in the plain between Dartmoor and the sea. Dergind is probably the Devonshire Dart.

One Patrician text, however (TT 13; ASH 571; vita 11, 24), states that Palladius died 'in campo Girgin, in loco qui dicitur Fordun'. Fordun, Kincardine, is on the edge of Chircind. Unfortunately, this life (Bieler, CPL, 22), which is one of the more important lives of Patrick, though extant in six MSS., remains unpublished, save for Colgan's unverified transcript of one defective MS. Until this text is properly published, there is no reason to take Munstermen to Perthshire.

DRUMCEAT. Dorsum Cete, Adomnán v. *Columbae* 1, 10-11; 1, 49, *cf.* 1,50; 2,6; *cf. Amra Choluim Chille*; Keating 2, 10 (3, 87) ff.; *Lismore Lives*, 309, etc.

Mullagh, or Daisy Hill, Roe Park, Newtown Limavady, in north-eastern Ireland, near the east shore of Lough Foyle, Reeves *Adamnan* 37, the site of a conference of Irish kings (*condictum regum*) called by Aed mac Ainmirech apparently soon after his accession, attended by Columba and Aedan of Dal Riada among others.

The *Annals* give two dates, 574 (AU) and 588 (AC). They are linked with alternative traditions about the date of Aed's accession, given both as 569 and 588. The source of these different traditions is the confusion caused by the joint kingship of 564 onwards. The probability is that Aed became king of Ailech in 574, high king in 588.

The evidence of the date rests on Adomnán's report (1,11) of Columba's prophecy about Scanlan, son of Colman, then a prisoner of Aed. He was to outlive Aed (who died in 601); 'post aliqua exilii tempora', 'after some time in exile', he would reign for 30 years and then be exiled again for a few days, recalled, and die after three days. Adomnán says that the prophecy was fulfilled; and it would hardly have been reported if it had not been.

Scanlan was king of Ossory. The record is confused because there were two, perhaps three, contemporary Colmans of Ossory in the late sixth century, two Scanlans in the early seventh. The king Colman, whom the *Annals* knew died in 608, is distinguished in the genealogies from his uncle, Colman the Elder (Mór), said to be Scanlan's father. Scanlan's exile therefore probably ended in 608, his reign in 638. Since he was already adult at Drumceat, the later date, 50 years before his death, is more probable than the earlier; and the convention is more likely to have been convened after Aed became high king than when he was king of Ailech. Aed's son, Domnall (died 643), whose blessing is mentioned, evidently because his grandson presided over a similar conference years later when Adomnán himself secured the passage of his law curbing military violence, was *adhuc puer*, 'still a boy', at Drumceat (Adomnán 1,10). If he were 10 or 12 in 588, he would have been nearly seventy at his death. If the date were 574, both he and Scanlan would have died as octogenarians; such advanced ages are more common in sheltered monasteries than in the strenuous and dangerous careers of kings. Both *Annals* and genealogies distinguish Scanlan mac Cennfaelad (died 646) from his distant cousin Scanlan mac Colmain, though Irish stories confuse them (cited Reeves, *Adamnan* 38).

The *Amra*, Keating and many other tales single out the three items on the agenda of the conference with which Columba was most closely concerned. He interceded for Colman; he persuaded King Aed, who was his cousin's son, to remit tribute from the Dal Riada colonists, though Dal Riada was still required to send contingents to the king's hosting; and he defended the poets. The large class of learned secular Irish were under attack for three main reasons. Many of the older generation of monks (e.g., *Vita* 'Colman of Dromore', 15 [*Sal.* 832], cited Reeves, *Adamnan* 80) feared and detested secular learning, for in their youth the druids had been redoubtable enemies of the Christians. Kings feared the satire of the poets. But the whole body of the professions was large; scholars made large demands, and were expensive to maintain. Secular hostility is noticed in the *Annals* record of the 'plundering of the poets' by King Brandub of Leinster, said to be half-brother to Aedan of Dal Riada, in 600. The annalist did not explain whether the plundering was as wholesale as Henry VIII's plundering of the English monasteries, or was merely a curtailment of their privileges; but whatever steps he took, they were drastic enough to merit a record in after ages. At Drumceat Aed is said to have proposed the abolition of their order, for 'nearly a third of the men of Ireland were attached to the *filid*'; but Columba's counter-proposals, that their numbers and stipends be limited by precise legal enactment, were accepted.

DUNNICHEN (*Dun Nechtain*). Watson (CPNS, 239) says 'Nechtan or *Neachdan* gives Dunnichen in Forfarshire'. This means 'Nechtan's fort'. He also suggests that Bunachtan in Stratherrick is from *Both Neachdain* = 'Neachtain's dwelling'.

See Marjorie Anderson, *Kings and Kingship in Early Scotland*, Edinburgh, 1973, 171-3.

R.B.W.

ECHWYD (*Yrechwydd*). BT 57, line 1: Uryen yr echwyd, haelaf dyn bedyd. 'Urien (of) yr *Echwyd*, the most liberal man in Christendom.'

Age (p. 232) gives: 'Urien of Echwyd, most liberal of Christian men', and notes the *Echwyd* is 'possibly Solway'.

But *echwyd* is the counterpart in Welsh of Latin *cataracta* (CATRAETH, *q.v.*), 'waterfall', this can be seen in another of the Taliesin poems, BT 68 (J. Morris Jones, 'Taliesin', *Y Cymmrodor* 28 [1918] 75.1).

Wylhawt eil echwyd yn torroed mynyd = 'Will weep like a cataract on the breasts of a mountain'.

Further BT 57, line 18: ends *rac vy yr echwyd*, meaning 'against the lord of *yr echwyd*' (*Udd yr Echwydd*).

This is equivalent to Latin 'princeps cataractae'. That this can be taken as the same *Catraeth* as that in the Gododdin poems is perhaps unlikely, for the north of Britain abounds in lively fast-flowing rivers, but the possibility remains. In any event Taliesin's *yr echwyd* is not in strict terms a place-name or territorial division; it is also very unlikely to be a reference to the Solway because the Solway is salt water and *echwyd* directly implies fresh water.

Source: Ifor Williams, *Canu Taliesin*, Cardiff, 1960, xxvii, revised J.E. Caerwyn Williams, *The Poems of Taliesin*, Dublin, 1968, xliii-xliv. R.B.W.

EIDYN (*Eitin*). In the *Gododdin* of Aneirin, *Eidin*, *Eidyn*, *Dineidin*, but *Caereidin* does not occur, thus disposing of any attempts to see the name in the Roman fort *Carriden* (which is stressed on the first syllable in any case). The author of the *Life* of St Morwenna tells us:

'*Dundene que Anglica lingua dicitur Edineburg*' (CA XXXVIII; FAB 1,85).

'*Dineidin* is in English *Edin-burgh*', and the name has nothing to do with Edwin as some have suggested.

ELMET (1). The southern portion of the West Riding. Bede *HE* 2,14. When the Mercian pagans burnt the royal vill at Campodonum (Slack, north-west of Huddersfield, *SE 0817*) in 632, its stone altar survived to be preserved at Thryduulf's monastery '*in silva Elmete*'. The returning English kings built a new vill '*in regione quae vocatur Loidis*'. The battle of the River Winwaed (location uncertain, perhaps the Went; *cf.* EPNS WR 7,35) was fought '*in regione Loidis*', and '*civitas Loidis*' was recovered by the British in the tenth century, v. *Cadroe* 17 (ASH 497, reproduced CPS 116). King Dynfwal (Donald) of Cumbria escorted Cadroe '*usque Loidam civitatem quae est confinium Normannorum atque Cumbrorum*' and handed him over to Gunderic, who took him to York to King Eric (Blood-Axe, 952-4, SC 952 MS. E [Laud] only; 954 E and D). The place is Leeds (as Stenton, *Anglo-Saxon England*, 357 note, and others) not the Lothians, which were neither a *civitas* nor the boundary of Eric's kingdom of York; the territories of Earl Oswulf of Bamburgh then separated Norse York from the Lothians. The British may have retained the reconquered territory for some time, since the English recovery of York in 954 was immediately followed by the long uneventful reign of Edgar. The king of Cumbria was among those who are said to have acknowledged the supremacy of Edgar 20 years later, and to have rowed him on the Dee. Since Edgar was only 12 on his accession, and the accounts of his reign give no hint of northern wars, the British will either have lost their Yorkshire lands at the time of Eric's fall, to an unrecorded local Northumbrian expedition, or retained them.

In the Tribal Hidage (BCS 297) the Elmed Saetna were reckoned at 600 hides (*cf.* **T**). The Leeds-Loidis names stretch south-east from Leeds to the Aire, the names Barwick, Sherburn, etc., in Elmet north-east from Leeds towards York, summarised EPNS WR 7,26, where the Becca Banks between Leeds and Tadcaster may mark its north-eastern border. The Loidis are probably a people, Elmet the region they inhabited, which is likely to have comprehended the whole of the southern West Riding, later restricted to the country between Leeds and the Roman north road.

During Aethelferth's supremacy, an exiled Deiran prince, Edwin's nephew, Hereric, father of Hilda, was there sheltered, but poisoned (Bede *HE* 4,23). On his return, Edwin 'occupied Elmet and expelled Ceretic, king of that country' (Nennius 63; *cf.* ACm 616, *Ceretic obiit*). It is likely that a British-speaking population remained a considerable time.

(2) The district name Elvet is recorded elsewhere. Elfed was the name of the easternmost commote of Demetia (Dyfed) (HW 266, *cf.* 751). The Elvet of Madauc in the Gododdin (CA 1179) better fits a northern context. In place-names, Elvet is identical with OE *elfetu*, swan, and is normally so treated by EPNS, except for the West Riding Elmet. But Altham, Lancs. (*SD 7732*), between Burnley and Blackburn, Elvetham in 1150, cannot be, as DEPN 8, 'a homestead inhabited by swans' (Ekwall emends to *hamm* [meadow] to avoid the absurdity, but hardly correctly, since *hamm* has 'no clear example at all in the north country', EPNS 1,230). Similarly, Elvet in Durham, parish name (*Aelfetee* SC 762, *Aelvet, c.*1085, *Elvete, c.*1195, *Elvet*, 1225, containing Elvet Hall from the fourteenth century) without suffix cannot be 'Swan'; the single added -e does not make it Elfet-ea, 'swan island', any more than Bede's 'Elmete' makes the West Riding Elmet an island; nor is the parish an island. Gwallauc, apparently of Stirlingshire, was a 'judge' in Elvet. The meaning of a word that named a district in several parts of Britain is unexplained.

ETELICIAUN, the cantref between Gwynnlliauc and Gwent, LL 247, 273; *cf.* LBS 2, 20, 5, 4. Etelic and Eteliciaun occur in v. *Kebi* 6-8, in the later fifth century, and therefore placed earlier than Paul(inus), Merchiaun and Gwynlliw. The personal name Etelic remained in use, and is, for example, borne by several different persons in LL (158; 179 b; 191). The cantref includes the two places (*ST 3796*) and nearby Llan Deverguir (probably Tredunnock, St Andrew's [*ST 3794*]), said to have been given by Etelic to Cybi. No other rulers are named; the cantref later formed part of Gwent. Whether it passed early to Gwent, or was at one time obeyed by Gwynnliw, is unknowable.

FETHANLEA. 'Ceawlin and Cutha fought the British at the place called Fethanlea; and Cutha was killed; and Ceawlin, having captured many *tuns* and much booty, returned to his own (territory) in anger.' SC 584.

Stenton, *Anglo-Saxon England*, 29, cautiously observed that 'A wood called *Fethelee*, mentioned in a twelfth-century document relating to Stoke Lyne (*SP 5628*) in north-east Oxfordshire bore the only name so far observed which corresponds to the *Fethan leag* of the *Chronicle*'. Ant. 17, 1945, 61, etc., make the identification positive. But the archaic OE *Fetha* is not easy to parallel in place-names, and other names can be observed. The old name of Hereford and its territory (HW 282) was Fernleag, and the difference between Feanleag and Fer(a)nleag is scribal.

If Ceawlin fought the British near Oxford in 584, then the British of the Midlands or of Gloucester had recovered their strength; or he faced invaders from the midland Cornovii. But since the English are said in Welsh texts to have campaigned on the Wye about the years 580-5 Hereford seems the more probable identification.

FINN'S BURG (Finns-buruh, *Finnsburg Fragment 36*).

Scene of the battle between Finn Folcwalding, king of the FRISIANS (*q.v.*) and the Danes, headed by Hnaef, and after his death by Hengest, *Beowulf*, 1086 ff; *The fight at Finnsburg* (editions and translations listed in the bibliography to R.W. Chambers, *Beowulf*, third edition, Cambridge, 1959, 557 ff; 585 ff; 599 ff).

The interpretation of the saga is fully discussed in Chambers' *Beowulf*, 245 ff, *cf.* 288-9, and 543-6; *cf. Age*, 266.

Beowulf summarises the entire saga, while the *Fragment* preserves 48 lines from the middle of the story. Though much of the detail presents unsolved problems, the outline of the story is clear. Finn had in his service a body of Jutish (Eoten) settlers. He was visited by his brother-in-law, Hnaef, son of Hoc, king of the Healfdene or Half-Danes. Fighting broke out between Finn's men and Hnaef's. Hnaef was killed, and his thane Hengest assumed command of his men, but the majority of Finn's men fell, and the Danes retained possession of the hall and *burh*. The *Fragment* describes an unsuccessful Frisian counter-attack that failed to recover the *burh* after five days' assault. The two sides then reached agreement: the Danes evacuated the Frisian *burh*, but were given a hall, on similar terms to the Jutes, and entered Frisian service, receiving the same gifts as the Frisians themselves received from Finn; and any Frisian who jeered at the Danes for entering the service of the leader who had killed their king was to be killed, as a potential author of renewed hostilities. The Danes then dispersed for the winter to the homes and hall (*hea-burh*) assigned to them, but Hengest remained with Finn, secretly plotting revenge. Two of the Danish leaders, Guthlaf and Oslaf (Ordlaf) sailed home, reported the struggle, and returned with reinforcements headed by their nephew, Hunlafing, who killed Finn in his hall, in the next year, and returned home, taking with them Finn's Danish-born widow. The story does not relate whether or not Hengest accompanied them.

The texts do not indicate whether Finn ruled the Greater Frisians about Leeuwarden and Groningen or the Lesser Frisians between the Rhine and the Zuyder Zee, or both; and therefore gives no indication of where Finnsburg was. Chambers created a non-existent problem by a strange misinterpretation: the text states that after the fighting the Danish warriors left Finn's hall to see Friesland, their homes and high-town (*hea-burh*), the individual farmsteads and collective hall that had been assigned to them by the treaty; but, for reasons unexplained, Chambers understands their *hea-burh* to be Finn's burg, in flat contradiction to the text, and therefore assumes that Finn's Burg lay outside Friesland.

The location is suggested by the archaeological evidence. In the neighbourhood of Leeuwarden, among the Greater Frisians, a few graves contain early cruciform brooches, including the Beetgum-Dorchester type, also found in Jutish and Anglian graves in Schleswig and Denmark, but which has not been found in any Anglo-Saxon graves in England, whose earliest cruciform brooches are of the next typological stage. These brooches therefore date to the decades immediately before the migration of Hengest to Britain, within the period 390×430, and probably fell later rather than earlier within that period, since the Jutish Leeuwarden burials also include types found in Britain.

Jutish settlement is not attested in any other part of Frisia. The texts assert the presence of Jutes near to Finn's Burg in Frisia in Hengest's youth, immediately before his migration to Britain, at a date in or about the 420s. The brooches locate Jutish settlement, about the period 410×430, in the Leeuwarden area. It is therefore probable that Finn's Burg lay in or near Leeuwarden, and that Finn ruled the Greater Frisians. He may or may not have ruled the Lesser Frisians as well.

FORTRENN, Fortriu. One of the seven provinces of the Pictish king-lists, CPS 4, 25, 323, 396; Strathearn, the valley running eastward to Perth. It appears to have included Menteith, the upper Forth, whenever that region, in British 'beyond Bannauc', the territory at Cauus, was in Pictish possession.

The name is plainly that of the Verturiones, applied by Ammianus to the southern PICTS (*q.v.*); Watson, CPNS, 48, 68, *cf.* 113.

From the time of Bruide f Bili (670-91) the kings of the Picts are regularly called kings of Fortrenn in the *Annals*; *cf.* also references in CPS index.

FRISIANS. The name has many meanings. Tacitus distinguished the Frisii Maiores of the north, between the Zuyder Zee and the modern German border on the Ems, from the Frisii Minores, between the Zuyder Zee and the northern arm of the Rhine, about Utrecht. In Carolingian times, the Frisii Minores appear above all as traders centred on Dorstad near Utrecht, whilst the Frisii Maiores spread far to the east, so that their former home, west of the Ems, became Westfriesland, now in the Netherlands, with Ostfriesland in modern Germany. But the modern Dutch administrative system divides the region of Friesland into three administrative provinces: Groningen, near the German border on the coast; Friesland, centred about Leeuwarden, on the coast; and the Zuyder Zee, and Drente, stretching inland. The words are here used with these meanings: Friesland is a sub-division of Westfriesland, and not, as might more naturally be expected, a wider area including including Ost- and Westfriesland.

See especially, P.J.C. Boeles, *Friesland tot de 12de Eeuw*, 1951. The Roman 'Frisian period' ends *c.* A.D. 400, perhaps slightly earlier on the dating which German scholars assign to the same vessels. The Frisii were still regarded as part of the Roman province in the later second century (*cf.* e.g., *Année Epigraphique*, 1964, s.v.), but it is rarely possible to determine which Frisians are meant; and no frontier works are known to have defined or protected the borders of the greater Frisians. For the concentration of imports (especially Samian ware and figurines of the second century) see the map in Eggers' *Der römische Import im freien Germanien* (Hamburg, 1951). The Frisians were shortly followed by the Saxons and the Jutes.

The cruciform brooches begin slightly earlier than those found in the first cemeteries in England since they include series 3 (Witmarsum or Beetgum type), but not series 2 (Dorchester, dated 390×410), whereas series 4 (Åberg I and II) are the earliest found in Anglo-Saxon cemeteries in England. The Saxon pottery of Frisia covers a wider area than the brooches; it begins certainly no later, and probably slightly earlier. The Franks appear to have mastered Frisia by *c.* 500.

GIUDI URBS, *Iudeu*.

Nennius, Chapter 64: '*usque ad urbem quae vocatur Iudeu*', part of a probably confused and corrupt passage reporting an expedition by Penda *c.* 654 'to the city which is called Iudeu'. Bede *HE* 1,12 says (in a different context) that the Firth of Forth has *in medio sui urbem Giudi*, literally 'in the midst is the city of *Giudi*', but *medio* in this case could be translated as 'halfway along', giving, as P. Hunter Blair suggested ('The Origins of Northumbria', *Archaeologia Aeliana*, fourth series, 25 [1947] 27 f.), Cramond or Inveresk. On the other hand, and perhaps more persuasively, Castle Rock, Stirling, from a distance appears to be an island arising from the midst of the Forth; thus *urbs Giudi* is perhaps Stirling.

See Angus Graham, 'Giudi', *Antiquity*, 33 (1959), 63-5; K.H. Jackson, 'On the Northern British Section in Nennius', *Celt and Saxon*, ed. N.K. Chadwick, Cambridge, 1963, 36-8.

GWYNEDD, north Wales.

'Cantiori(x) hic iacit venedotis cive fuit consobrino magli (e)t magistrati' (ECMW 103, CIIC 394, Penmachno).

The name is an adjective (Jackson, LHEB, 188, n.1), the substantive being Veneda (LHEB 655) for the country, for the citizen Venedos, Latin Venetus. The Veneti also lived in north Italy, to name Venice, and in Brittany, to name Vannes. Connection of the name with the Irish *fine*, family (HW 40), is dubious. The name is confined to the north, not found in other areas settled by the Votadini, and is therefore unlikely to have been imported by them.

The full extent of medieval Gwynedd is from the Dee to Anglesey, divided into Gwynedd *uwch* Conwy and *is* Conwy, beyond and this side (east of) the Conway. The name attaches more strongly to the western portion, Snowdonia; the alternative name of the eastern portion, the 'middle country', implies that it lay between Powys and Gwynedd proper.

The principal people of Roman north Wales, the only *civitas* known to Ptolemy, were the Ordovices. Their name probably survives in the commote of Ardudwy, south of the mountains, and Traeth Mawr, in the north of the modern county of Merioneth. It probably did not include Cardigan. ECMW 126, CIIC 354 Penbryn, between Cardigan and Aberystwyth 'Corbalengi iacit Ordous' commemorates an Ordovix (Jackson LHEB, 618, 637), and when a man's nationality is inscribed on his tombstone, the usual reason is that he was a foreigner. It probably did include much of Caernarvonshire, surviving in Rhyd Orddwy, Din Orddwig, etc.: John Rhys, *Celtic Britain*, London, 1882, 299-300.

The large Roman *civitates* commonly included numerous smaller constituent peoples: Ptolemy's place-names mention a couple of peoples within Brigantian territory; Caesar names a few small peoples in the Catavellaunian area; and Tacitus, *Annales* 12, 32, names in eastern Gwynedd the Decangi (*cf.* Decanti, ACm 822; *cf.* the Decantae of Ptolemy's Scotland, of modern Degannwy; and Tegeingl, Flintshire). The names of most of these early smaller peoples are not recorded. The Veneti were probably the earlier, pre-Roman natives of all or part of Snowdonia, incorporated by the Roman administration within the territory of the Ordovices. The Penmachno inscription (late fifth-century) might normally be held to imply that Cantiorix was a foreigner, but its emphasis on citizenship and magistracy is probably intended to distinguish a native citizen from the immigrant Votadini; the Penbryn inscription, however, comparatively early fifth-century (LHEB 619), was probably set up before the Votadini recovered the area. It is unlikely that either stone needed to distinguish natives from Irish settlers; the name and Latin characters sufficed for that purpose.

[But *see* T.M. Charles-Edwards, 'Some Celtic Kinship Terms', BBCS 24 (1970-2), 117 ff, where he argues that *Gwynedd* is indeed from Brythonic *wenya*, an exact cognate of Old Irish *fine*, 'kindred'. The Ordovices have little to do with it, and indeed they may not have been in north-west Wales at all: *see* R.B. White, 'Excavations at Brithdir . . . ', *Monographs and Collections*, 1, Cambrian Archaeological Association, Cardiff, 1978, 46.]

ICELAND. The *Vita Prima Sancti Brendani*, which is earlier than the celebrated *Navigatio* (voyage), has the saint searching for a place to withdraw in retirement rather than voyaging in search of an Earthly Paradise. That other monks or saints also did this is shown by the number of them recorded on islands, including Iceland. The *Landnámabók* speaks of Irish books, bells and bachalls (para. 41) which were left behind in Iceland by the monks when the Norsemen expelled them, and at least

one monk (Ailbe) expressed the desire to withdraw 'ad insulam Tile', to the island of Thule (Shetland).
Source. Charles Plummer, *Vitae Sanctorum Hiberniae*, Oxford, 1910, Vol. 1, cxxii.
R.B.W.

ICHT. *Muir nIcht*, the Ictian sea, is an Irish name for the English Channel. Niall Noigiallach is said by the 10th-century Irish poet Cinaed ua hArtacain to have been slain on the last of his seven raids on Britain *os muing Mara Icht* ('above the waves of the Ictian sea'). Icht (*pace* Morris, *Age*, 155) is not Wight (*Vectis Insula*), but St Michael's Mount (*Ictis Insula*). Diodorus (5.22.2, 4) says that the people of Belerium (*Land's End*) took wagonloads of tin at low tide to the island Ictis.
See *The Oxford Classical Dictionary*, second edn., ed. Hammond and Scullard, Oxford, 1970; Byrne, F.J., *Irish Kings and High Kings*, London, 1973, 87. R.B.W.

JUTES. The inhabitants of Jutland, modern mainland Denmark, probably the Eudoses of Tacitus's *Germania* 40. Of Kent, Wight and the coast opposite Wight, Bede *HE* 1,15; of the New Forest, Florence of Worcester, '*in provincia Iutarum in Nova Foresta*' (ed. Thorpe, 1, 276; *cf*. 2, 44-45 *s.a.* 1100). The ornament of the Isle of Wight cemeteries contains much that is proper to Kent and to Sussex; and this ornament extends after *c*.550 to the Salisbury area and East Shefford, near Wantage.

Thirty years ago it was widely held that the Jutes came not from Jutland, but from the middle Rhine. This view, ably argued by J.E.A. Jolliffe, *Pre-Feudal England*, Oxford, 1933, rested on a disregard of archaeological data: since the most striking ornaments of Kent are of Frankish origin, therefore Bede was mistaken (or else the Angles and the Saxons must be transported to the Rhine in saying that their home lay beyond the Angles). It was not appreciated that the Frankish ornament first appears in quantity early in the sixth century, nearly a century after the arrival of the Jutes in England. The novel fashions affected by young women at the beginning of the sixth century do not prejudice the nationality of their great-grandfathers. The theory was backed by the fact that partible inheritance prevailed both among the Franks and the Jutes, with a wide range of agricultural and social habits that derive therefrom; but it was not observed that similar customs also prevailed among the British, and are traceable in English Norfolk. It is natural that indigenous British customs should be most prominent in the areas that were taken over earliest by the English, as going concerns, their native economy not disrupted by the fifth-century wars. It was also stressed that both Kentish and Frankish laws reckon wergilds by the short hundreds, in contrast to the Saxon long hundred; but not adequately stressed that the earliest extant Kentish laws were set down after two generations of Frankish influence in Kent, and put into writing by clerics trained in Frankish lands, at a moment when coinage was a recent novelty, itself derived from a Frankish model. Like many short-lived views, the 'Rhineland Jutes' have survived the basis on which they were built; for they were adopted in Sir Frank Stenton's *Anglo-Saxon England* in the Oxford History (second edn., 1947, p.15). More recent attempts to people southern England with fifth-century Franks seem unlikely to be so widely endorsed.

LANGOBARDI, Long Beards, Lombards.
Located on the Lower Elbe in the first century B.C. and A.D., Strabo 7,70. Tacitus, *Germania* 40; *Annales*, 2,45; 11,17, etc.; Ptolemy 2,22,9;17; Velleius Paterculus 2,106, etc. Originally emigrants from Scandinavia, Paulus Diaconus, *Historia Langobardorum*; *cf*. Jordanes, *Getica*.

The fiercest of the German peoples, though small, according to Valleius and

Tacitus; all early-empire sources agree in placing them on the Elbe above the estuary, but disagree about the extent of territory they ruled, and on which bank of the river it lay. These contradictions may reflect the extent of their dominion over the Cherusci and other neighbours at different periods rather than movements of their own. They long retained the marks of their origin among the Anglo-Saxon group of peoples: as late as Carolingian times, their laws and their language were closer to the English than to the continental Germans, and contemporaries remarked that their costume was Anglo-Saxon, unlike that of Germans of Europe (Paulus Diaconus 4,22). The names of their best-known kings, latinised as Audoin and Alboin, appear in their native Germanic in the familiar spelling of Eadwine and Aelfwine (*Widsith* 70, 74, 117). A part of the population, traditionally a third (Paulus 1,2), emigrated in the second century to Bohemia and Moravia, Pannonia and (568) Italy, their movement spanning four centuries; in each of these areas, pottery and brooches akin to those of the Anglo-Saxons, but diverging from the common stock, are reported at the right dates. To Bohemia and to Italy (Paulus 2,6; 3,5-7; Greg. Tur. *HF* 4,42) they summoned substantial contingents of Saxons. They also shared the Saxon gods. Nothing further is heard of the remainder who did not emigrate in the second century; some may have reinforced the emigrants at a later date; others may or may not be equated with the Heathobarden, Hundingas, or other named peoples of the lower Elbe, but it would appear probable that the remnant merged in the general body of the Saxons.

LEITHRIG. Battle of Aedan of Dal Riada, 593. The site is unidentified; a possibility is Carleatheran in the Gargunnock hills (*NS 6891*). The village of Gargunnock looks as though it may conceal a British Conoc; since the name is not usual among the north British, it is more likely to be that of a saint than of a settler chief.

A principal residence of Urien of Reged, CT 4,21; 7,19; 8,27; 9,10; 10,8. The name is identical with Lyvennet, now the name of a small river that runs north to join the Eden (*NY 6126*) a mile and a half from the Roman fort of Kirkby Thore, south of Penrith: *cf.* Hogg, Ant. 20, 1946, 210, whence CT, p. 47, Jackson Ant. 29, 1955, 83, EPNS Westmorland, etc. Kirkby Thore seems a more likely centre for a king as powerful as Urien than any of the uncomfortable villages and earthworks near Crosby Ravensworth *NY 6214*, higher up the river, Ewe Close, Cow Green, etc., suggested by Hogg. It is possible that the site straddling the Roman road at Ewe Close (*NY 6013*) might prove to be more substantial, but its position makes it a place of refuge for an insecure leader rather than the seat of the king of a large territory.

LLYDAW, latinised Letavia, normally Brittany, Armorica. Medieval imagination held that the people were 'silent' because the British killed the men, and cut out the tongues of the women lest they should corrupt their speech (*Dream of Maxen*, conclusion, etc.). Silent, or dumb, is a normal description of foreigners who do not speak one's own language; Nemets is the normal word for German in the Slavonic language, from *nemoe*, dumb. The Irish occasionally used Letha for Gaul and Italy; *Bordgail Letha*, Bordeaux, *Bethu Phâtraic* (VT 238); Auxerre in southern Letha, Fiac's Hymn 5 (VT 404) glossed in the Notes (VT 418) as *Letha in Latium qui Italia dicitur'*, as well as for Brittany '*Bretnaib Armuirc Letha*', Notes (VT 412), Britons of Armorican Letavia. The commentator tied himself in knots because he knew that Auxerre was in Gaul, not Italy, and devised a strained explanation, implying that the word was ill understood, and therefore a British usage. The British usage implies that the native Armorican language was not intelligible to the British.

LONDON. In the enormous quantity of Roman objects discovered in London, the proportion that belongs to the later fourth century is exceptionally small. Their absence is not adequately explained by the removal of later levels by medieval and later cellars and pits; no later interference was governed by a set rule that it should halt at a mid-fourth-century level. The absence of late finds is not confined to the city. On the Verulamium road, the intervening town of *Sulloniacae* (Brockley Hill) ended as soon, or sooner on the Ermine Street. Extensive excavations at Braughing have uncovered great quantities of early fourth-century material, nothing later than *c*.350, and the chance finds at the three Roman towns between Braughing and London have also ample early fourth-century objects, nothing later. But from Wimpole and Baldock northward, even small quantities of finds regularly include a few later fourth-century coins. This very local lack of late objects cannot be attributed to enemy raiders since even on the coastal sites exposed to enemy attack the towns and villages continued to use late fourth-century objects after the open country villas ended.

Natural causes are evidenced. From the middle of the fourth century onward, profound changes occurred in the water table of the Atlantic and Mediterranean coasts. Exact dates are not known, but the Thames level rose by a dozen or more feet; the trouble began in the later second century, and was at first overcome (R. Merrifield, *The Roman City of London*, London, 1965, 46-7). In Norfolk, and perhaps on the Dutch coast, severe floods date to the fourth century. A necessary consequence of the rise of the Thames level was a corresponding spread of the River Lea, whose bank the north road follows. London, of course, continued to exist, but no longer with its past affluence. Economic changes contributed to lessen its importance. The sharp increase in Cotswold wealth in the fourth century shifted the centre of economic strength to the west. Though the port of London remained an important outlet to Europe, internal communications no longer depended so much on London.

To some extent, Colchester seems to have benefited from the troubles of London. It has many late objects. On the road westward from Colchester to Bishops Stortford, all known Roman towns and villages have a number of late coins and, more emphatically than on any other road, all the Roman sites became modern towns and villages – Coggeshall, Braintree, Dunmow, Takeley – and no Roman sites are known except the modern towns. The north road shows evidence of continued use only after the Colchester road joins it. It is therefore likely that much of the trade despatched to the north passed through Colchester, while much of the rich country trade will have been attracted to Poole. London will have henceforth depended mainly on trade between the Thames Valley and the north Downs and the continent, while the astonishing wealth of late Roman Richborough suggests that much of the passenger and light goods traffic was diverted there. The communication of Kent and Sussex with the north may have been diverted through Richborough and Colchester.

The fate of London is not known. Negative evidence is strong enough to show that though the English were numerous in Surrey, eight or ten miles south of the city, they did not yet inhabit London. If any people lived there, they were British. It is not yet possible to recognise the archaeological traces of the sixth-century British, except in the west, where they imported foreign pottery, or used other artefacts that can be associated therewith, and the absence of archaeological evidence gives no indication as to whether London was densely populated or totally uninhabited. Any view on sixth-century London is therefore necessarily a guess founded on no positive evidence. Since the British were still able to put armies in the field in Wiltshire and Bedfordshire, and possibly to attempt a feeble defence of

Colchester, it is not unreasonable to guess that at least a small population survived and remained independent until English armies appeared in 568. Since the archaeological evidence suggests that London was already in decline in the fourth century, it would not be reasonable to suppose a large population in the sixth. It has been argued that the early medieval episcopal boundaries perpetuate a Roman *territorium*. If so, some kind of urban authority must have survived until the second Saxon revolt to preserve them, but the assumption of a continuing *territorium* is itself a guess.

LUITCOET. Identified as Lichfield and perhaps more closely as the Roman station at Wall. The words mean 'grey wood', and this is thus a topographical description and not a specific habitation site name. Some early forms are:

	Letoceto	4th cen.	Antonine Itinerary
	Lyccidfelth	c.730	Bede
	Luccidfeld	c.730	Bede
	Liccetfield	c.890	OE Bede
(Caer)	Luitcoet	9th cen.	Canu Llywarch Hen.

Modern Welsh Llwyd = 'grey'; coed = 'wood'; and the English element 'feld' means 'open ground'; and so the present name Lichfield means 'the open ground in the Grey Wood'. Other 'Letoceto' names in England include Litchett (Hants.) and Lytchett (Dorset).

See Margaret Gelling, *Signposts to the Past*, 1978, 40, 58-9.   R.B.W.

MAES COGWY. Nennius 65 says in his account of Penda that '*ipse fecit bellum Cocboy in quo cecidit Eoua*'. This is the same battle called *Maserfelth* by Bede (*HE* 3, 9) at which Oswald was killed. The name Oswestry (modern Welsh Croes Oswallt) means 'Oswald's tree' ('Oswald's cross'). The fort 'Old Oswestry' on the outskirts of the present town is called *Caer Ogyrfan* by Thomas Pennant (TW 1, 258) which he notes as 'from Ogyrfan, a hero co-existent with Arthur'. Perhaps a local tale used some form of Cogwy, assuming it to be a personal name and associating it with the hillfort?

Nennius's *Cocboy* presents no difficulty as it would give *Cogfwy* or *Cogwy* in Middle Welsh (Ifor Williams, 'A Reference to the Nennian Bellum Cocboy', BBCS, 3, 62). The poet Cynddelw (fl. 1150-1200) writes of *Gweith Gogwy ... pann gyrchwt ... yg gyuranc Powys, pobyl degyn ac Oswallt uab Oswi aelwyn.* 'The battle of Cogwy when attack was made in the conflict between Powys, a stubborn people, and Oswald, son of the fair-browed Oswy'. The poet here mistakes Oswald as son rather than brother of Oswy.

See K.H. Jackson, 'On the Northern British Section in Nennius', *Celt and Saxon*, ed. N.K. Chadwick, Cambridge, 1963, 39.   R.B.W.

MAGIOVINIUM. Dropshort, near Bletchley, Buckinghamshire, named in the Antonine Itinerary in two forms, viz. *Magiovinio (iter vi, viii)* and *Magiovinto (iter ii)*. The first element is straightforward: *magio 'great' (*cf.* Latin *magnus*). The meaning of *vinio*, *vinto*, is obscure, but may have something to do with *Vinovia*.

See A.L.F. Rivet, 'The British Section of the Antonine Itinerary', *Britannia*, 1, 1970, 76.   R.B.W.

MAG ROTH, or Mag Rath. Moira (*J 1560*), south-west of Belfast, on the borders of Down and Antrim. Battle of 639. Domnall, king of Ireland beat Congal Caech of the Ulaid and Domnall Brecc of Dal Riada, in Adomnán v. *Columbae* 3,5. The story of the battle exists in many MSS., three of which were published by John O'Donovan in 1842 (*Fled Duin na nGed and Caith Muige Rath*). A shorter version, without translation is printed in *Ériu* 5, 1911, 323-327, and substantial extracts from the longer versions were printed by Anderson, *Sources*, 1, 162-3, and by A.S. Green, *History of the Irish State to 1014*, London 1925, 167-70. Despite accurate facts, it remains a romance. The causes of the war London 1925, are the negligence of Domnall's bee-keeper, and Congal's offensive table manners.

MANAU (*Manaw*) **GODODDIN**
Manaw Gododdin (*Nennius* ch. 62), i.e., a part of *Gododdin* was particularised as *Manaw* and qualified by the more general territorial unit *Gododdin*, perhaps to distinguish it from Manaw itself ('The Isle of Man'). The connection, if any, between *Manaw* and *Manaw Gododdin* remains obscure.

See K.H. Jackson, *The Gododdin*, Edinburgh, 1969, 71 ff. R.B.W.

METCAUD. *cf.* **A** 635 Inis Medgoeth (Metgoit) founded by Aedan (bishop of Lindisfarne), FM 627.

MEVANIAN ISLANDS. A late Roman *Periplus* (I), MHB xix, '*Huic (Hiberniae) etiam Mervania insula proxima est, et ipso spatio non parva, solo commoda, aeque a Scotorum, gentibus colitur*'. The meaning is clearly the Isle of Man. Bede *HE* 2,5, *cf.* 2,9: '*Mevanias Brettonum insulas quae inter Hiberniam et Britanniae sitae sunt*'. The plural probably means that Bede applied the name Mevania to Anglesey as well as Man, doubtless through similarity of spelling, perhaps with Mon (*Menaw*), latinised as Menavia.

MIATHI. Cassius Dio, 75, 6, 4 (*c.* A.D. 200): 'The two most important peoples of the (north) British are the Caledonii and the Maeatae; the names of the other peoples have almost all been absorbed into theirs. The Maeatae live near the wall that divides the island into two, the Caledonii beyond them. Both inhabit rough mountains with marshy ground between them; neither have walled places or towns or cultivated lands. They live by pasture, hunting and on a kind of fruit with a hard shell. They eat no fish, though their waters are full of many species. They live in tents, unclothed and barefoot. They have their women in common, and raise all their children. Their government is democratic, and they delight in raids and plunder. They fight from chariots, and have small fast horses. Their infantry move fast, and are enduring. Their weapons are a shield and a short spear with bronze knob on the butt end . . . '

'They can stand hunger, thirst and all other hardships. They dive into the marshes, and can hold out for several days with only their heads above water. In the forests they live on bark and roots; and, in particular, they prepare a food that saves them from hunger and thirst, if they eat a piece no bigger than a bean.'

Aedan of Dal Riada lost two of his sons in the '*bellum Miathorum*', Adomnán, v. *Columbae* 1,8-9; the same sons were killed at a battle in Circinn, **A** 599. The name is preserved by the hill named Dumyat (Dun Myat) (*NS 8397*), north-east of Stirling, and Myot Hill (*NS 7882*), west of Denny, five or six miles south of Stirling, Watson CPNS 59. The Miathi are therefore the principal people of the southern 'Picts'. In Dio's time and in Adomnán's the name probably still comprehended all Circinn and Fortrenn. Since they had absorbed other peoples, and are themselves not known to Ptolemy, they may have originally been the inhabitants of a smaller area. The names indicate that the Stirling area was not in, but on the borders of, their territory, when the names were first given; such ethnic names for places of isolated hills normally indicate that the people who held the hill were strangers to those who gave the name.

MOEL FENLLI. The name of a hillfort in Clwyd, near Ruthin. Moel (literally 'bare, rounded [hill]') is a common element in hillfort names (Moel Hiraddog, Moel-y-Gest, Moel-y-Gaer, etc.), but not exclusively so (Moel Faban, Moel Siabod). Benlli Gawr (Benlli the Giant) is a prominent figure in Middle Welsh Arthurian tales, but whether the traditional name of the hillfort embodies a genuine 'historical' connection or not remains doubtful indeed. Arthur, for instance, can be found in the names of a whole range of features of the Welsh landscape:

Ogof ('cave'), *llech* ('slab'), *maen* ('stone'), *carreg* ('stone'), *bwrdd* ('table'), *buarth* ('enclosure'), *bedd* ('grave'), *cist* ('chest') + *Arthur* are all common, as well as *Moel Arthur*.

See M. Richards, 'Arthurian Onomastics', *Transactions of the Honourable Society of Cymmrodorion*, 1969, 250-64.　　　　　　　　　　　　　　　　　　　　　　　R.B.W.

MOEL-Y-GERAINT. See Moel Fenlli (above) and reference cited.　　　R.B.W.

MYRGINGAS, *Widsith* 4, 23, 42, 84, 96, bordered the Angli on the south, on the Eider, at least near its mouth; and should correspond to at least the western part of Tischler's *Ost Holsteinischergruppe*, Genrich's *Fuhmlsbutteler Kreis* and the southern half of his *Ursaechisches Gebiet*. The name is plainly a patronymic, and the people who use it will have had an ethnic name; the name of the Maurungani given in the 'Ravenna Cosmography' and of Morungen (*cf.* Malone, *Widsith*, 176) is not near enough to warrant identification.

NORTH BRITONS. In the two centuries which lie between the last consular of Britannia Maxima and the first king of a united Northumbria, the political geography of northern Britain must be deduced from the names provided by the genealogies of the Men of the North, the dates set down by the annalists and hagiographers against their names, and the indications of place afforded by the poems and remembered in the Triads.

Bonedd Gwyr y Gogledd lists six dynasties derived from Coel Hen, followed by five derived from Dyfnwal Hen, with a note of an apparently unrelated Cornish prince thrown in to make the round dozen. Annals and poems provide secure dates for most of the princes who ruled in the last quarter of the sixth century, and locations for some of them. The regions and places named refer to the centres of their authority, but only exceptionally give any hint as to its wider extent. From what we know of the history of Wales and of Europe in the same age, and the bewildering series of battles involving the rise and fall of more powerful rulers and dynasties in northern Britain, it is to be assumed that the extent of territory varied from generation to generation, almost from year to year. It would be quite idle to transpose to this age the concept of stable kingdoms with defined frontiers proper to earlier and later ages. The territory which obeyed a ruler was that in which he could demand entertainment or tribute from his warband without arousing effective resistance; and that varied with his own standing at the moment of the particular demand, and with the degree to which external or internal dangers impressed upon the lesser lairds the wisdom of unity and obedience.

The location of Dyfnwal's power is quite certain. His was the long-lived dynasty of Strathclyde, whose seat was the formidable and fantastic rock of Dumbarton below Glasgow. His grandson, Tutagual Tutclit, seems to incorporate the name of the river in his nickname, and Tutagual's son Riderch is explicitly described by Adomnán, born some 20 years after his death, as ruler of the Rock of Clyde. From another son of Dyfnwal descend the long line of well-recorded kings of Strathclyde, down to the end of the kingdom in the tenth century.

The later kings do not figure in the northern genealogy, whose record ceases in all cases before the end of the sixth century. They are set down in **G** Harleian genealogy 5, which, unlike the northern list, traces the ancestry of Dyfnwal to his fourth-century ancestors. Dyfnwal's father or grandfather was Ceretic Guletic whose fleet raided across the narrow seas to northern Ireland in the mid-fifth century in the time of Patrick. Dyfnwal's own date is the late fifth century, and he ruled at Dumbarton at the time of Arthur's triumph or not long before.

Other traditions in the Harleian and Jesus College genealogical collections trace Dyfnwal's ancestry back to Magnus Maximus and give him a 'brother', also named Tutagual. This chieftain is presumably the Tuduvallus who was believed to have granted Ninian the site of Whithorn in Galloway early in the fifth century. The location has some support from another genealogy (Harleian genealogy 16), wherein the name of his 'grandson' is replaced by the name Cathen, elsewhere recorded only as the name of the subordinate of king Morcant who expelled Kentigern from the region of his early labours in the mid-sixth century. This area ranges from Cumberland and the Carlisle region north-eastwards to the Lothians. At the end of the century Cathen's grandson, Run, seems to have lost Dumfries to the rulers of Carlisle. These traditions enshrine a belief that the line of Tutagual was dominant in the extreme south-west of Scotland from Galloway to Dumfries.

These dynasties lie beyond the Cheviots. The main weight of the house of Coel lies in northern England, within the Roman diocese. Under his sons, about the time of the Saxon revolt, when the Saxon genealogists remembered that Soemil first separated Deira from Bernicia, his line split into two, the dynasty of Keneu and that of the Morcants. A century later Keneu's inheritance was split among half-a-dozen different rulers. Some of them are indisputably located. Urien ruled Reged, a territory which included Carlisle and Catterick, but only later acquired Dumfries. How far south it stretched is not known. Urien's father, (Kyn)March, son of Merchiaun, was one of the three princes who owned a fleet together with Geraint of Cornwall and the unknown Gwenwynwyn. The ports on which this fleet was based must have included either the Cumberland harbours, or Lancaster, or both. Kynvarch's brother Elidir was killed in a raid, apparently without allies, on north Wales, and it may therefore be that Elidir's territory was south Lancashire, bordering on the north Welsh power, their father Merchiaun's territory including the whole east coast from the Mersey to the Solway. Elidir's son, Llywarch, boasted a lifelong guest friendship in the Cornovian territory of Shropshire and Cheshire.

The collateral line of Keneu's other descendants includes two prominent 'brothers', Eleuther and Pabo. Eleuther of the Great Army, apparently also called the Sorrow of Deira and Bernicia, father of Peredur Steel Arms, (son) of York, was evidently originally remembered as a prince whose seat was York, heir of the greater part of what remained of the command of the *Dux Britanniarum*. The genealogist certainly regarded the common ancestor of the kings of Reged and of York, Coel Hen, as a ruler of both territories. Such a ruler controlled virtually the whole of the lands which had once obeyed the Roman *dux*, at least as far north as the wall. The misty recollections of medieval Wales preserve the outline of a man who took over that command when the government of Ravenna refused to appoint more regular officers thereto. In the political climate of the time, there is little doubt that 'Coel' himself used the title *Dux Britanniarum*, later rendered into Welsh as *Guletic*, and into Anglo-Saxon as *Bretwalda*. Nor is there any reason to doubt that such a ruler at that time would have endeavoured to bequeath as much as he could of this authority to his sons.

The indications of Coel Hen's date are not very precise; no Saint Patrick wrote to him or his father any document that posterity preserved. The genealogies, both of his ancestors and his descendants, place him certainly between 400 and 450, with a heavy bias towards the quarter century 400×425. Since his daughter was married to Cunedda, he was clearly held to be slightly earlier than him. He may have controlled the land south of the wall before Cunedda moved to Wales (about 425×430); the poems celebrate Cunedda as a hero who defended the wall before his move southward, and Coel's association with the wall rests on the names of his mother and daughter, Stradwawl and Wawl, 'Street-Wall' and 'Wall'. It may be that Coel took over the command of York in or soon after 410, perhaps after some short-lived and unremembered commanders, and assumed responsibility for the wall and its outposts when Cunedda took his warriors southward.

The dynasties of Dyfnwal and Tutagual in Scotland, and of the two main lines that flow from Coel, in England, are reasonably clearly located, Dyfnwal's certainly, the other two with a high probability. There are other sets of names which occur, with varying and uncertain descent in both lists. Where the memory of descent is confused, it is well to suspect that, though successive rulers of the same area may be accurately remembered, the statement that one man was literally son of the other is a great deal less convincing. The most remarkable confusion is in the rulers of the Edinburgh region: the names Cinuit, Cinbelin and Clinog Eitin or Clytno Eitin occur in the same order in both the Dyfnwal and the Coel genealogies, with considerable variants in their exact relationship to each other. The name Eitin is a safe enough indication of their seat; Caer Eidin is Carriden, Edinburgh a nearby fort sharing the name. But that the rulers of the Glasgow region and the York command both claimed to sire the princes of the Edinburgh area contains a strong hint that neither claim is true. Moreover, the ancestor who gives his name to the line, Cinuit, is placed in the Coel pedigrees later than the other ancestors, in the second half of the sixth century, while in the previous generation the ruler of Dinas Eidin is Lewdwn, claimed by neither dynasty, listed only as a maternal ancestor, again in the claims of both Glasgow and York. He is real enough, for his name survives in the Lothians. The suspicion is reinforced by a note to the Northern Genealogies of Coel (*Bonedd Gwyr y Gogledd* 6):

'300 swords of the Kynverchyn, 300 shields of the Kynnwdyon, 300 spears of the Coeling . . . never failed'.

The note implies a threefold division in which Reged and Edinburgh were distinct from the 'Coelings' of York. It may be that Merchiaun and Kynvarch of Reged were in fact subordinate chiefs, who in the sixth century repudiated their allegiance to the *dux* at York, rather than literally descendants of the blood of Coel.

There can also be little confidence in the claim that Guallauc, son of Lennauc, was a descendant of Coel. The claim is made explicitly only in the Jesus collection (**G**), though 'Masguic Clop' of the Harleian genealogy 9 may be a corruption of Mar. Here again the location and date are secure: Lennauc's name survives in Lennox, the hills and plain west of Glasgow, and Guallauc ruled 'from Caer Clut (evidently some fort on the Clyde, if not Dumbarton itself) to Caer Caradawc', presumably a fort somewhere between the Campsie Fells and Edinburgh, and extended his arms southward to Maw (? Peebles).

The location of the house of Keidyaw is fairly clear: Guendoleu fought and died at Arfderydd. The Knows of Arthuret lie on the Esk some ten miles north-east of Glasgow, and nearby is Carwinelow which sounds very like Caer Guendoleu. There is no indication of how far or in what direction his authority spread; he was destroyed by an alliance of three main powers: Alclud, Eitin and the sons of Eleuther of York are named. Urien of Reged, who ruled Carlisle, is notably absent. It does not, however, follow that he ruled Carlisle before the battle; tradition makes Taliesin the bard of Guendoleu, and ascribes to Taliesin the greater part of the songs sung in honour of Urien. It may well have been that Keidyaw and his sons controlled the western end of the wall, with Carlisle and the lands to north-east and east, while the centre of Reged lay to the south. Carlisle may have been the reward won by Urien for his absence from the battle, and Taliesin was the bard of Carlisle.

There remain two principal chiefs of whose location the sources give no hint, Pabo Post Prydein and Morcant, son of Cledawc, son of Morcant. There remains one large area whose rulers are not known, the north-east coastland from the Tees to the Tweed. This area divides naturally into two, with the Tyne as a hard frontier between its halves. A very little is known of the two rulers. Pabo was a brother of Eleuther of York; his title *Post Prydein* (Pillar of Britain) was later used by Taliesin for Urien. Urien is said to have conquered Bernicia, and Pabo's son Dunawt was the chief of the alliance which eventually destroyed Urien.

The inference of these slender signposts is to make Pabo's territory somewhat more happily lie south of the Tyne, bordering on the Vale of York and on the Pennine frontier of Reged, than north of the river. What can be gathered of Morcant is even less substantial; he joined the alliance against Urien and, according to Nennius, did so because he was jealous of Urien's supreme command; apparently during an expedition Urien was besieged by Theodric, son of Ida, or was besieging Theodric, in Lindisfarne. It may therefore be that Lindisfarne lay within Morcant's territory. The line of Morcant split off from the main line of Coel's descendants in the middle of the fifth century, when 'Deira was first separated from Bernicia', a hundred years before the separation of Pabo's line from York. It would be more probable that the country north of the Tyne, the former Votadinian territory beyond the Roman frontier, should separate out so early; and it is theoretically possible that Morcant's name survives at Morpeth.

The major territorial areas therefore which seem quite securely to be deduced from the genealogies, poems, and annals are the regions of Glasgow, of Edinburgh and of Reged in north-western England. The dynasties of York, of the Cumberland-Scotland border and of Galloway-Dumfries have evidence enough to make their approximate location probable; the location of the rulers and territories of the north-east coast are no more than probable. But though it is possible to reconstruct some idea of the main centres of power, and to form some conception of how they devolve from the fragments of Roman administration, there must in the conditions of these centuries have emerged very many petty lords, comparable with multiple clans who claimed descent from the Scottish royal house, who left no mark among the genealogists or in the epic literature. The very numerous little forts of the northern shires on both sides of the border cannot but have attracted little local tyrants obeying the greater rulers only when they were so constrained by superior force, induced by hope of greater gain, or perhaps occasionally inspired to join in a wide alliance against the Saxon enemy. Beyond stating the possibility, as a warning against too easy over-simplification of what we know, nothing can be assumed. It is known that at the close of the Roman period there were many Germans on the northern frontier, and that the Frisians among them were numerous, but nothing is known of their relation to the Saxons save what may be inferred from the casual distribution of a few Saxon brooches on Roman sites, and the marked absence in the north of the Saxon cemeteries characteristic of the Midlands, the south, and the Yorkshire Wolds. It is certain that Briton fought Briton and Saxon fought Saxon as often as, if not more often than, the two races combined against each other. The little lords may have included Teutons as well as Celts; and in the uncertainty nothing may be safely inferred beyond the broad outlines of the names, the wars, and the territories of the greater princes, and their method of fighting and ruling.

PADSTOW. *Sancte Petroces stow* SC s.a. 981, the name means 'St Petroc's Church'. In one of the versions of *Vita Sancti Ciarani de Saigir*, the saint travelled to Cornwall just before his death, and visited Padstow: '*quiescit autem in Cornubia supra mare Sabrinum, a Petrokstowe miliaribus xv* . . .'
See C. Plummer, *Vitae Sanctorum Hiberniae*, 1910, Vol. 1, 233, n 3.

PENSELWOOD (Som.)
Ekwall (DEPN) gives

Peonnum	658	SC
Peonnan	1016	SC
Penne	1086	Domesday
Penne in Selewode	1345	Episcopal Register.

Brit. *Pen* = 'a hill' and *Selewode* ('sallow wood') was added presumably to distinguish this *pen* ('hill') from any other. R.B.W.

PENYCHEN. The cantref west of the Taff. Paul (Poulentus) Penychen occurs in the lives of Cadoc (8, 19), Illtud (2, 3), where Illtud served him in his youth as a *miles*) and Docco. Paul Aurelian's father (v. 1) was *comes* Perphirius who lived in Penn Ohne, either a follower or a predecessor or a successor of Paul(inius). But Cadoc's Llancarfan is in Penychen, and he inherited the secular government from his father, who evidently annexed it.

PICTS. The word is purely Latin, meaning 'painted people'. In the late first century, the poet Martial derided the current fashion of ladies' handbags, '*barbara de pictis veni bascauda Britannis*' (14, 99), 'a barbarian basket from the painted Britons'. It then meant the British as a whole, and referred to Caesar's descriptions of British warriors who painted themselves blue, *cf.* Martial 11, 53, 1, '*Claudia caeruleis cum sit Rufina Britannia edita*', the 'blue Britons'.

'Painted Britons' became a literary epithet and was applied to tattooed northerners from the late third century. Claudian's dying Picts in 368 '*ferroque notatas . . . figuras*', 'bodies marked with iron', tattooed. Cicero (*de Officiis* 2, 7.25) and Ammianus (31, 2, 14) use *nota* for the tattooing of Thracians and Agathyrsi; *cf.* Isidore of Seville, in the early seventh century (*Origines* 19, 23, 7), '*nec abest gens Pictorum nomen a corpore, quod minutis opifex acus punctis, et expressus nativi graminis succus inludit, ut has ad sui specimen cicatrices ferat, pictis artubus maculosa nobilitas*' ('the name of the Picts relates to their bodies, which a specialist craftsman decorates with tiny pinpricks, and juices squeezed from native plants, so that it bears these wounds as a mark of honour, and the nobility is disfigured by painted limbs'). *Figura* includes the whole body, and is not limited to the face.

The word is used only in Latin texts; and *Picti* is used only of the peoples of northern Britain. The Irish, however, commonly call them *Cruithin*, an early Irish transliteration of *Britanni*. They use the same word for earlier inhabitants of Ireland; the name there survives into the eighth century among the Ulaid, into the early fifth in Munster, and is occasionally found elsewhere as a territorial description. The Irish usage evidently echoes a once extensive immigration of British in the long-distant past. There is no reason to suppose that the Cruithin of Ireland spoke any tongue but Irish in the fourth and later centuries. In referring to Cruithin of Britain, *Picti* in Latin, Irish usage always restricts the word to the Picts, never extending it to any of the British. The country is termed *Alba*; the word is used with reference to all Britain as far as the Channel, including the south-west, in texts relating to the fifth century and perhaps the sixth. Thereafter, when Britain was divided into Saxonland and British territories, *Alba* was retained for the north, modern Scotland and, from about the tenth century expanded to *Albania*. Albany was used for southern Pictish territory.

Roman usage knew of two main divisions among the Picts. By the late first century, CALEDONII (*q.v.*) served as a general term for the northern barbarians. Ptolemy lists the separate smaller peoples who then lived in their territory. Cassius Dio (75, 6, 4) (*c.* A.D. 200) described the northern barbarians as divided into the Maeatae nearest to the frontier, Caledonii beyond them, who between them had absorbed almost all the other names of peoples. Eumenius in the late second century knew 'Dicaledones and other Picts', Ammianus in the fourth (27, 8) knew Picts divided into two peoples, Dicalidonae and Verturiones (FORTRENN, *q.v.*) Bede in the eighth century wrote of '*septentrionalium Pictorum, hoc est eis quae arduis atque horrentibus montium iugis ab australibus eorum sunt regionibus sequestratae*', *HE* 3, 4 ('southern Picts, separated from the northern districts by a range of high and horrible mountains'). The meaning is plainly the Grampians, whose spur, the Mearns, reaches the sea south of Aberdeen.

All these notices concern the central region of Scotland, between the Forth-Clyde estuaries and the Great Glen. None of them is interested in the north-west, beyond the Inverness coastal region. Almost nothing of the archaeology and no more than five per cent of the place-names associated with the Picts are found in this region. Orkney is described as '*ultra Pictos*', 'beyond the Picts', and therefore not Pictish, in the fourth- or fifth-century *Periplus* (Nennius 8: see **T**). It is therefore unwise to include the north-west and the islands in the territory of the Picts, as do some modern writers. Present indications suggest that the ATECOTTI (*q.v.*) were the inhabitants of the north-west. The native records were collected by W.F. Skene, *Chronicles of the Picts and Scots*, Edinburgh, 1867. From the mid-ninth century, some chronicle information is entered. The earlier notices give little more than the names of kings and the number of years they reigned.

The principal archaeological monuments of the Picts are their symbol-stones, probably grave-monuments, incised with vigorous naturalistic animals and precise geometrical patterns admirably executed. The symbols plainly had a meaning; suggestions for their interpretation have been advanced by Charles Thomas, Arch. Jl., 120, 1963, 31 ff. The stones are published by J. Romilly Allen and J. Anderson, *Early Christian Monuments of Scotland*, Edinburgh, 1903, and are conveniently illustrated by F.T. Wainwright, *The Problem of the Picts*, 1955, 102-3, and I. Henderson, *The Picts*, 1967, 104; 107; 113, mapped Figs. 15, 16, pp.109, iii; S. Cruden, *Early Christian and Pictish Monuments* (Ministry of Works Guide, 1964); M. Dillon and N.K. Chadwick, *The Celtic Realms*, 1967, Plates 91-3, etc.

The stones have been classified into three groups, of which class III is late. The essential difference between classes I and II is that class I stones are roughly hewn, class II are well dressed and often carry a design of an interlaced cross. The dates assigned by Anderson (seventh to eighth centuries, class I; ninth to tenth, class II), are probably too late, *cf.* Henderson, 115 ff.; and there is nothing to suggest that one class ended before the other began. It is, however, unlikely that class I began much before the sixth century, probable that class II began somewhat later; and likely that both styles remained in use for a long time. The unique class I motif is closely datable. The two circles on the Dunnichen stone (Henderson, Plate 28, etc.), found close by the royal residence of the southern Picts, are in their detailed treatment exact copies of the Saxon sixth-century six-scroll saucer-brooches. The motif began in Sussex, early in the sixth century, and spread later in the century to the Midlands, and has not been observed in any context that looks later than the sixth century. There is, however, no obvious connection between Picts and southern English in the sixth century. The motif is therefore likely to have struck the eye of the Pictish artist who saw a single brooch in chance circumstances; it was incorporated into his stock of symbols. It should have remained in use for a long time, and therefore gives no date to the stone other than that it should not be earlier than the sixth century. But the ability of the artist to make use of an alien design suggests that his symbols were then still in an early stage of development.

The class I stones predominate in the north, between Aberdeen and the Inverness region by Dornoch, with a score among the southern Picts, three or four outliers on the east Caithness coast and in the Orkneys, a couple south of the Forth; but the great majority of class II stones are in or about Strathmore, among the southern Picts, with half-a-dozen in the Aberdeen region, a dozen in the Inverness region in the north, with a couple of outliers in Caithness and a couple on Largo Bay, across the Forth from Edinburgh. The distribution argues that the difference is more one of regional styles than of date, though doubtless the northern stones began earlier. The suggestion (Henderson, 112) that the northern style developed in the time of Columba and of Bridei son of Maelgwn, at the end of the sixth century, when the main royal residence is known to have been near Inverness, seems sensible; the kings of the Picts are called kings of Fortrenn, by Perth, from Bridei son of Bili in the late seventh century, when the southern style may have developed.

A few other archaeological objects match the division of the stones between northern and southern Picts (*Problem of the Picts*, ed. Wainwright, 34, 36, etc.). The scatter of forts in both northern and southern Pictish territory echoes this; but few are dated, and their numbers are very much fewer than those of the Votadini on their south. The striking fortresses called 'brochs' and the galleried duns belong to the north-west (ATECOTTI, *q.v.*); less than one per cent of the brochs are found in southern Pictish territory, none among the northern Picts, though a concentration of duns is located in the south of the main mountain mass, between the Tay and the Trummel, in territory where the name of the Caledonii survives, but which Ptolemy ascribes to the Vacomagi. These fortifications are conveniently mapped in IANB (map in pocket). It is probable that many of the small ring forts built over larger earlier earthworks (e.g., *Problem of the Picts*, 74 ff.) belong to the fifth or later centuries. The so-called 'Galloway Picts' seem to be a medieval fancy (Henderson, *The Picts*, 72), as also the 'Irish Picts' of Wales.

The language of the Picts was a form of Gaulish, akin to British. The evidence is discussed and mapped by K.H. Jackson, in *Problem of the Picts*, ed. Wainwright 147 (names in *Pit*), 150 (other P-Celtic names). Ninety-five per cent of these names are found in the territory of the northern and southern Picts, a very few in the north-west; like the symbol stones, they are not found in Argyle, or west of a line from Fort Augustus to Glasgow. The element *Pit-* derives from Gaulish, the word meaning 'piece of ground', hence modern French '*pièce*' and English 'piece', but is not found in British place-names. Most of the other elements, Aber- and the like, also occur in British. The British language was itself brought to Britain from Gaul, probably at much the same time as the migration of the ancestors of the Picts. At least one word was dropped from British place-name usage, but it is not easy to say how far the language devolved over many centuries; it may be that Pictish was quite close to the British speech of the Clyde, or it may be that greater difference had arisen.

There are a few signs of elements of other languages among the Picts. Bede *HE* 1,12, says that *Aebbercurnig* (Abercorn), the east end of the Antonine Wall, was in his day called '*sermone Pictorum Peanfahel, lingua autem Anglorum Penneltun*'. The word *Peanfahel* is a hybrid of British and Irish (Watson, CPNS, 346) and is evidence that the Picts used foreign borrowed place-names.

There are also a small number of inscriptions in Irish Ogam characters, with an outlier found on the sites of a Roman town in Norfolk. (R.A.S. Macalister, *Feilsgribhinn Eoin mhic Neill*, ed. J. Ryan, Dublin, 1940, 184-226, also published F.C. Diack, *Inscriptions of Pictland*, Aberdeen, 1944; *cf.* J. Rhys, PSAS 26, 1891-2, 263 ff.; 27, 1892-3, 411-2; 32, 1897-8, 324 ff.) They are found mostly in the north, and, if the strokes of the ogam alphabet are meant to have the same value as in Ireland, their transcription is for the most part meaningless. If the letters so spelt out are intended to be ordinary words and names in a language, then that language is neither Pictish nor Irish; if it is a language, then it is evidently a relic of a pre-Celtic language, perhaps not Indo-European. The only other evidence for such a language is Adomnán's story (1, 33) that, when a dying old man, '*Geonae cohortis primarius*', was brought to Skye, Columba had to converse with him through an interpreter; *Geona* is unlocated, but was probably not far from Skye. The man's language was clearly not Irish; nothing suggests that Pictish was spoken in the islands. It is therefore possible that they also spoke an old language, perhaps that of the inscriptions, perhaps also of the Atecotti.

A few place-names may be non Indo-European and pre-Celtic; but such place-names do not argue that such a language was spoken there in historical times. The name of London is British, of the Thames perhaps pre-Celtic. But the names do not argue that the modern inhabitants of London speak ancient British or earlier languages, though they have adopted an ancient name into English.

The ancestors of the peoples whom the late Romans called the Picts used ethnic names which suggest that many of them migrated from Gaul in the same epoch as the British farther south. Their dominant language, like British, derived from Gaul. The Irish called them by a generic term (Cruithin) which means British, the Welsh called them Prydyn; and the Roman writers of the late first century included them among the Britanni. It is probable that they were British, their difference from the British farther south stemming only from the fact that they were never conquered by the Romans. Since they had no other collective name, the British of the Roman province and its border protectorate, who used the word British for themselves, had to find a different term for the barbarians. The term Picti, 'painted people', perhaps first devised by the army, first came into use because the people it described had none of their own and to distinguish them from the Roman provincials.

The striking peculiarity of Pictish society is their law of inheritance. All inheritance passed through the women. Later Pictish texts insist upon the custom. 'In the right of mothers they succeed to Lordship and all other successions' (CPS 319); 'territorial succession derived from women' (CPS 126); 'the dominion of the land from women and not from men' (CPS 328); 'from women the royal succession' (CPS 329); 'the royal succession on the mother's side' (CPS 45); 'from the mother's nobility the right to kingship' (CPS 40).

These texts assert that both kingship and property were inherited through the mother; and in most societies the rules that determine the succession to political power are closely akin to those that govern the inheritance of individual property. The succession of kings is amply confirmed by other testimony. The long record of Pictish kings includes the name of each king's father, in Irish, English and British records as well as in the native lists. In over 400 years no king is ever succeeded by his son in any record; and all kings are recorded. From the sixth century onwards, the fathers of Pictish kings were frequently foreigners, British, Irish, or English. None of these kings' fathers, whose ancestors are known, had a paternal claim to the Pictish throne.

The practice is also noted by Bede (*HE* 1,1), '*ubi res veniret in dubium, magis de feminea regum prosapia quam de masculina regem sibi eligerent; quod usque hodie apud Pictos constat esse servatum*' ('whenever there was doubt, they chose their king rather by the female royal ancestry than the male; which custom is still observed among the Picts today'). Bede's qualification, 'whenever there is doubt', is his own, added perhaps because he found it difficult to believe that so odd a custom could be normal, or perhaps because doubt was normally removed by naming the heir in his predecessor's time, the scrutiny of a new king's claim arising only when no heir had been named. The record of the actual successions discounts the literal implication of Bede's words, that female successions arose only in cases of doubt, presumably exceptional: had the succession through the women arisen only in cases of doubt, at least one or two kings in four centuries must have been succeeded by their sons.

The custom of matrilinear succession to monarchy is not recorded as the rule of any other documented European dynasty. But it recalls the succession to some states in southern Britain noted by Roman writers in the first century A.D. When the king of the Iceni in Norfolk died in A.D. 60, he expected his daughters to succeed; his widow, Boudicca, commanded the armed forces of the Iceni when the Roman government refused to accept the succession, but the texts do not say whether or not the king also had sons, or whether the daughters had husbands. In the same generation, among the Brigantes of the Pennines, the king was whoever was the consort of queen Cartimandua for the time being. These were both earlier Iron Age peoples; the Belgae observed patrilinear succession. The earlier custom is not necessarily identical with that of the Picts, but it indicates that royal power might pass to daughters, or be vested in a queen's husband.

PORTH MAWR. The name means 'Great Port'.

REGED. The territory of Urien and his son Owain, CT 2, 27; 3, 4; 6, 4; 7, 1; 7, 44; 10, 3; CLH 3 *passim*; 7, 8; *cf.* TYP 518, etc.

Rochdale (*SD 8913*), Lancs., is Reced Ham in DB; Ekwall DEPN 389 connects the name with OE *raeced*, hall, not found in any other place-name, and offers an improbable Welsh alternative of *rac coet* ('against the wood'); EPNS 81-82 also suggests the alternative of a British regional name, with greater reason.

Other references point farther north. The thirteenth-century poet Cynddelw makes a horseman ride night and day from Maelienydd in Radnorshire to Lliwelyt (Carlisle) (MA 198 b, *cf.* YC 28, 1918, 67). Martyrology of Oengus, Nov. 24, *cf.* p. 246, places Colman Dub Cuilenn both in Leinster and in *Din Reichet in Rennaib*, probably Dunragit (*NX 1557*) at the head of Luce Bay, between Glenluce and Stranraer, on the edge of the Rinns of Galloway; though Hogan, *Onomasticon Goedelicum*, 580, understood the Rinns in Ardcarne, Roscommon, Connacht.

Of places that Urien controlled, Aeron might be Ayr, and Llwyfenydd was probably by the Lyvennet, near Penrith. *Yr Echwydd* (discussed at length, Sir Ifor Williams, *Armes Prydein*, Cardiff, 1955, 62-5, *cf.* CLH 117; Morris-Jones, YC 28, 1918, 68-9; *cf.* Watson CPNS 156) remains unlocated. Argoed Llwyfein was probably in Reged. Urien was also 'lord of Catraeth' (Catterick), CT 8, 9, but probably did not annex territory east of the Pennines until after the English destruction of the British kings of York in 580.

Jackson's conclusion (LHEB 218) that Urien's Reged 'seems to have included Galloway and Cumberland' accurately summarises the slender evidence.

But Urien's father had a brother, Elidir, and it is probable that they shared a territory previously united under their father. Elidir invaded north Wales and was there killed. It is possible that his territory was Lancashire, that the kingdom of his father included all the western Pennine country from Carlisle to the Mersey, and that the whole of this territory, including Rochdale, bore the name of Reged, Urien's share being northern Reged. Southern Reged may in the late Roman empire have been the province of Valentia.

The term *Teyrnllwg*, applied to Cheshire and south Lancashire (*Iolo MSS.*, 86) between Gwynedd and Deira and Bernicia, etc., hence some modern writers, is not found in the earlier sources, and appears to be late antiquarian fiction, coined from the epithet Durnlluc of Catell of Powys.

REINAWC. The name of two distinct districts in south Wales.

(1) *Regnum Seisil* was the episcopate of Padarn, *regnum Rein* the episcopate of David, *regnum Morgant* or Eliud (Teilo), v. *Paterni* 30, plainly meaning southern Cardiganshire with Carmarthenshire, Demetia and Morgannwg. The same division of Wales, into Gwynedd, Powys and Deheubarth (the south) which comprised Rieinwg, Morgannwg and Seissyllwg is given in ALW 5, 2, 1. This Reinawc will have been named from Regin of Demetia in the late eighth century and will also be the territory of Margedud, *rex Reinuc* (v. *Cadoci* 41), Regin's father who raided Morgannwg. It is a name of Demetia in use in and about the ninth century.

(2) *Rein o Rieinawc*, whose daughter Guensased is married to Sawyl Bennuchel, by *ByS* 13 cannot be so late, for none of the parents of saints named in *ByS* is later than the sixth century. He is likely to be identical with king Rein, contemporary with sixth-century kings in LL 118. Cinan Carguinn, described as *rex Reinmuc*, who also invaded Glamorgan, was king of Powys in the sixth century. The territory ruled by a king of Powys cannot be Demetia, but a Powys king who came by way of Brecon is as likely as a Demetian to reach Glamorgan by the Neath. The text requires a district on the borders of Powys, that its more powerful kings might seize. The *Vastatio Reinuch ab Offa* in 796 (ACm MS. B) also fits better with a location nearer Powys. This Reinawc is likely to have been named from the later sixth-century Rein of Brecon, who is said to have invaded Gwynlliog, while his brother, Clytwin, invaded 'all south Wales', leaving his own name in Carmarthenshire and Glamorganshire, his son's in southern Herefordshire. Rein is the only king of Brecon, after its founders, whose exploits were recorded, and evidently extended his frontiers. This Reinawc is likely to lie between Brecon and Powys, open to Mercian attack, in or about Radnorshire and southern Herefordshire, possibly an alternative name for Buellt.

ROSNAT, in Britain. '*Vade in Britanniam ad Rosnatense monasterium, et esto humilis discipulus Maucenni, magistri illius monasterii*', v. *Endei* placed *c*.460. Faecha dispatched Enda from Rossiry, co. Fermanagh, in northern Ireland.

Darerca of Killeevy, by Armagh, died 516, careful for the future of her pupil, Brignat, '*eam in Britanniam insulam, de Rosnatensi monasterio conversationis monastice regulas accepturam, misisse perhibetur*', v. *Darerca* 25.

'*Nennyo qui Maucennus dicitur, de Rosnatensi monasterio*' obtained the liberty '*a rege Britannie*' of Eugenius, a Leinsterman, and Tigernach of Clogher in Airgialla in the north, who were captured and enslaved together in Ireland by pirates who took them to Britain, v. *Eugenii* 1, *c*. 500. '*Puer libertati restitutus, sancti Mo Nenni disciplinis et monitis in Rosnatensi monasterio, quod alio nomine Alba vocatur, diligenter instructus*', v. *Tigernach* 4, *c.* 500.

'Magister suus Mugentius nomine, qui in vicitate quae dicitur Candida liberales disciplinas eum docuerat', v. *Finnian* of Moville (Frigidian) *1*, 1 (ASH 634; *cf.* v. 2, 6 ASH 638), *c.*550. Finnian studied at the *Magnum monasterium* of Nennio in Britain, NLA 1 = ASH 438; at *Futerna*. Preface to the Hymn of Mugint, *Irish Liber Hymnorum* 1, 97.

All five mentions of Rosnat relate to saints who were sent, or taken, from northeastern Ireland to Britain. The name *Alba, Candida* (white) is given by Bede to the church built by Nynia '*qui locus ad provinciam Berniciorum partinens vocatur ad Candidam Casam, eo quod ibi ecclesiam de lapide, insolito more fecerit*', in Bede's time the episcopal see of Whithorn (Whitern), Galloway, *NX 4440*. *Futerna* is an Irish transliteration of Whitern.

A small simple early church, with altar to the west, and therefore probably of the fifth or early sixth centuries, has been excavated at Whithorn.

No text connects Rosnat with the monastery named, and probably founded by Maucennus in Pembrokeshire, *cf.* Maucennus *Rosina Vallis* (*Glynn Rosin* in *Buchedd Dewi*), v. *Cadoci* 69, v. *David* 3; 15, 16, v. *Paterni* 20, '*quam vulgari nomine Hodnant Brittones vocitant*' (v. *David* 15) is the valley in which St David's lies, now called Merry Vale, and is used as a synonym for St David's. It is neither 'Rosnat' nor the Pembrokeshire monastery of Maucennus, as some modern writers have hazarded, misled, no doubt, by the identity of the first three letters of the two names. Rosnat is not spelt Rosnant.

Rosnat, Whithorn, was regarded as a major teaching centre for Irish, Pictish, and British youth in the fifth and early sixth centuries. Since the daughter of a Pictish king was a pupil, it was co-educational, under the saints cited above, and Ninnian, and the two later abbots, Maucennus and Mugentius.

[*See* WHITHORN, below.]

SAXONS. The origins of the continental Saxons are obscure (*cf.* e.g., the long inconclusive discussion by Tischler, *Sachsenforschung*, 174-94). The territorial name is confusing: up to the fifth century, *Saxonia* meant the coastal lands whence the Anglo-Saxons sailed to Britain; but throughout the Middle Ages, Saxony was centred farther south, in the territory still called Lower Saxony, in later times comprised within the electorate or kingdom of Hanover, including the Elbe mouth. Modern Saxony, between Bohemia and Prussia, the Saale and the Neisse, was in the Middle Ages the Marks of Thuringia and Meissen.

The name is first found used by Ptolemy (2, 11, 7), located 'about the neck of the Cimbric Chersonese', whose most natural interpretation is north of the Elbe, in much the same area as Tacitus's Reudigni. The Saxons of *Widsith* 62 are named after Angli and Suevi, before various small peoples of Jutland and Scandinavia.

Wherever they lived, they mastered and named the whole of the northern coastal peoples beyond the Franks in the fourth century: Zosimus, 3, 6-8 (reproducing Eunapius), whose fragment 12 is evidently a portion of the same account, calls the Chamavi (so Eunapius; Zosimus, wrongly, Quadi), who had lived for centuries in and about Gelderland (on the modern Dutch-German border north of the Rhine), a part of the Saxon people. They were not, in any archaeological or ethnic sense, but Eunapius and Zosimus mean that they were under Saxon political control.

In Carolingian times the term Saxon was used for and by the Germanic peoples on the left bank of the Elbe north of Thuringia, and of those north of the Elbe. The area was later known as Lower Saxony, and in modern times as the kingdom of

Hanover, but there are no grounds for peopling Hanover with Saxons before the middle of the sixth century.

The coast west of the Elbe estuary was occupied by the Chauci in the time of Tacitus and Ptolemy; their name occasionally recurs commonly as sea robbers till the end of the fourth century, when Claudian (*in Laude Stilichonis*, 1, 225), perhaps with poetic freedom, locates them on the Lower Rhine. It is quite uncertain whether they were absorbed or evicted by the Saxons.

Modern archaeological convention attached the name of Saxon to pottery and brooches that appear on the coasts of the Chauci about the beginning of the third century, and the name will do as a trade term, as long as it is not pretended that written evidence assigns this name to this region, for it locates the homes of Angle and Jute. The evidence shows that the Saxons lent their name, by domination or eminence, to the whole of the coastal barbarians in the fourth and fifth centuries; but it does not suffice to pinpoint the portion of the area that was properly theirs.

Archaeologically, Saxon pottery and ornament is clearly identifiable to the end of the fifth century on the coasts, but, when it there ends, it continues in Britain, with no area of comparable sixth-century cemeteries being found anywhere in Germany.

Bede *HE* 1, 15 divides the '*Angli vel Saxones*' into the three main groups of Angli, Saxones and Iutae, from among whom the Saxons from 'Old Saxony', named the West, East and South Saxons. This is the terminology that had hardened by the eighth century. The archaeological evidence extends and qualifies Bede. The clear pattern of burial rite marks off three regions from the first migrations of the earlier fifth century. Later, this distinction is less clear: most of the cemeteries that first came into use in the sixth century practised inhumation, including those in mixed and cremation areas, although the original communities retained their earlier rites with little change to the end of the sixth century. In each area, the appropriate ornament predominates from the beginning but, in the earlier sixth century, distinctions are absolute: Anglian cruciforms are found only in Anglian areas, saucers only in Saxon areas, while Kent develops its special jewellery. The distinction between Angle, Jute and Saxon is more marked in early sixth-century Britain than in fifth-century Germany but, after the second revolt of the later sixth century, the barriers break down. It must be noted that the division of the Saxons into western, eastern and southern groups arises in Britain after the earliest settlement, and that, because of their situation, the men of Sussex soon adopted much Kentish ornament. The Saxons south of London formed the *Sudergeona*, southern district, Surrey (EPNS 1) by the eighth century; the names imply a former 'Norrey' north of the Thames, the two presumably being sub-divisions of the *Middelseaxan*, first attested in 704 (BCS 111; EPNS 1), and thenceforth restricted to the north of the Thames. Much of the earliest ornament of Essex looks to Kent, rather than to the Saxons or Angles, and the name first occurs in Bede. Middlesex has a few pre-Christian place-names, but no burial grounds away from the river-bank area. There is no reason to suppose the separate existence of either Middle or East Saxons before the mid-sixth century. It is also to be observed that Bede's simplified geography omits Lincolnshire, where Frisian pottery is more than usually common. In the fifth century, Bede's tradition makes Hengest leader of all the English, not merely the men of Kent.

In England, pagan 'Saxon' ornament is not confined to the areas termed Saxon. In the fifth century, the cemeteries of the Icknield Way from the Cambridge to the Oxford regions practised a mixed burial rite, and used mixed ornament. The future Wessex came into being during the second Saxon revolt in the 570s, at first centred in the Oxford region, its chief town Dorchester, and its best excavated pagan cemeteries at Abingdon and Long Wittenham. The earliest name of the people was the *Gewissae*, the probable meaning of which is 'confederates'. The name West Saxons is adopted in preference in the laws of Ine in the 690s, and may not have been many generations older.

Usage varied. The general term used by the whole of the immigrants was *Englisc*, and this term is used by Ine for his West Saxon subjects. To Bede they are normally all *Angli*, occasionally glossed as 'Angli vel Saxones', including Angles, Saxons, Jutes, Frisians, etc. But to the British and Irish the general term was and is 'Saxon', Angli used only rarely in the north. The British and Irish regularly describe individuals as 'Saxon'; the English even in Wessex virtually never use the term of individuals. Its adoption by the seventh-century *Gewissae* may have been influenced by British usage; or by a desire to find a word distinct from the Mercians and Northumbrians; or perhaps because a large proportion of the original settlers had originally come from 'Saxon' lands west of the Elbe.

The term 'East Saxons' meant those living east of Wessex. Neither the archaeology nor the personal names connect the East Saxons any more closely with the west of the Elbe than they do the men of Wessex. Its principal connotation is a distinction from the Angles, a term coined out of English political experience. The Middle Saxons are not distinguished from the East Saxons until later Mercian expansion set a frontier to the East Saxons east of London.

On the continent there is no archaeological continuity. The English called the later European Saxons the 'Old Saxons', implying that they believed them to be the descendants of Saxons who stayed at home. But the continental tradition knew only Saxons who left Britain. One party returned to the Lower Elbe about 531, and were transferred to Thuringia, where ultimately a large part of them perished after adventures in Italy. Though there is ample evidence for Angli and Varni in Thuringia, evidence of Saxons is slighter but strange: for example, a simple urn that would pass for fifth-century Saxon was buried, grave 1, at Grobzig (Schmidt, Plate 83), with a Salin-style 11 S brooch that cannot be earlier than the mid-sixth century; and the Thuringians developed a cast saucer brooch whose size, shape and technique are Saxon, but whose ornament is unrelated to England (e.g., Mildenberger, Fig. 126; Schmidt, Plate 42 a-e, with animal designs hardly earlier than the mid-sixth century). But there were doubtless other unrecorded moves from Britain to Lower Saxony.

The old Saxon homeland by the Weser has almost nothing of the sixth century, but contains a number of cemeteries assigned to the seventh or possibly very late sixth century, whose rough plain urns Tischler (*Sachsenforschung* 79 ff, Fig. 28, p.83) rightly compares with urns from Northamptonshire and Lincolnshire and Cambridgeshire (Fig. 30, p.87, *cf*. p.89) while some of the urns from Sievern (Plate 2, p.90) are best matched in the late Sussex cemetery of Hassocks. The *Hessen-Schortens* vessels of the Weser are comparable, though not identical, with the English urns, which in England were the ancestors of the later 'St Neots ware'. Similar burials, with urns of similar shape, but better manufacture, and weapons that could be English occur in the seventh and eighth centuries (distribution map, *Harburger Kreiskalender* 1959, 2; *cf*. 1960, 1ff). Possibly small initial sixth-century return migration was reinforced by others who sought escape from the rule of the Mercians or of Aethelbert.

The Carolingian *Lex Saxonum* is primarily concerned with Westphalians, Eastphalians and Angr(iv)arii. Carolingian writers traced the origin of these people to immigrants from Britain (Adam of Bremen and the *Translatio Sancti Alexandri* for example). It may be that these people had in the fifth century accepted the general appellation of Saxon; and revived it on the arrival of immigrants from Britain. But as yet they have little archaeological connection with any of the vessels or ornaments termed Saxon. At present our understanding of the Saxon peoples in sixth-century Europe is summed up in Genrich's comment on their East Holstein neighbours. It will not be possible to explain their further history more certainly until we can establish a clearer picture of the characteristic forms of this period, and of their distribution, than the literature at present makes possible.

The Saxons were among the few Germanic peoples who had no kings. Among some 40 German peoples named in *Widsith* 18ff, 57ff, the Saxons, with a few Norwegian and north Jutland peoples, are the only ones not credited with a monarchy. The Old Saxons were still without kings in the eighth century and later: *cf.* Bede *HE* 5,10 '*non enim habent regem Antiqui Saxones, sed satrapas plurimos suae genti praepositos*'; and in war time a single leader is chosen, his authority lapsing *peracto bello, cf. Poeta Saxo*, 1, 23 (*MGH Poetae Latini aevi Carolini*, 4, 8) '*plebs omnis habebat quot pagos tene pene duces*'. Gregory of Tours, Einhard and related Carolingian chronicles regularly complain of the 'perfidy' of the Saxons: agreements made with one *dux* were not respected by the *plebes* and other *duces*. Stable monarchy also took longer to establish in Wessex than in other English states.

SCOTLAND. Scotland, like Gaul, is divided into three parts: south of Clyde and Forth separate the lowlands from the central highlands called the Grampians; Loch Ness and Glen Mor mark off the northern and western highlands.

Their history, population and culture are and always have been markedly different. The lowlands were British in speech and culture throughout the Roman period, assimilated to the Roman province even after the abandonment of the northern Antonine Wall. Roman and British writers applied to the peoples beyond Forth and Clyde the general term of PICTS (*q.v.*), a Latin word meaning 'tattooed people', and the national sentiment of later Scotsmen, from the eleventh century onward, preferred to keep the generic unity. But the general term covers four main distinct populations. Throughout the low-lying country that skirts the mountains from Argyll by Stirling, Perth and Aberdeen to Inverness, British place-names abound. These fertile lands were and are the homes of a relatively dense population, the heartlands of the Picts, and their inhabitants were known to the Irish as *Cruithin*, which is simply Old Irish for British. Apart from the consequences of their successful resistance to the suzerainty of Rome, their language and culture differed little from the southern British. These are the southern Picts, the Maeatae of Fortrenn and Caledonii of the mountain foothills; the name of the latter is preserved at Dunkeld, where the Tay debouches from the mountain.

Beyond the Great Glen the only numerous people were the builders of the brochs. There are 200 of these towers in the Orkneys and Shetlands, with another 160 in the Caithness lowland and the glens that lead to the Sutherland coast and 50 in the western isles, half of them in Skye, with a dozen scattered outliers farther south, by the Tay and Forth, and in Galloway. They were in use during the first three centuries A.D., possibly also a little earlier and a little later. On some sites in the west they came after the builders of 'duns', which are confined to the west coast, and to the heartlands of the Maeatae and Caledonii about the upper Forth and upper Tay, with few outliers. The distribution of the brochs almost exactly corresponds with the area of Norse settlement a thousand years later; they continue the pottery traditions of the 'dun' builders, whose origin lies in southern Britain. We do not know whence they came. They clearly came south from the Orkneys and feared attack, for the stupendous labour expended on their massive castles was done because it was needed. The outliers along the north-west coast are strategically sited to hold the main landing places, Tongue, Eriboll and Durness, Eddrachillis, Assynt, and Broom, against seaborne enemies who might attack their main settlements in Strathnaver and on the east coast from the rear; and the few outer Hebridean brochs screen the main settlements on Skye. The numerous references in the *Annals* to Gaelic and Pictish attacks on the Orkneys may have been the native Cornovii of Caithness, evolving new techniques to meet new dangers, or may have been invaders who overran the Cornovii: heavy Scandinavian settlement has obliterated almost all trace of earlier place-names, though one Pict-name survives near Dornoch.

These are plainly the core of the northern Picts, centred on Caithness and Orkney in easily habitable lands. The rest of the farther highland divides into two areas: equally barren of people, they are separated by their ancient and modern communications north of Stromeferry and Inverness, and a coast road surrounds the modern counties of Caithness, Sutherland, and Ross and Cromarty. The inland population today, outside the brochland of Caithness, barely exceeds 2,000 people, spread over an area of 3,500,000 acres, half of them concentrated in the township of Lairg. Some half-dozen mountain roads link coast to coast, but apart from the east coast road, all but a few miles are tracks too narrow for cars to pass except in passing places, and there is no land communication with the rest of Britain save through the town of Inverness. It follows that at all periods a ruler who holds Inverness holds all northern Scotland. South of Stromeferry and Inverness the western highlands are as empty and still worse off for roads. Two passes only lead westward from the Great Glen, commanded by Forts William and Augustus, branching to half-a-dozen ferries to the islands, but no coast road links the ferries to one another. It is plain that in earlier centuries as today the highlands beyond the Great Glen consisted only of the brochland and a number of tiny isolated coastal settlements, each widely separated from its neighbours. They cannot have formed at any time an effective political unit or fielded a formidable army. Their glens were not the nuclei of peoples, but routes through which the denser and stronger populations of the islands and of Argyll might penetrate to Inverness and the central highlands; and they are therefore wholly ignored in the Pictish list of provinces.

In Bede's time the border between northern and southern Picts was not the Great Glen, but the Mounth or Mearns, the hills that reach the sea by Stonehaven, south of Aberdeen. Either the broch people held Inverness and the coastlands eastward, or Bede disregarded them. These rich lands between Aberdeen and Inverness are among the most fertile in Britain, and even today a well-sited Aberdeenshire farm will support more capital investment than a farm of the same size in Lincolnshire or Dorset. Throughout their early history, the northern centre of government has resided not at Aberdeen but at Inverness.

This is the geography that governed the early and the medieval history of Scotland. Beyond Firth and Clyde are two centres of power, one in the Fortrenn Perth-Stirling area controlling Strathmore, the other at Inverness controlling the central highlands and the fertile coastlands to Aberdeen. Roman writers distinguished the highland Caledonii from the Maeatae of Fortrenn. Bede knew southern and northern Picts, and the native tradition of the king lists reports the ultimately successful attempts of strong rulers to combine both under a single government. Beyond the Great Glen the peoples of the islands and of Caithness might raid, but could not influence, the south unless they either seized and held Inverness or allied with its ruler.

The Gaelic colony in Argyll established a decisive third power. Within a century, it taught the Picts of both kingdoms to embrace the religion of Britain and the Continent, and to fashion a political state on the Irish and British model. The Christian religion brought with it a written language, Irish, that was also a living spoken tongue. The Irish religion and the Irish language speedily spread to the British-speaking southern Picts, to the western isles and Inverness, ultimately to the barren northern and western highlands, probably also to the brochlands of Caithness, though there is no evidence to show decisively what language these people spoke before the Norse invasions. But political unity was less easily achieved. The earlier Irish attempts at conquest were repelled in Fife and Fortrenn in the seventh century, and the Pictish territories divided. The peculiar succession system of the Picts, through the woman, ensured that a fair proportion of Pictish kings were sons of foreign fathers, once the Picts had established a monarchy comparable with those of the south and of Ireland, whose daughters made dynastic marriages with neighbouring princes. Ultimately the Gaelic kings overrode the ancient custom, and paternal succession prevailed during the course of the ninth century. But ancient geographical division forbade unity. Though the Irish language now prevailed, Norse invaders took over the old brochland in Caithness and the western islands, where the independent Norse-Irish kingdom of the Lord of the Isles controlled the west coast; and the ruler of Inverness, the old territory of the northern Picts, asserted a factual independence as the Mormaer of Murray; and Marr and Buchan, dependent on Aberdeen, became debatable borderlands. The effective kingdom of Scotia was limited to the territory of the southern Picts and of Argyll, though the actual government of Argyll passed to rulers who claimed the same ancestry. The name of *Alba*, hitherto used by the Picts, gave way to *Scotia*. The past traditions of Pictland gave the kings of Fortrenn a traditional claim to suzerainty over the rulers of Inverness and Aberdeen, and the Irish ancestry of the dynasty secured its suzerainty over Argyll.

The Gaelic kings of Fortrenn found strength in the south. The lands to their south had been British and Roman. The eastern seaboard as far as Edinburgh and beyond was overrun by the Northumbrians in the seventh century, and permanently settled by the English. The Northumbrians also annexed Dumfries and the northern Galloway coast after the collapse of Reged, and it remained part of the kingdom of Strathclyde till the end of the eleventh century. The Gaelic kings profited from the destruction of Northumbria. They expelled the English from the former British kingdom of the Lothians, and they acquired Strathclyde by dynastic marriage, appointing younger sons to rule it as a separate state. With a powerful reservoir of southern subjects to reinforce their armies, they turned south. The crisis came early in the seventh century. The northerners rebelled, resentful of growing southern influence. In 1040 Macbeth, the Mormaer of Murray, in alliance with Caithness, overthrew king Duncan, and restored the sovereignty of Inverness, reviving the ancient traditions of Bridei son of Meilchon whom Columba had converted centuries earlier. Macbeth ruled 17 years, while Duncan's son, Malcolm Canmore, lived in exile in England. The English made full use of an exiled pretender. He was married to an English princess, and in 1054 Earl Siward recovered the British kingdoms of Edinburgh and the Clyde, installing Malcolm as their king. Three years later, with the help of Siward's successor, Tostig, brother of King Harold, Malcolm invaded Scotland, killed Macbeth, and occupied the throne.

Southern influence thereafter predominated. Nine years later, in 1066, William the Norman took Harold's kingdom, and Norman feudal rule swept over England. William's son secured Carlisle and southern Cumbria, fixing permanently the present border, and the strong rule of feudal Norman kings in England overshadowed the kings of Scotia in Fortrenn. Under Malcolm's successors the castles and institutions of a feudal baronage spread rapidly in his chief dominions.

Scotland was thenceforth divided in two. A southern dynasty with its capital at Scone in Fortrenn secured permanently the title of kings of Scotland. To the northerners, they appeared as a dynasty enslaved to foreign Anglo-Normans. Their secure territories comprised the lands of the former southern Picts, and the former British kingdoms of Clyde and Forth, the latter heavily settled by Northumbrian English, and Irish Argyll. The rulers of Aberdeen and Inverness, each a *mormaer* in native speech, accepted the appellation of *comes* in Latin, rendered in English by the Anglo-Norse title of Earl, and acknowledged a grudging allegiance to the half-foreign kings of Scone. The southern kingdom was an artificial grouping of peoples of different nationality, speech and culture, whose common language was English. It was welded into a nation by the wars of the next three centuries against the English; in victory or defeat, kings who defended the border against the foreigner attracted the loyalty of all who lived north of it. Beyond the Great Glen, however, where the English threat was remote, their authority took long to win acceptance. Caithness was recovered late in the thirteenth century, and the Lord of the Isles did not finally succumb to the Scottish king till the fifteenth century. The Orkneys and Shetlands were not formally ceded until the sixteenth century.

The feudal institutions of the south were close copies of the Anglo-Norman. Those of the north were compelled to accommodate the traditions of the Pictish, British and Irish past, and took the highly original form of a contrived artificial blood relationship, known as the clan system. The term 'clan' first appears in the twelfth century, at the same moment as the feudal earldoms of David I. Hitherto the unit of government had been, as in Ireland, the '*tuath*'. The chief of the *tuath*, called '*rí*' ('king') in Ireland, accepted in Scotland the humbler appellation of '*toíseach*', chieftain; the provincial king was content with the title *mormaer*. As in Ireland, chieftainship was hereditary, and special privileges attached to the chieftain's family. In particular, the heir, or tanist, was chosen in Ireland from among those whose great-grandfathers or nearer male ancestors had been chief. It is not known whether similar rules had prevailed in Scotland; probably not, since, outside Argyll and the islands, genealogies were not preserved, as in Ireland, before the twelfth century, and the links between twelfth-century chiefs and their supposed remote Irish ancestors are wholly fabricated. The dynastic genealogies of Ireland use the term '*Uí*' or '*Cenél*' to denote paternal descendants, the term '*mac*' meaning strictly 'son of'. From about the tenth century, Irish pedigrees begin to employ frequently an additional word '*clanna*' (children of), with the same meaning as '*Uí*' or '*Cenél*'; but in Ireland these king terms are always followed by the name of the founder, never with the qualification '*mac*'.

The earliest use of 'clan' in Scotland is in a twelfth-century grant in the Buchan, recorded in the Book of Deer (Skene, 3, 303), where the names emphasise the artificiality. Donnachach mac Sithig, Toíseach of Clan Morgan, signs with Mormaer Colban and his wife Eva, daughter of Gartnait. His name is Irish, his father's Norse, his clan British; and the Mormaer's wife has a Norman name, but her father's is Pictish. The text does not explain what was understood by 'clan', but two centuries later, in the privileges claimed on the alleged law of the Clan MacDuff, the term clan was still held to mean the descendants of MacDuff to the ninth degree. The word still meant what it meant in Irish, descendants of a man, in direct provable male succession. At the beginning of the fifteenth century, the word was still confined to the collateral male relations of a chief (Skene, 3, 310).

SILCHESTER. The Roman town of Calleva, meaning '(the town) in the woods'. The English name may preserve this word, influenced by OE *sele* ('sallow copse'), *see* PENSELWOOD.

In the nineteenth century a broken Roman pillar, perhaps a balustrade, was found in the fill of a Roman wall bearing an ogam inscription in two lines reading (CIIC 496)   EBICATO
S MAQI MUCOI ...
commemorating an 'EBICATOS a son by dedication to ...'. The formula is common in Irish ogams and may be compared with the Wroxeter CUNORIX MACUS MAQUI COLINE, 'CUNORIX a son by dedication to the holly'. The name of the eponymous ancestor of EBICATOS was presumably cut in a part of the pillar now lost.

See G.C. Boon, *Silchester*, second edn. (1974); S.S. Frere, 'The Silchester Church', *Archaeologia*, 105, 1975, 277ff.   R.B.W.

SLAVS in northern Germany. The term Slav means the peoples who spoke a Slavonic language. The westernmost modern Slavonic peoples are the Poles, Czechs and Yugoslavs, with the small pockets of Sorbish, Wendisch, Lusatian, etc., that are still spoken in parts of Germany. To the writers of the sixth and succeeding centuries they were commonly known under the generic name of Sclaveni, which included a large number of peoples with their own individual names. Their language already gave them a cohesion, distinctive pottery styles and burial customs, that separated them from the Germanic nations though each people was as much an entity as Goths, Franks, Angles, etc., among the Germans.

During the migration period Slavonic peoples advanced westward to a frontier that ran roughly due south from the neighbourhood of Kiel and Hamburg to the Danubian lands. Their territory included eastern Hanover and Magdeburg, Leipzig, Halle and Jena, but not Erfurt and Weimar; farther south it followed the hills that form the present border between Germany and Czechoslovakia, parallel to the Danube, about 20 to 30 miles from the river.

The early Slavs were pagan and illiterate, and have no written record of their own. Their frontier is known from the chronicles of the Frankish emperors who engaged the Slavs from the late eighth century onward, and from the abundant record of their archaeology and their place-names. This evidence does not, however, give any clear indication of when the Slavs first reached various stretches of their ultimate frontier.

Recent discussion of the date and nature of Slav settlement has suffered from modern national prejudice and assumption, from a desire to exaggerate the antiquity and importance of the forbears of modern populations. At one extreme, Professor F. Kavka of the Charles University in Prague makes the Stone Age inhabitants of Bohemia the ancestors of the modern Czechs, surviving through Celtic and Germanic occupation, 'reinforced' in the migrations of the fourth century, so that the impact of the fifth-century Huns 'in no way broke the continuance of firm Slav rule over the territory in which they had lived from the remotest times' (*Outline of Czechoslovak History*, Prague, 1960, pp.14-15, *cf.* 10). Such interpretations are not endorsed by Czech archaeologists, but, at the other extreme, they are matched by the very late dates assigned to the arrival of the Baltic Slavs, placed in the seventh, eighth, or even ninth century, leading to conclusions no less patriotic. To Hermann Aubin (*The Cambridge Economic History of Europe*, vol. 1, 2nd edn., ed. M.M. Postan, 1966, p. 449), 'the Western Slavs ... percolated ... into lands that Germans had abandoned', occupying 'lands which Germans had formerly tilled. But they were not numerous enough to occupy them all at once ... They may have learnt something about the arts of daily life from the few Germans who remained behind'; while Richard Koebner, in the same volume, pp. 53-4, pictures their 'economic carelessness', their thin settlement, and their 'superficial use of the land'.

Such simplifications create a powerful climate of opinion which tends to cloud and inhibit the judgement of the archaeologist, who has to face the inherent difficulties of weak and fragile evidence.

Dates must be deduced from what is known. The nature of the evidence is that the Danubian Slavs are datable, since they lived near the Roman frontier, are mentioned on particular occasions by Mediterranean writers, and have left archaeological remains associated with Roman and Germanic objects, whose approximate date is known. But no direct evidence dates the Baltic Slavs, whom no texts mention, and whose material remains have no such associations. The Baltic Slavs can only be dated by the comparison of their relics with those of their southern relatives. The comparison has been hindered by modern tendencies to study the archaeological cultures within the frontiers of modern countries in preference to the study of ancient peoples in the territories in which they lived.

The earliest Mediterranean notice of the northern Slavs is Procopius's account (*de Bello Gothico* 2, 15) of the migration of the Heruli after their defeat by the Langobardi (*cf.* Paulus Diaconus 1, 20) which he dated to 494 (some modern views, e.g., L. Schmidt, *Geschichte der Langobarden* 53, argue a date as late as 508 but no later). A part of the Heruli returned to Sweden. Starting from somewhere north and east of Bratislava, where the Moravian and Slovak rivers reach the Danube, they traversed 'all the nations of the Slavs in succession, crossed a large deserted land, and reached the VARNI (*q.v.*), thereafter the Danes, whence they came to the Ocean, and crossed to the island of Thule (here Sweden) where they remained'. Procopius wrote about 50 years after the event. In general he is well informed on the geography of the barbarian lands, and in this account the northern geography is fully confirmed. In 500, the Danes had recently moved into Jutland, but had their main centres in Seeland, about modern Copenhagen. The Varni lay immediately to their south; immediately south of the Varni is Angeln, the home of the Angles, with whom the Varni are regularly associated. Thirty years later, they had left their old home to rejoin the Angles, but in 500 the Angles had recently deserted their homeland, and the Varni had not accompanied them. Bede, and the extensive archaeological evidence, attest that the country immediately south of the Varni was deserted in 500. The deserted territory was 'large' and probably reached considerably farther south than the Angeln. The route of the migration is not closely described between its terminal points: the defeated Heruli are likely to have avoided Langobard territory, and to have passed through Silesia and thence between the Oder and the Elbe. In describing their passage through 'all the nations of the Slavs', Procopius understood an extensive territory inhabited by a number of independent Slav peoples, whose southern boundary must have been some distance from the Danube, beyond the Moravian Langobards. He therefore means that a large region in and north-west of Silesia was already peopled by Slavs. A further notice of Procopius (3, 35) suggests that the Slavs were pushing rapidly forward: about 530×540 the exiled Langobard prince Hildechis took refuge with the Varni, and fled thence to the Slavs. The implication is that the Slavs were then close neighbours of the Varni. The migration of the Varni is not dated but was probably not much before 530; the regions to which they are said to have moved are the Lower Rhine, far removed from Slavs at any time, and the Middle Elbe below Magdeburg and Thuringia.

These notices attest considerable Slav pressure close to the German borders in the first years of the sixth century. Their advance in the middle of the century is more exactly described. A new Hunnic people, the Avars, first heard of by the Caspian Sea about A.D. 400, overwhelmed the Slav Antes of Moldavia and Wallachia, and pushed on with subject Slav allies to the Langobard and Gepid lands of Moravia and Pannonia. The essential evidence for their early career is Menander (FHG 282; 302). Paulus Diaconus (2, 10; *cf.* Greg. Tur. *HF* 4, 23; 4, 29) described their attack on the Franks on the accession of king Sigebert (561-75). After their attack began, Sigebert approached through Thuringia to meet them on the Elbe: the first battle was a Frankish victory; the second, a year or two later, a Frankish defeat ending in a permanent treaty. Gregory's order of events suggests that the second battle was not later than 567. In 568 the Langobards left Pannonia for Italy, handing over their Pannonian lands to the Avars and their Slav allies. In northern BOHEMIA (*q.v.*) extensive Frankish settlement ends suddenly about or just after the middle of the sixth century, and is replaced by Slav burials. Northern Bohemia is the only region where Frankish territory touched the Elbe. These texts therefore give exact dates for the wholesale Slav and Avar settlement in northern Bohemia and Langobard Pannonia, after 567.

The Slavs threw off Avar domination in 623, under the leadership of Samo (Fredegarius 4, 48, MGH SRM 2, 144-5: *cf.* MGH SS 11, 7, ch.4). Before the end of the sixth century the Slavs had pushed south into Carinthia, and westward up the Danube, where their advance was halted by Tassilo, king of the Bavarians, in 596 (Paulus Diaconus 4, 7). Recent work on the Austrian cartularies (L. Havlik, *Stari Slovane v rakouskem Podunaji*, Rozpravy Ceskoslovenske Akademie Ved, 73, 9, 1963) has located the limits of this settlement: it runs the entire length of the Austrian Danube, from Bratislava upstream to Aschach, 15 miles short of the modern Austrian-German border.

The Bavarians had settled Salzburg before the end of the seventh century; in the middle of the eighth century Carinthia, centred on the Klagenfurt area, was Slavonic (*Conversio Bagoariorum et Carantanorum*: MGH SS 11, 4 ff., *cf.* 1, *cf.* 5 ff.).

These are the principal texts from which Slav archaeology in the middle Danube basin acquires its dates. A few brooches derive from sixth-century Germanic models, but the principal evidence is the pottery. Much cannot be closely dated, but it has been possible to locate some types that belong to the earliest settlement, known from the places where they were first identified as Koblice Type, Prague Type, etc. The Prague Type is the most widespread, brought from the Lower Danube and beyond. It is a rough and simple vessel, whose shape strikingly recalls much earlier Celtic vessels. It is found in quantity in Moravia, sometimes together with Germanic vessels, and in the empty uplands of southern and central Bohemia that were not cultivated by the Germanic peoples, as well as in the Prague area. The Germanic and Roman objects found with these vessels argue that substantial groups of Slavs were settled in the area long before the arrival of the Avars and their allies. After much discussion and disagreement, the conclusions suggested by the evidence now available are summarised by the south German scholar, H. Preidel, *Slavische Altertumskunde des oestlichen Mitteleuropas*, Muenchen, 1961, 2, 14-16, that 'it is probable that the earliest Slav graves began in the fourth century', and that the Prague Type dominates in the fifth and sixth centuries. It is, however, very rare in the areas first occupied by Slavs in the late sixth century, in Carinthia and the Austrian Danube, and seems to have passed from use before the end of the century.

This is the Danubian evidence with which the Baltic material must be compared. In Mecklenburg and Pomerania, the latest Germanic burials are Anglian; the latest cemeteries end by the middle of the fifth century, though some individual burials may be later. The next settlements are Slavonic. Widely different views are advanced on their initial date. For R. Beltz and P. Diels (RV 12, 251-92) the Slavs 'pressed forward immediately behind the departing Germans'. The pottery has been classified into three successive groups I, II, and III by A. Gotz, who starts group I, c. A.D. 600, maintained by E. Schuldt, *Die Slavische in Mitteleuropa*, Berlin, 1956, 7, as 'still valid', put back by H.A. Knorr (*Die slawische Keramik zwischen Elbe und Oder*, Mannus-Bucherei 58, 1937) to 700. The most important westward sites are Hamburg Altstadt and Farchau bei Ratzeburg, Lausenberg, regarded by H. Jankuhn, *Geschichte Schleswig-Holsteins*, 3, 1957, 100, as a Slavonic site of the late eighth or early ninth century. To Jankuhn, however, Czech research has succeeded in recent decades in isolating early Slavonic pottery, to be dated to the seventh, eighth, or ninth centuries, perhaps as early as the sixth. This dating is in fact much later than that normally advanced by Danubian scholars, and is scarcely compatible with the evidence of Procopius and Paulus Diaconus. The material from the Lower Elbe Slav sites is not easily available. Tischler, however, *Sachsenforschung* (RGKB 35, 1954, Abb. 29, p. 85), illustrates a plate of vessels from Hamburg Altstadt giving them the same date as Jankuhn, c. 800, but calling them 'late Saxon'. The largest vessel illustrated is, in the opinion of such Czech scholars as I have been able to consult, an ordinary Prague Type, its accompanying vessels late Roman derivatives of the fifth and sixth centuries. The Prague Type would, in the Danube, be of the same date. Prague Type pots are also found on other Baltic German sites, e.g., Prytzke, Brandenburg, though dated by J. Herrmann, *Die vor- und fruehgeschichtlichen Burgwälle Gross-Berlins* (Deutsche Akademie der Wissenschaft zu Berlin, Schriften der Sektion fuer Vor- und Fruehgeschichte 9), 1960, 27, citing W. Unversagt and J. Hermann, *Ausgrabungen und Funde* 3, 1958, to the late seventh century (*cf.* e.g., B. Schmidt, *Die spaete Voelkerwanderungszeit in Mitteldeutschland*, Halle, 1961, Plate 27, especially G and H). Occasionally in the border regions Slav and Germanic burials are found in the same cemetery, e.g. Stossen by the Saale, south-west of Leipzig (K. Zeigel, *Nachrichtenblatt fuer Deutsche Vorzeit*, 11, 1935, 133, cited in Schmidt, above), where at least grave 106 in a long-lived Germanic cemetery contains Slav pottery (*cf.* Beichlingen, Sommerdar, Thuringia [G. Mildenberger, *Mitteldeutschlands Ur- und Fruehgeschichte*, Leipzig, 1959, Figs. 126-7]): a Thuringian cast saucer brooch probably of the mid- to late sixth century, and a Prague Type urn.

It is theoretically possible that a common pot-form might have been retained by Baltic Slavs for several centuries after it had ceased to be used on the Danube, but no evidence suggests such a discrepancy. No adequate corpus of the material exists, and no thorough comparison of the Baltic and Danubian material has yet been undertaken. In its absence, the dates advanced in north Germany, disagreeing by several centuries with one another, most of them centuries later than the corresponding Danubian dates, do not appear to rest upon evidence. They appear to be influenced by the assumptions of the economic historians cited above that 'careless' Slavs infiltrated into areas long relinquished by the Germans. The principal present hindrance to close study of the available evidence is the modern difficulty that faces north German scholars in presenting evidence from which the dispassionate inference is that Hamburg was founded by the Slavs in the sixth century.

The archaeological evidence is supplemented by that of the place-names. Place-name evidence cannot by itself give absolute dates. It can show differences between regions, and suggest relative dates. Where evidence is available, as in England, marked variations in distributions normally coincide with the dates when regions were first settled. The terminations -worth, -worthy, -wardine, are dialect differences; but the form -worth prevails almost universally in the areas of fifth- and sixth-century settlement, the others, in Devon and on the Welsh borders, in areas first settled in the seventh and eighth centuries. The termination -tun is evenly spread through all areas, and was in use from the beginnings of English settlement until after the Norman conquest, but the forms in -ingas, -ingaham, etc. are very rare in areas first settled after the sixth century.

The Slavonic place-names of Germany present similar features. They have not been studied comprehensively, and no survey of place-names exists. It is therefore not possible to ascertain early forms. Enquiry is necessarily limited to those which appear upon modern maps; and must therefore be restricted to terminations which are not liable to alternative origins. The commonest terminations, as frequent as English -tun, -ham, etc., are those in -ow, -in, -itz. Names in -ow must be ignored, since -ow is often spelt -au, and German -au has an independent existence, equivalent to English -ey; but names in -in and -itz have no such complications.

The distribution of these names is markedly different. Names in -itz run in very large numbers up to the farthest frontier of Slavonic settlement, without significant variation within, as evenly spread as English -tun. Names in -in, however, are found in a more restricted region, as English -ingas, etc. They reach the frontier of Slavonic settlement in the north about Kiel, and follow it closely, in considerable numbers, as far south as the Madgeburg region. Their southern limit then runs westward, south of Berlin, to the Oder, and then curves southward into Bohemia, skirting and slightly penetrating the northern Bohemian territory of earlier German settlement, overrun by the Avars and Slavs about 567, but occurring rarely therein. Outside that area they are common in the southern upland, but not in the border mountains and their foothills.

In England, comparable distributions can be matched against the evidence for the advance of the English given by texts and large numbers of well furnished graves. The Slavonic distributions have no such supporting evidence to show that the difference they mark is a difference of date, save that the area where -in names are common roughly corresponds with the area of distribution of the Prague Type, and that in the area where the -in names are not found, Germanic graves appear to last a generation or two longer than elsewhere, notably about Dresden (*cf.* e.g., B. Schmidt, *Die spaete Voelkerwanderungszeit in Mitteldeutschland*, Halle, 1961, Fig 8, p.23), mid-sixth century, as late as the Frankish sites in Bohemia.

The most reasonable interpretation of this complex evidence is that the habit of using -in names in areas of new settlement, and the use of the Prague Type vessels died out at much the same time, and that time was approximately the second half of the sixth century. This frontier suggests that the Slavonic peoples advanced at more or less the same time both along the Baltic coast and up the Danube, filling in the area between later on. The particular frequency of -in names in the Bohemian upland, in contrast to the Prague area, and in Holstein and in the Lauenburg area east of Hamburg, indicates that these regions may have been reached somewhat earlier towards the beginning of the sixth century. These indications match the statement of Procopius, who reports a considerable deserted area in and perhaps south of Schleswig Holstein, south of the Varni, *c*.500, but suggests that the Slavs were nearer neighbours of the Varni 20 years later. These inferences rest on the accessible available evidence. They are liable to modification as and when further evidence becomes available.

TAILTIU (Teltown) (*N 87*), Meath.
The Synod of Tailtiu excommunicated Columba in 561/2, Adomnán v. *Columbae* 3, 3.

The *Fair* of Tailtu is concisely described by Keating 1, 39 (2,249); the Fair was annual at the end of the seventh century (v. *Moling* 18: VSH) and continued till the disruption of the Scandinavian invasions in the later ninth century, with short-lived revivals in the tenth and eleventh (*cf.* Binchy, *Ériu*, 18, 1958, 115 ff.).

TARA (*N 95*), Meath, seat of the high kings of Ireland. The Feast of Tara was discussed by Binchy, *Ériu*, 18, 1958, 127 ff. Whether or not it was a 'primitive fertility rite' (p. 127), connected with Beltaine, or any other feast, or with the 'apotheosis' or 'inauguration' of kings, the *Annals* record it of three fifth- or sixth-century kings, and three only. In none of these references is there any suggestion that it had anything to do either with religion or with the inauguration of kings, let alone with the deaths of the predecessors; and in each case it is dated long after the king's accession. An 'assembly to regulate the laws and customs of the country' was held at Tara about 660 (v. *Geraldi* 12), another at Drumceat about 574. I know of no suggestion in ancient sources to warrant the modern hypothesis that the Tara Feast was disliked by Christians because it had pagan associations. Tigernach and the seventeenth-century Annals call Diarmait's Feast in 560 the 'Last Feast of Tara'; whether the word in Tigernach is part of the original text or a late gloss I do not know. Diarmait appears to have been the last king of Tara who was able to enforce the effective obedience of the 'nobles of all Ireland'. The Feast may have involved hostages, for Diarmait's fateful execution of the king of Connacht's hostage-son seems to have taken place during the Feast.

TRAPRAIN LAW (*NT 5874*), East Lothian, between Edinburgh and Dunbar. Dunpelder in British, Kepduf in Gaelic (Watson, CPNS 345). In the early sixth century it was the residence of Leudonus of the Lothians, father of Thynoy, mother of Kentigern, and many other saints. A hog-back hill, whose fortifications enclose 32 acres. Excavated 1914-19; see PSAS.

The fortress contained numerous round and oval houses, with much undressed building stone, Roman coins from the first to the fifth century (Nero to Arcadius), some other Roman material from the second century onward, and much of the latest Roman pottery, rare elsewhere north of the frontier. It was clearly the residence of a ruler who was in treaty relations with Rome, probably in or after the second century, with a marked increase in Roman connections in the later fourth century. The site is one of two large fortified centres north of the wall, situated in northern Votadinian territory, matching Yeavering Bell, near Wooler, among the southern Votadini. One of these fortresses is likely to have been the residence of Paternus Pesrut, probably appointed by Valentinian I. Since comparable Roman material is not reported from Yeavering Bell, Traprain Law is the more probable royal centre of Paternus.

The site contained a rich silver treasure (A.O. Curle, *The Treasure of Traprain*, Glasgow, 1923), much of it bent and broken, apparently ready for smelting; the hoard contained four coins, of Valens, Valentinian II, and Honorius (died 423; probably minted *c.*400). Much of the silver seems to have been of north African and eastern Mediterranean origin; the treasure contained an army officer's belt with fittings (Plates 32-3, pp. 84, 88) in *Kerbschnitt*, with Christian A and Ω decoration, and a Gothic brooch of the late fourth or early fifth century. It was presumably a gift to the ruler, or booty, and perhaps originally looted from the Continent rather than Britain; but such treasure is likely to have passed through several hands before the Traprain ruler received or seized it, from Pict, Briton or Saxon.

Traprain Law may have remained a royal centre until the English conquest, since Modwenna is said to have founded a church there, probably in the middle of the seventh century, soon after the English conquest. It is extremely probable that someone built a church there at that date, as Paulinus established a primitive timber church at Yeavering immediately after the conversion of Northumbria, which in 627 controlled Yeavering, but probably not yet Traprain Law.

VALENTIA. It is theoretically possible that this new Late Roman province was the territory between the two walls, and that Quintilius Clemens and Tacitus of Ceint, in the Alclud and Gododdin genealogies, were its first two governors. But it seems highly improbable that the territory from which troops had been evacuated after centuries of occupation should be described as 'recovered', even in language that flatters the reigning emperor's father, and equally improbable that territory abandoned, on the enemy side of the most advanced Roman military position, should be given the status and title of a province. It is much more probable that this was part of the territory not recovered, and to which it was decided not to appoint a 'legitimate rector'. The institution of Roman *praefecti* seems to have been the alternative here. Unless and until there is positive evidence to the contrary, Valentia must be sought on the west coast, in the area exposed to Irish raids, rather than in the north.

VARNI. Suevi, among the peoples who worshipped Nerthus, in Jutland, between the Angli and the Eudoses (Jutes?), Tacitus, *Germania* 40 (Varni). Ptolemy distinguishes the Pharodini (2, 213), probably Tacitus's Varini and the Viruni (2, 12, 17), apparently on the Baltic coast, *cf.* Pliny *NH* 4, 28, a branch of the Vandals, who perhaps named Waernemunde; apparently two branches of the same people. Waerne, *Widsith* 59, the king Billing Wernum, 25.

Tacitus locates them about the eastern end of the modern Danish-German border. There is no trace of them in England. About 494, Heruli, returning from Sweden, passed through a deserted territory between the Slavs and the Varni, which presumably included Angeln, Procopius Gothic Wars, 2, 25 (see SLAVS). About 505 Theodoric the Great urged the kings of Heruli, Guarni and Thuringi to deter Clovis from attacking the Visigoths (Cassiodorus, *Variae* 3, 3); about 510×520 a Langobard refugee fled from the Varni to the Slavs, evidently not far distant; *see* on this Procopius, Gothic Wars 3, 35. In the reign of Theudebert (534-47) the king of the Varni on the Lower Rhine, evidently on the north bank in the Utrecht-Leiden area, made a marriage alliance with the Angli, but changed to a Frankish alliance, and was subdued by an invading force of Angli from England. By the eighth century, Varni (Werini) were located with Angli in Thuringia, and had evidently long lived there.

Their law code is extant in a Corbie MS., and, in somewhat better shape, in the *editio princeps* by J.B. Herold, Basel, 1557, whose MS., perhaps of Fulda, is lost. The Corbie MS. entitles the text '*Lex Thuringorum*', while Herold gives '*Lex Angliorum et Uuerinorum, hoc est Thuringorum*'. The title has troubled some modern writers, who did not expect Angli in Thuringia; occasionally, the Thuringi, along with the Angli, have been transported to a semi-mythical 'Torangia' in the Low Countries, on the strength of Procopius's account of the presence of Varni on the north bank of the Rhine estuary in the 530s.

The evidence of archaeology and place-names is decisive. A sizable proportion of the vessels recovered from Thuringian graves of the late fifth and perhaps earlier sixth centuries, preserved in Weimar and Halle regional museums, are Anglian, and are there so described. A few cruciform brooches of Åberg group 11, of *circa*

500, are also preserved in central Germany, and similar vessels and brooches of the same general date occur in Bohemia. In all contexts, the Varni are named as immediate neighbours and associates of the Angles, but no distinctive pottery can be ascribed to them.

Whatever they used is included in what we call Anglian. Immediately north of Angeln in Schleswig is a group of place-names ending -leben, found on both sides of the modern German-Danish border, and is probably those of the Varni. Names ending in -leben are elsewhere found only in Thuringia. There they are very many, numbering many hundreds, entirely associated within the borders of the greater Thuringian kingdom, both in the northern portion, overwhelmed by the Franks in 537, and in the southern portion that remains Thuringian. On the western border of this northern portion is also a tiny dense concentration of -buttl names, north of Brunswick.

A considerable part of the population in Thuringia consisted of Angli and Varni who had immigrated in the fifth century. The end of their pottery roughly coincides with its end in their homeland. Whether or not any large part of their wares was imported, or made by potters who emigrated, the grandchildren of the first immigrants were clearly content with local Thuringian products, in place of the ornament of their ancestors. It does not of course follow that they therefore immediately merged their identity with the native Thuringians. The title of the laws, written down probably in 802, suggests that they were in origin the laws of the Angli and Varni within Thuringia, rather than of the Thuringians themselves. Their principal content is the statement of composition payments in monetary prices; the payments themselves, and their relative worth, will of course be much older than these payments. Some sections appear in Kentish law almost 200 years earlier.

VOTADINI. *See* GWYNEDD, TRAPRAIN LAW. Ptolemy, Nennius. *See* K.H. Jackson, *The Gododdin*, Edinburgh, 1969, 69 ff.

WALES. Evidence for the administration of Wales during the Roman empire is still extremely thin. Inscriptions, notably RIB 311, attest a normal civilian government of the *civitas Silurum* with a capital at Caerwent. A similar government is probable among the Demetae, though their capital, with whatever inscriptions it may contain, is completely buried under the modern town of Carmarthen, as yet virtually unexcavated. The territory of the Ordovices in north Wales is dominated by the Roman fort of Segontium (Caernarfon). Theirs is the only name known to the geographer Ptolemy, and the Decangli, known to Tacitus and probably preserved in the place-name Degannwy, near Llandudno, may have been a subordinate constituent part of the Ordovices, and were in any case overshadowed by Chester. A number of villages of the Roman period, some on hilltops, have been excavated, but there are no signs of civilian capital towns or country houses (villas). The continuing military presence, the absence of the normal signs of civil government, and the post-Roman inscription boasting relationship to a *magistratus* (ECMW 103) suggest that the basis of civilian government will have been through *magistri vici*, as in the north, local magistrates appointed with the approval of the central Roman government. It is theoretically possible that in some areas one or more families were important enough for *magistri* to be chosen from among them, but the excavated native sites show no sign of a social differential that would encourage the view that there were outstanding families. Eastern Wales appears to have been divided between the lowland *civitates* of the Cornovii in the upper Severn and the Dobunni in the upper Wye valleys, though it is not known how far west either extended; and nothing is known of the political administration of Cardiganshire. But nowhere in the north or centre is there any sign of monarchs or chiefs in the Roman period. The two southern *civitates* contain a number of villas, and their government will have been in the hands of a normal landed aristocracy. It is quite possible that in the fourth or early fifth century concentration of property may have led, as elsewhere in the Roman west, to the emergence of one or two families rich enough to overtop the rest with a quasi-monarchical authority, and that the fifth-century dynasties of Gwent, perhaps also Glywysing, may have evolved from such families. But there was no monarchy in the Roman period.

Most of the evidence comes from northern poems. They incorporate broken traditions of Maelgwn, but may attribute to him the normal features of a northern ruler without independent tradition. But Gildas credits Maelgwn with retainers who bawl Bacchanalian songs in his honour, which implies poets to compose them and musicians to accompany them. Cynddylan of the Wroxeter area and the Powysian kings in the poems had halls on defended hilltops. There was post-Roman occupation at Caernarfon and Caerhun, the Roman fort on the Conwy, which bears the name of Maelgwn's son, Rhun.

Welsh tradition assigns the later north Welsh royal capital of Aberffraw in Anglesey to Maelgwn, and it might have been one of his centres. It is evident that the north Welsh kingdom was divided in the later fifth century and largely reunited under Maelgwn; and its several sections will have had their own political centres. But the initial base for Cunedda's reconquest of north Wales must have been Chester. Chester has no independent place in northern or Welsh tradition. Had it formed a separate state with its own kings, it is scarcely possible that it could have avoided playing some part in the well preserved traditions of either Powys or the north or both, and it is therefore probable that it formed part of one of the known kingdoms. In the later sixth century, under Maelgwn's son or grandson, the monastery of Bangor-on-Menai was able to found a large daughter house at Bangor-on-Dee, and St Beuno at the end of the century founded Tegeingl (Flintshire) under the authority of Maelgwn's descendants. It is therefore likely that Chester formed part of his kingdom, and remained within his successor's dominions until the English conquest in 613. But for a king who had to fight to retain control of both 'Wild' Wales and Wales east of the Conwy, Chester was a remote normal residence. Caerhun or Conwy are better sited. The evidence of post-Roman occupation, however, in defended sites, whether of Roman or pre-Roman origin, is still too imprecise to establish which were royal residences when. There is, however, a marked absence of defended homesteads. Such sites are by contrast very common in the south, some moderately small, some tiny; one, Dinas Powys, near Cardiff, has been thoroughly excavated and fully and clearly reported (Leslie Alcock, *Dinas Powys*, Cardiff, 1963), and for the present is a type site. The smaller sites, whatever their date and appearance, are called *Rath* in Demetia, but not in Silurian territory; the vast majority are unexcavated, and it is not yet possible to say which were occupied or re-occupied or first constructed in the post-Roman centuries.

WALLOP. '*Et a regno Guorthigirni usque ad discordiam Guitolini et Ambrosii anni sunt XII, quod est Guoloppum, id est Catguoloph.*' ('And from the reign of Vortigern to the quarrel of Vitalinus and Ambrosius are 12 years, which is Wallop, the battle of Wallop.') (Nennius 66.)

WANSDYKE (Wodnesdic, Woden's Ditch). The name of two massive dykes with banks, defending Somerset and Wiltshire against an enemy on the north. West Wansdyke runs for seven and a half miles, overlooking the Bristol Avon, from the Horsecombe Valley south of Bath to Maes Knoll (*ST 6066*), overlooking Bristol;

east Wansdyke for 12 miles from Morgan's Hill, north of Devizes, to Savernake by Marlborough, near the Roman town of Cunetio, Mildenhall. Almost all the interval is filled by the Roman road from Cunetio to Bath. A number of shorter sections of dyke with different names extend eastward, to turn sharply southward, just west of Silchester, some 70 miles east of Maes Knoll.

The Wansdyke was first proved to be later than the Roman period by the excavation of Pitt-Rivers (*Bokerley Dyke and Wansdyke*, 1892); surveyed by O.G.S. Crawford, *Archaeology in the Field*, 1953, 252 ff. Both sections are of similar construction (photographs, Ant. 6, 1932, 349; G.J. Copley, *Conquest of Wessex*, 1954, 80-1, etc.). Both parts with the Roman road had been dug out to construct a similar embankment along its length. In disproving the digging-up of the Roman road, Sir Cyril Fox (Arch. Jl. 115, 1958, 1 ff.; *cf.* A. Clark, Ant. 32, 1958, 89) argued that the two Wansdykes were separate works constructed on separate occasions, an inference rightly rejected by J.N.L. Myres (*Essays . . . to Sir Keith Feiling*, ed. H.R. Trevor-Roper, 1964, 1).

Both sections bear the name of Woden, and they cannot have received that name after the pagan period. The name means that the pagan English did not know who built the massive earthwork, and ascribed it to the gods, that it was built before the English reached the area. It is not reasonable to assume that the Saxons had anything to do with building it; the English did not reach its western end until about the time of the conversion of Wessex, probably not until some years later. The eastern end was reached in the 550s, but it is not probable that they then built it, and their grandchildren forgot who had built it. The earthwork is a British construction of the fifth or sixth century. Eastward to Marlborough, with the Roman road, it is a virtually continuous frontier; farther east, construction differs, and consists of a series of short ditches, separated by land that was presumably forested when it was built. No part of it makes any sense as an English frontier, since even in the later sixth century it cuts between the related cemeteries of Salisbury and East Shefford; but it closely corresponds with the northern frontier of the Roman *civitates* of the Belgae and the Dumnonii, which are likely to have been united under a single Dumnonian king after the battle of Badon.

The earthwork is not a 'defensive' earthwork in the sense of a Roman wall or modern military wall manned by a permanent garrison. It is a frontier work which enables a small force to move rapidly along with clear vision, spot and catch cattle raiders, or march parallel with an invading enemy who seeks an easy crossing point, and choose its own ground for battle, forcing the enemy to delay slightly in crossing. For this purpose the Roman road from Cunetio to the neighbourhood of Bath was deemed an effective frontier; and might have been protected by a wooden fence on the north.

WELSH LAND-MEASUREMENT. The Welsh unit of land measurement in the LL texts is the *uncia* (twelfth part, evidently then connected with the Irish *gniom*), which was, according to Columella, in *De Re Rustica*, 5, 1, in early Roman reckoning 2,400 (square) feet, approximately half an English acre of 12 *modii* (i.e., the area that requires 12 *modii*, the area requiring sowing by a *modius* of corn, in Classical reckoning, one third of an *iugerum*, about 10,000 square feet). The terms do not correspond to their Roman areas. One text, LL 164, placed in the mid-seventh century, gives the unequivocal boundaries of Ballingham, Herefordshire (*SO 5731*), an area of about two square miles, or 1,300 acres, almost entirely enclosed by the Wye, which it rates at two-and-a-half *uncia*. On this occasion, an *uncia* contained a total superficial area of about 500 acres. Four other texts (LL 201, 203,

209) all placed in the mid-eighth century give the value of estates, ranging from 20 cows an *uncia* to 60-80 cows an *uncia*. The figures, however, are a rash of uncertainties; one defined estate is no basis for a general calculation, and may be corrected when exploration on the ground of the numerous boundaries detailed in LL provides other equations; although plainly the compilers and transcribers of the LL texts, whatever their dates, intended precise figures with a meaning that served their purpose, the value of land varied with its worth. The figures, however, invite further study.

WHITHORN. Three main Irish traditions, relating to two distinct periods, send Irish saints to train at Whithorn. Those of Finnian of Moville in the mid-sixth century name a monastery at 'Futerna' (a late Irish transliteration of the English name Whithorn), 'Candida', and 'Magnum Monasterium', the monastery of 'Nennio' or 'Mugentius' (*Irish Liber Hymnorum*, Preface to Hymn of Mugint, 1, 97; Colgan, ASH 633 ff.). One text treats 'Nennio' as the living abbot rather than the founder, much as accounts of visits to the monastery of St Martin of Tours sometimes make visitors meet St Martin in person. The title 'Magnum Monasterium' means that northern Irish tradition regarded Whithorn as the 'great monastery' and contains no allusion to Tours, where Martin's monastery was also called 'great'. Traditions of an earlier period in the lives of Enda and the related lives of Eugenius of Ardstraw and Tigernach of Clones call the monastery 'Rosnat, otherwise Alba', under Nennyo or McNennus and Maucennus. The place-name is here less decisive, being equated with 'Alba', white, an alternative for 'Candida', but in theory it might be argued that the equation misunderstands an original 'Rosnat in Alba (Britain)'. The place-name ROSNAT (*q.v.*) is not otherwise known; nor is the geographical name of Whithorn, whose English and Latin appellations both refer to Ninnian's church, and do not preserve the name by which the site was previously known. Save for the equation with Alba, there is nothing to show whether Rosnat was or was not the name of the site on which Ninnian built.

The personal names are, however, more decisive. The forms Nennyo and Mo-Nenn indicate the monastery of Ninnian. No tradition locates this monastery anywhere but at Whithorn. There are, however, possible connections with south Wales. Maucennus is one of the spellings of the name of St Mawgan. His dedications are unusually widespread, from north Wales to Brittany, but his principal centre appears to have been in Cemais, south of Cardigan. No Life survives, and there is no direct evidence to give his date, or to connect him with the northern Maucennus; but there are some hints. About the 490s, the parents of Samson visited a 'magister librariusque' who lived 'in longinquam terram aquilonis' (in the far north), but was then staying ('commanebat') three days' journey from their Demetian home. At about the same date, the parents of David gave gifts 'ad Maucanni monasterium, quod nunc usque Depositi monasterium vocatur'. Deposit or pledge is in Welsh 'gwystl' and the monastery was doubtless that of Guistilianus, whom the Life of David makes abbot Vetus Rubus and 'uncle' of the saint. Both stories concern hopes of a child yet unborn. The Life of Samson made use of the recollections of the saint's mother, and is good evidence that a distinguished ecclesiastic from the far north visited Demetia, then still under Irish rule, towards the end of the fifth century. The later traditions suggest that he was Maucennus of Whithorn, and that he founded in Irish Demetia one or more daughter houses, whose fame was later eclipsed by David. There may have been more than one. David's principal monastery, the modern St David's, is said to have borne previously the name of

Rosina Vallis (Glyn Rosin in *Buchedd Dewi*). Though Ricemarchus identifies it with Hodnant, he made heavy weather of the confused names in his sources, and it is theoretically possible that the native name was Rhosnant, corrupted in Ireland to Rosnat. David, of course, is not involved, for he was not yet born when Enda was schooled, and was at best a child in the time of Eugenius and Tigernach; but the monasteries may have existed. The confused accounts of David's life suggest that his severe discipline prevailed in a number of pre-existing houses, which later tradition turned into new foundations.

It is therefore uncertain whether Rosnat is to be identified with Whithorn or St David's. In either case, Enda, Eugenius and Tigernach were held to have been trained in a Ninniac house headed by abbot Maucennus of Whithorn, and Irish tradition sharply distinguished him from abbot Mugentius, who lived half a century later.

WINWAED. The encounter between Oswy and Penda in 654, when the latter was killed, is placed by Bede '*prope fluvium Uinued* . . . in regione Loidis' (*HE* 3, 24). The River Winwaed cannot be identified with any certainty, but *Loidis* is certainly the area round Leeds. R.B.W.

YEAVERING BELL (*NT 9229*), Northumberland, west of Wooler, near the head of a tapering valley with no inland access, secure, but uncomfortably situated amid winds of unusual vehemence. The site had a stone wall eight or more feet high, 10 to 12 feet wide. With an area of 13½ acres, it is half the size of Traprain, but four times as big as any other southern Votadinian fort, or of any other prehistoric fort north of the Humber, with the exception of Almondsbury, 16 acres, and Roulstone Scar, 53 acres, both in the central Pennines. The entrenchments of Stanwix by Scots Corner belong to an entirely different context. The interior contained a large number of round and oval huts with diameters of about 15 to 30 feet.

Immediately after the English conquest, Aethelferth constructed a royal vill at the foot of the hill. It is difficult to perceive any reason for constructing the vill on such an inconvenient site, unless it was still a principal British residence at the time of the conquest. There was some native occupation over the remains of the English vill after the English moved their centre to a more convenient site in the middle of the seventh century.

Paulinus spent 36 days baptising the Bernicians in the River Glen (now Beaumont Water) at Ad Gefrin (Yeavering in Glendale), in 627, Bede *HE* 2, 14; and it is probable that one of the excavated structures is a temple converted to a church by Paulinus. The name is British, *DEPN* 544.

YORK(H). Vita *Meven 1* reads 'Orcheus pagus' for Ercig, Archenfeld, Herefordshire, south of the Wye, later incorporated into the Gwent territories of the Morgannwg kings. Vita *Meven 2* (AG 323) translates its source as '*une ville aux quartiers de (G)Went qui s'appelloit Orkh*' whence came the family of Samson's mother, and makes Samson '*archevesque d'Yorkh*'. In the earlier lives Samson was bishop of a district north of the Severn, that might have included Ercig ('Yorkh') or been so interpreted. The life used by AG was presumably a Breton version of a British original. The British original was doubtless the source of the late antiquarian Welsh pretence that Samson was 'archbishop of York'. The authors of this transmutation of names may or may not have been aware that one church in York had an ancient Samson dedication. The late south Welsh fable cannot, however, have contributed to the reasons which caused a church in English York to bear Samson's name. Unless a plausible occasion for the honouring of Samson in York after the English conquest can be discovered, the probable inference is that a church on the site bore the name of Samson before the conquest; its likely origin is a small monastery or school established by a pupil of Samson's shortly before the fall of British York, in the years about 550×580.

SAXON ARCHAEOLOGY

The Chronology of Early Anglo-Saxon Archaeology*

The Anglo-Saxon Cemeteries of Caistor-by-Norwich and Markshall, Norfolk (Reports of the Research Committee of the Society of Antiquaries of London, no. 30). By J. N. L. Myres and Barbara Green. 20·5 × 27 cm. xx + 262 + 5 pp., 71 figs., 24 pls., 3 maps. Oxford: Society of Antiquaries of London, and Thames and Hudson, 1973.

This long awaited volume reports the patient study of excavations undertaken forty years ago by the late F. R. Mann. 439 urns are illustrated from Caistor, with the grave-goods, from a total of 496 known cremations and 60 late inhumations; from near-by Markshall 101 urns are illustrated from an estimated total of several hundreds. A map and a gazetteer list 156 Saxon burial grounds in East Anglia, E. of Royston and N. of Harwich, though space excludes references. The late Rainbird Clarke describes earlier Roman use of the future cemetery site, and the last years of Roman Caistor are discussed.

The volume is much more than a site report. Caistor is at present the most important of the great English urnfields, for it is the best published. In time it will be overshadowed by the more numerous urns of Elmham, Loveden and other sites; but the reports and interpretations of these sites are bound to draw heavily from the Caistor evidence. Myres has therefore classified and dated the Caistor urns, and his volume will serve as a basic reference work.

The relative dates stand foursquare; and so do most of the continental parallels, showing whence the English came. The main conclusions are likely to endure, for, though Myres himself makes limited use of associated grave-goods, their evidence firmly endorses his main inferences. Myres' *Caistor* and *Anglo-Saxon Pottery and the Settlement of England* (Oxford, 1969) much advance the frontiers of knowledge, for they have systematized the evidence, enabling future workers to identify vessels with greater precision.

More troublesome are the absolute dates, especially of the earliest period. Myres' introduction gives much space and heavy emphasis to his view that English burials in Britain began much sooner than his colleagues have supposed. In 1969 he suggested "say 360". Now he considers it "quite possible" that the Caistor cemetery came into use in the 3rd century, and asserts "that it was so used on an increasing scale from at least the middle of the 4th century can be taken as certain" (p. 13). The 4th-century "increase" assumes that prior 3rd-century use was not merely 'possible', but probable, if not 'certain'.

This view matters, for it entails a radical reappraisal of how and why the English came to Britain, and also of the recorded policies of successive late Roman governments towards the employment of barbarian troops. If it is silently accepted and then proves mistaken, it will mislead a generation; for many will read the conclusions set forth in the introduction and quote them as gospel, but far fewer will have the means or the experience to scrutinize the evidence which purports to justify them. This evidence must therefore be the main concern of a short review. Enquiry cannot begin with the Caistor report, for much is there taken for granted. It must go back to square one, and look at the nature of the evidence upon which all datings of the Germanic migration period rest, and at the ways in which modern scholars have used it.

The starting point for all archaeological datings in western and central Europe in the early centuries A.D. is Roman literature. Most Roman pots and sites are dated either because they are found with the coins of emperors, whose reigns are dated by surviving writings, or because the foundation or destruction of sites is reported by writers; and most barbarian objects are dated by association, direct or indirect, with datable Roman

---

[4] 'Der Stand der Sachsenforschung archäologisch gesehen', *35. Bericht der Römisch-Germanischen Kommission*, 1954, 66–7.

* Review reprinted from *Medieval Archaeology* 18 (1974) 225–32, by kind permission of the Society for Medieval Archaeology.

objects, or by notices which report the dates at which various barbarians moved in and out of particular regions.

A single statement by one contemporary writer concerns the migration of the English to Britain. In 441 or 442 Britain passed *"in dicionem Saxonum"*, "under Saxon control".[5] The words were written ten years after the event by a northern Gaul, who could not know that in the future 'Saxon control' was to be overset, and not permanently reasserted until the 570s. Before then Gildas, writing about 540, just within living memory of the event, describes (ch. 23) the overthrow of the constituted government of Britain by rebellious Saxons, who had previously been invited peaceably into Britain by a 'proud tyrant', whom later texts call Vortigern, some years after Italy had abandoned Roman Britain; the first settlers had been few, but they had been followed soon by large reinforcements, in the time of the same ruler. The contemporary notice places the first arrival of the English not later than 441; Gildas, who was born about thirty-five years after Vortigern's death, places it after Italy had abandoned Roman Britain, in 410. Other evidence argues that the main migration was over, and much of the homeland deserted, by about 500 A.D.

These are not dubious texts, at variance with archaeological evidence. On the contrary, it is upon these texts that modern German scholars have based their dating system, and they still remain today its ultimate criteria. The essentials of their dating have endured, robust because they are firmly built upon contemporary written evidence, not only upon typological speculation. The fundamental survey of the evidence is the seventy-page thesis of Alfred Plettke, completed in tragic haste; his preface is dated 4 August 1914, and a few weeks later he was killed. His work was published in 1921 by his father, the director of the Morgenstern Museum and excavator of Westerwanna, who added two pages of important cautionary notes.[6]

Plettke recognized, more clearly than many others, that in N. Germany and Scandinavia there is no independent native date criterion whatever. For the Roman period he used and extended the work of his predecessors, O. Almgren and others, whose main guide to dating had been Roman imports or imitations thereof, especially brooches. For the migration period he anchored his dates upon the statements of the Gallic Chronicler and Gildas, which he found through the historical work of L. Schmidt. His argument is clear. "After 407 . . . Prince Vortigern took a band of Germans into his pay . . . But more and more Germans pressed in . . . The Germans were victorious in 441/42 . . . Not until the battle of *Mons Badonicus* was the advance of the Angles and Saxons halted" (p. 65). He was as clear about the consequence for the homeland, emphasizing that "I know of no Anglo-Saxon cremation cemetery in north-west Germany . . . that lasts beyond . . . the 5th century" (pp. 69–70).

These texts gave him a simple and effective yardstick. Types found in both Britain and Germany are in principle 5th-century; those found in Germany alone are 4th-century or earlier, and those found in Britain alone are 6th-century or later. The yardstick is used repeatedly. The A7 urn-type (*Buckelurnen*) is 5th-century "because it is particularly plentiful in England" (p. 45); the date of the early cruciform brooches is fixed "because their presence in England indicates the period about 400" (p. 15), but, in contrast, their predecessor, the *Armbrustfibel* "is still missing in England . . . which argues . . . a typical 4th-century form" (p. 17). Similar judgements recur again and again.

The researches of half a century have adjusted Plettke's conclusions in detail, but have left his main fabric untouched. Myres still uses his categories to describe German pots. In Germany in 1954 Tischler's thorough reappraisal of the evidence emphasized that "in the last analysis, my chronology deviates only slightly from Plettke's", and in 1969 P. Schmid's discussion of Feddersen Wierde opens with the assertion that Plettke's "arrangement of the material still today forms the starting point for chronological evaluation . . . in the North Sea coastal area".[7]

Plettke was a starting point. Later work has modified much detail. Though it has confirmed that most sites ended in the 5th century, a few burials on a few sites are later.

---

[5] *Monumenta Germaniae Historica, Auctores Antiquissimi*, IX, *Chronica Minora* I, 615 ff.
[6] A. Plettke, *Ursprung und Ausbreitung der Angeln und Sachsen*, (Hildesheim, 1921).
[7] F. Tischler in *35. Bericht der Römisch-Germanischen Kommission*, 1954, 21 ff.; P. Schmid, 'Feddersen Wierde', *Neue Ausgrabungen und Forschungen in der Niedersachsen*, IV (1969).

Some types that Plettke did not know in England have now been recognized here, and therefore on this criteria "extend into the 5th century". But the most important modification was already printed in his book. His father's notes (p. 84) drew attention to Brenner's important article, published in 1915, warning that many dates should be up to half a century later.[8] War-time publications and small print are easily overlooked, and it was forty years later that Tischler worked out this redating in detail; in particular, he shifted the A3 and A4 urns from the 3rd century to the 4th, and the "early 4th century" A5 urns moved with them, extending into the 5th century. But not everything moved automatically later. It is still true that no *Armbrustfibel* has yet been found in England; and though one or two may be found in the future, their rarity would still mark them as characteristically 4th-century. But they are often found in urns indistinguishable from those that contain their successors, the early cruciform brooches. Similar urns persisted through the decades about the turn of the 4th and 5th centuries, in which the new brooch fashion ousted the old.

Fruitful new considerations have also emerged. Myres has convincingly argued[9] that earlier classification concentrated too exclusively on the shapes of vessels, too little on their decoration, and also that imitations of much earlier forms, or anticipations of later forms, are natural and normal. German scholarship has also tended to avoid overprecise dating, for even the abundant material of late Roman pottery can rarely be pressed to a closer date bracket than half a century, and has emphasized periods or stages. As B. Almgren and D. M. Wilson have shown, a period cannot normally be less than a generation of thirty or forty years, the working life of a craftsman and the adult life of his customers; and the shorthand symbol of 'the time about 400' cannot mean more than the limits of about 380/420.

German datings have stayed steady, and have not faced serious challenge to the fundamental arguments upon which Plettke based them. The study of the English material has been more erratic. Until about twenty years ago almost all scholars, including Myres, accepted Bede's mistaken date of 'about 450' for the first arrival of the English without critical enquiry, and ignored the evidence on which German dates were founded, while German scholars paid no attention to Bede. Confusion naturally followed. In particular, the important double grave at Dyke Hills, Dorchester-on-Thames, which contained a late Roman officer's belt and a woman's brooch of a prototype cruciform type, paralleled in Germany but not in Britain, was squeezed back to about the mid 5th century, and the early cruciforms that followed, in Germany and England, were dated mid or later 5th century.[10]

English studies also suffered from an unfortunate division of labour. Leeds studied the brooches, Myres the pots. Leeds' sensitive perception of detail was thwarted by his curious assumption that the 'invaders' should have buried their earliest brooches near the coast, and left progressively later types as they slowly 'penetrated' inland by recognizable 'routes'. The notion was never explained, or even discussed, but was maintained against overwhelming contrary evidence, which placed many of the earliest burials deep inland, especially in the Abingdon region, and showed no 'routes'. The imaginary puzzle confused a generation.

English attitudes began to change after 1954, when Kirk and Leeds republished the Dorchester double grave, dating it firmly to the end of the 4th century, with the consequence that the first pagan cemeteries, whose earliest brooches are of slightly later types, might reasonably be assigned to the early 5th century. In the same year Tischler revised the German evidence. Later German dates and earlier English dates for the grave-goods of the first English in Britain removed the main cause of confusion, and Myres then undertook the rethinking of the pottery dates. But the unfortunate division of the material persists, for no comparable reconsideration of the brooches has yet appeared. Its absence hinders estimates of date, for brooches and other metalwork survive in quantity from inhumations, pots principally from cremations; and all evidence agrees that the first immigrants practised both forms of burial simultaneously in various

---

[8] E. Brenner in 7. *Bericht der Römisch-Germanischen Kommission*, 1915, 253 ff.
[9] *Anglo-Saxon Pottery and the Settlement of England* (Oxford, 1969), 23 ff.
[10] N. Åberg, *The Anglo-Saxons in England* (Uppsala, 1926), 13.

regions. No satisfactory conclusions can therefore be drawn from studying a section of the evidence on its own, either pots or brooches.

This is the context in which Myres' analysis of the pottery and his report on Caistor appear. The report begins with the historical background. At Caistor, "Romano-Saxon pottery, late Roman military equipment, and early Germanic cemeteries have all been recorded in close association . . . It is most natural to suppose that these finds represent two aspects of the same phenomenon . . . Germanic mercenaries who . . . defended the walls . . . and . . . were buried . . . outside" (p. 32). The factual statement is formally true in the sense that pottery, equipment and cemeteries were all found in and about the same town; but they are no more 'in association' with each other than they are with earlier Roman material on the same site. The supposition is not 'natural', for it confuses unlike evidence.

'Romano-Saxon' ware was identified by Myres in 1956.[11] A tiny proportion of the output of late Roman kilns imitated decoration popular in NW. Germany. Its purchasers lived and died chiefly in civilian towns, large and small, in East Anglia and the E. midlands; and it is also reported from four Saxon Shore forts and three or four rural sites, mostly farther to the W. The status of its users can only be guessed. It is probable that people who favoured German ornament over successive generations were of German origin, and remained in Germanic communities, not assimilated into Roman society. They may therefore have been a British equivalent of the *gentiles* and *laeti*, descendants of Frankish and Sarmatian prisoner-of-war families settled under military control as dependent cultivators on the estates of some towns and some landowners in Italy and Gaul. It is not probable that they were authorized to wear military insignia, or entrusted with the defence of town walls; but garrisons and citizens needed subject cultivators to feed them, and perhaps to discharge some minor police functions. Their wares are not found in pagan English cemeteries, at Caistor or elsewhere.

Myres is however seeking to explain supposed 3rd and 4th-century burials at Caistor. He therefore holds that "the military belt fittings . . . were undoubtedly used by barbarians in Roman service . . . When the Roman military command withdrew, the 'regular' barbarians may have . . . joined their irregular compatriots . . . It seems certain that some . . . settlers were established before the breakdown of centralized Roman rule in the first decade of the fifth century" (p. 33).

Though many units were doubtless posted to other frontiers in the late Empire, no 'command' was ever 'withdrawn', and there was no early 5th-century 'breakdown'. From 407 military and civil officials were appointed and paid by a Roman government in Britain, no longer in Italy. The devolution of sovereignty did not affect military or other equipment. But other causes brought a change. The belt (*cingulum*) was the badge of rank of civil and military officers, whatever their nationality. Surviving examples have been thoroughly studied by Riegl, Behrens, Bullinger, Mrs. Hawkes and Dunning, and others. They extend all along the European frontier zone, from Britain to the Black Sea, with a few in the interior and a few in German graves, either loot, or the property of former officers. Their fittings range from large ornate plates, often decorated in chip-carving, fit for the highest dignitaries, to the simple buckles of other ranks. They are held to be of Balkan rather than Germanic origin[12] and to have disappeared from the West very early in the 5th century, after the fall of the Rhine frontier. They were not buried in the Caistor cemetery, and are found in Britain only on Roman sites, apart from a few survivals and imitations of simple buckles.

The notion that belts were barbarian stems from a modern belief that most of the late Roman army was German. The information available to the late Empire Prosopography records a German origin for about 15 per cent of the known western 4th-century officers, and suggests that German other ranks were proportionately fewer. But whatever their numbers and national origin, enlisted men issued with belts were quite distinct from the large forces of federate allies raised for particular campaigns in the 4th century, often in civil wars. Both differed from the 5th-century federate settlers, legally established with

---

[11] 'Romano-Saxon Pottery' in *Dark-Age Britain: Studies presented to E. T. Leeds*, ed. D. B. Harden (London, 1956), 16 ff.

[12] H. Bullinger, *Spätantike Gürtelbeschläge* (Dissertationes Gandenses, XII, Bruges, 1969), 69–70, 74, 78.

their families on Roman soil. under their own laws and rulers. They used their own cemeteries, and when they were pagans, like the Franks and the Saxons, they practised their own burial rites and buried their own grave-goods. The first such federate settlement recorded in the West is that of the Visigoths in 418. It was a novelty, and there is no evidence to suggest that it had an unrecorded British precedent, though similar federate settlements soon followed. Among them were the Saxons, or English, in Britain. The wearers of belts, the purchasers of wheel-made Romano-Saxon wares, and the immigrants buried in pagan cemeteries were three different groups, not 'associated'. That is the simple explanation of the clear and abundant evidence, that neither the belts nor the wheel-made wares were buried in the cemeteries, either with cremated or with inhumed bodies. Direct statements, the record of Roman Europe, and the datings of modern German archaeologists agree in placing the first arrival of the English in Britain after 407, probably after 418, but well before 441. Later British tradition names a precise year, 428; its source is not known, but a date in or about the 420s fits the known evidence.

The known evidence would need to be reconsidered if it were sharply contradicted by the early Caistor urns. The hard evidence for their date is compressed into five pages of the report (43 ff.). The discussion is in two stages. First, a Caistor urn is matched with a continental parallel; then a date is assigned to the parallel. Space prevents illustration of the vessels compared, and the argument therefore turns on references to a multitude of publications, not all of them easily accessible. The authority for the date, when it is given, is usually the opinion of a modern scholar, but his evidence and reasoning is not always stated. Since not everyone will have the means or the time to scrutinize the dense argument and look up the parallels cited, some of the more important must be discussed here.

Footnote 9, p. 45,[13] compares eight Caistor urns with eight Westerwanna urns that contained '4th century brooches'. Six of the brooches are *Armbrustfibeln* and one is an early 'equal arm', all brooch types not yet reported in Britain. The eighth contained a *tutulus* brooch; its English parallel is not mentioned, Abingdon grave 106 (pl. xvi), which also contained an applied saucer brooch with five (?) running scrolls, of the 5th century. The urns have a general overall similarity; they are of types which overlapped the change of brooch fashion, from *Armbrustfibel* to early cruciform, in the late 4th and early 5th centuries. But within the overall similarity there are marked differences of detail. Three of the matched pairs are of identical shape, but three of the German urns are noticeably narrower in relation to their height, and two are considerably taller in relation to their girth. Three of the German urns are plain, but the English urns are decorated, all but one of them quite elaborately; Westerwanna decoration is however in all instances confined to the upper part of the vessel, whereas the English decoration extends well into the lower part. The brooches and the overall similarities confirm the general date horizon of 'the time about 400', meaning the date bracket of around 380/420; but the differences of detail do not warrant the inference that the urns were buried within thirty years of each other, and the differences common to the English group argue the work of a different potter, or potters, working in the same tradition, but separated by an interval of some years from the German potter(s).

Several other vessels instanced belong to the same date horizon, and might be supplemented by the evidence from Jutland, not discussed in the report. Arguments for dates significantly earlier than 'about 400' rely chiefly on the dates put forward by Albrectsen for his recent excavations on the Danish island of Fyn. The reasons for these dates are not discussed; but they are throughout too early, and Myres is compelled to revise them by a number of awkward corrections, as on p. 46, note 4, where he notes that corrugated urns, assigned by Albrectsen to date bracket 325/400, "persist into the 5th century in Schleswig". But similar vessels did not differ in date in these two regions; from Plettke to Genrich, German scholars have agreed that Fyn is "at one with north Schleswig", in "the same cultural region".[14] What is 5th-century in Fyn is 5th-century in Schleswig, and also in England.

---

[13] *Cf. op. cit.* in note 9, fn. 4.
[14] *Op. cit.* in note 6, 60; A. Genrich, *Formenkreise und Stammesgruppen in Schleswig-Holstein* (Neumünster, 1954), 30.

The purely typological arguments are as tenuous. "Hatched triangles" are a popular "3rd century fashion", and a Caistor example, N102, is "closely matched" on Fyn "by pieces datable before A.D. 325" (p. 44); but, "N102 contained part of a comb ... that can be dated with some certainty to the decades around 400" (p. 45, note 3; illustrated fig. 10). Y23, a "breakdown" of this style, "providing a direct link" with "corrugated technique which came in before the middle of the 4th century" is compared with a Suderbrarup urn (grave 5 is meant); but that urn is of quite different form, its decoration by no means so 'broken down', and the parallel leads nowhere, for the Suderbrarup urn is dateless. A more informative instance of the 'hatched triangle', not at all broken down, is Westerwanna 85, not cited, a 5th-century *Buckelurn*. The short answer is that this decorative motif lasted for a very long time.

One urn, P15, firmly asserts an early date (p. 43 f). It has plenty of 2nd and 3rd-century parallels. But it is also "somewhat similar" to a Hammoor bowl with an "early 5th century brooch". "Bracketed between these dates", it is therefore "no later than the second half of the 4th century",[15] not "as late as the closing years of the 4th century" (p. 44). Such splitting of the difference between several centuries gives no firm date, but the vessel is probably at least as early as Myres allows, for the Hammoor brooch, unparalleled in England, is 4th-century, probably well before 400.[16] It is wiser to endorse P. Schmid's view (cited *Caistor*, p. 44, note 4) that "P15 would not be in place much later than the 3rd century at Feddersen Wierde". It is also out of place at Caistor. This solitary urn underscores Myres' own warning that a few throw-backs, antiquities or imitations thereof, are to be expected in any considerable assemblage of pottery.

Myres' discussion does not support the view that burials began at Caistor before the 420s. But he has handled the urns for forty years, and intimate acquaintance teaches more than anyone can learn from words and flat drawings. It is, in theory, possible that if the dates were discussed at proper length with adequate illustration, a better case could be made; but on present evidence the possibility seems remote.

It is however likely that some of the earliest vessels were at the height of their fashion nearer 400 than 420, as are a handful of the earliest brooches from other sites. Any migration brings with it a proportion of elderly material. When the Romans landed in 43 A.D., they imported a quantity of Arretine ware, twenty or more years old when it reached Britain, most plentiful in London. But no one would argue that Arretine imports discredit Roman reports of the invasion date, or found London, without native wares, a generation before the conquest.

The prominence accorded to the argument for very early dating obscures the solid worth of the volume, and the important conclusions to which it points. As Collingwood observed long ago, what matters most is to get the questions right; for there can be no answers till the questions are posed. Though Myres' answers may be disputed, dispute is possible only because he has put the questions, drawn attention to Romano-Saxon ware, classified the pagan urns, and indicated their parallels. What his analysis spotlights is an abnormally high proportion of very early burials, firmly establishing Caistor as one of the few cemeteries that unquestionably belong to the first of the incoming English.

The matter deserves better presentation and publication. There is too much need of avoidable thumbing back and forth. The grave-goods, especially from inhumations, are meanly illustrated, and dismissed as "not of great interest" (p. 210), though to many scholars some are of high interest. But above all the unnecessary price is an impediment to scholarship. The volume need not have been priced above £3 or £4 at present costs, as Hull Museum's publication of Myres' Sancton has shown, half the length, issued at £1; its minor typographical faults could have been avoided by a more skilled compositor without extra cost, and its urns are as well illustrated, its grave-goods much better. Publication in this sumptuous coffee table form nowadays savours of vulgarity; it is a taunt to the many younger scholars who should buy the volume, but cannot.

The Caistor volume is a prelude to Myres' corpus of pagan English pottery. That corpus is likely to remain a standard reference work for a century or more, for it will embody a classification and a periodization that is likely to endure. It is to be hoped that

---

[15] *Op. cit.* in note 9, 72.
[16] From grave 72: *op. cit.* in note 6, 26, Taf. x, 1, and Genrich, *op. cit.* in note 14, Taf. 15E.

THE CHRONOLOGY OF EARLY ANGLO-SAXON ARCHAEOLOGY

it will be reasonably priced, and that views about the absolute date of the earliest period will be more judiciously expressed, as they are in the Sancton volume, the arguments for and against dispassionately balanced; for there is a risk that if our grandchildren are confronted with a reference work whose opening pages may seem to them to expound a buried error of the distant past, they may treat Myres' life's work with something less than the high respect which it deserves.

ANGLO-SAXON SURREY*

A. THE GAZETTEER

THE Gazetteer has been compiled from sites published in the *Surrey Archæological Collections* and relevant national periodicals; from the contents of the British, London, Kingston, Guildford Museums, and items in the possession of the local authorities of Croydon and Carshalton, and the records of the Archæological Department of the Ordnance Survey. It has unfortunately not been possible to make a thorough excerpt of all numbers of the Croydon Natural History and Scientific Society's *Transactions*, or of all reports in the *Croydon Advertiser*. It is clear that the gazetteer is incomplete; it can serve as a basis to which other items may in the future be added. References are given to the National Grid. The letters and figures of the 100 km. Grid Square are omitted. All references beginning with the figures 8 and 9 lie in square SU (41); all those beginning with the figures 0 to 3 are in square TQ (51).

A very considerable number of objects has been recovered at various times from the Thames, from the Surrey and Middlesex shores and from midstream. A few individual items have been published from the mass preserved in the Museums. These are all omitted, since they are the relics of people who crossed the river, rather than of those who lived on its banks. Most of the objects are weapons, and if their exact find-spots were recorded, it might be possible to suggest where battles were fought. Unfortunately the locations are with few exceptions too vague to permit such inferences.

Only objects of the pagan period, between about A.D. 400 and 650, have been included. The gazetteer is necessarily limited to the modern county, though Anglo-Saxon Surrey in the pagan period should probably be extended at least as far east as the Darenth and the Cray.

It is proper to record grateful thanks to the officers and officials of private societies and public bodies, whose help has made possible the compilation of this gazetteer.

ASHTEAD. 2000 5735. S.E. of Ashtead Park, near Stane Street.
    Anglo-Saxon *skeletons* found 1910, A. W. G. Lowther in *Sy.A.C.*, LI, 151, note 1.
    Small plain *urn* and *knife* in Guildford Museum (S6989–90), *Sy.A.C.*, XLV, 166.
    Undated.

---

* Reprinted from *Surrey Archaeological Collections* 56 (1959) 132–58, by kind permission of Surrey Archaeological Society.

At either Ashtead or Banstead may have been the meeting place of Copthorne Hundred *E.P.-N.S.* XI, 68.

BANSTEAD. 2410 6023. Near Banstead Railway Station, 1925.
Two skeletons (one 5 ft. 5 in. tall) with three *urns*, in Guildford Museum (S.6996–8), one illustrated (fluted globular vase with Kentish affinities), *Sy.A.C.*, XXXVII, 91, cf. 108; XL, 133.
Late sixth cent.

BANSTEAD. 2472 6120. Banstead Downs Golf Course.
Saxon inhumation with knife, found 1918. O.S. 19 N.E. 9., A. W. G. Lowther.
Undated.

BEDDINGTON. 3002 6548. A mile west of Croydon, 500 yards south of a Roman villa (*Sy.A.C.*, VI, 118), *V.C.H.*, I, 263. The area is now a sewage works.

At least 12 inhumations and at least 9 cremations were found in 1871–5, *Sy.A.C.*, VI, 122 (=*P.S.A.*,[2] V, 154); a sword, 8 spears, 5 shield-bosses and 8 knives are mentioned, together with 9 urns, a blue glass bead, a bronze bracelet, and "pieces of bronze," perhaps brooches. The urns included 2 "patterned Urns," one with "encircling lugs and impressed ornaments," and one with "markings like British urns."

Two spears and 2 bosses are illustrated in J. C. Anderson, *Prehistoric and Roman Croydon*, p. 41.

E. P. Loftus Brock twice exhibited objects from the site at the British Archæological Association; in May 1871 (*J.B.A.A.*, XXVII, 517) "an urn of rough description; a considerable quantity of bones; some other urns; a fine large circular cinerary urn . . . of dark colour, (which) has curious indented patterns . . . and another similar; and two spears"; in April 1874 (*J.B.A.A.*, XXX, 212), the skeleton of a tall man, 6ft. 6 in. high, with two shield-bosses, a sword and four or five spears (one 10 in. long), a coarse black urn, a glazed white drinking cup, and charred wood, as from "under a tumulus."

In the spring of 1875, three more skeletons were discovered "at oblique angles to each other, at six to eight yards apart"; with each was a shield-boss, spear, knife, "dagger," and "arrowhead." By the skull of one was "the rim of a helmet of some sort," possibly a bronze bowl, and also a "bronze ornament" and a sword. (*Sy.A.C.*, VII, xxxvii). The sword was 40 in. long, (J. C. Anderson, *Saxon Croydon*, p. 87).

From the site are a pair of *saucer brooches*, 1 in. in diameter, with a simple five-spiral design, one in Cambridge Museum (1871), the other in the Ashmolean, (donor T. H. Powell, 1912, 12). In the Ashmolean is also the base of an *applied saucer brooch*, 1⅝ in. diameter, with raised central boss, and traces of appliqué, apparently of a central cross with faces, similar to Croydon and Guildown types.

Forty years ago some objects were preserved in Croydon Public

Library (Baldwin Brown, IV, 631). The Croydon Society has recently discovered in the Town Hall a brown paper parcel labelled "Beddington, 1874." In it were 12 spears, of types A, B, C, D and E, one of them 17¼ in. long and another with a barbed point, rather too short to deserve the name "angon"; with them is part of a sword, a knife of type C, and a modern barrel lock. The extant objects account for most of the grave goods reported from the inhumations; the bosses, bracelet, bead and twelve urns are missing.

This was evidently a considerable mixed inhumation and cremation cemetery; the urns with "encircling lugs" sound like Saxon urns, perhaps Bückelurnen, perhaps of the fifth or early sixth century; the cast saucer brooches with five scrolls are probably fifth-century (cf. p. 81 above), the applied brooch sixth-century.

Fifth to sixth cent.

BETCHWORTH. 201 504. Between Dorking and Reigate, "Barley Mow" or Box Hill Sandpit.

Saxon *pots* on site of a Roman settlement, with Bronze Age and Neolithic pottery, *Sy.A.C.*, XL, xii, cf. xxi. (The Roman pottery is illustrated in *Sy.A.C.*, XLIX, 110).

Undated.

BROCKHAM. 19 49. Between Dorking and Reigate.

Merovingian *gold coin*, triens of Metz, moneyer Ansoaldas, *c.* A.D. 650. *Arch. J.*, XI, 69; *Sy.A.C.*, I, 5; *V.C.H.*, I, 272; C. H. V. Sutherland, *Anglo-Saxon Gold Coinage in the light of the Crondall Hoard*, 42, cf. 13, and 24–25.

CARSHALTON, four miles west of Croydon.

Bunkers Field, centre 2888 6502, in and around the grounds of Wallington County Grammar School, a fortified enclosure of the Iron Age, touching the bank of the Wandle, excavated thirty years ago, *Sy.A.C.*, XXXVI, 1925, 113–14, cf. also Rev. J. Williams, *Historical Notes on Wallington*, 1873.

The surviving material is in the possession of the Beddington, Wallington and Carshalton Archæological Society. The collection is cared for by the Carshalton Urban District Council, but for want of space is housed in boxes in premises used for other purposes, and could not be examined. A catalogue is however available, and was evidently compiled by someone who understood the objects. From Bunkers Field it lists 113 Iron Age sherds, 50 Roman sherds, and 13 pagan Saxon sherds. Among the Roman wares are listed New Forest products, a rosette-stamped sherd of the fourth century, and others listed as of the fourth century; no Samian, or other products of the early Empire are mentioned. It would seem that an Iron Age earthwork by the Wandle was reoccupied at the end of the Roman period, and that the occupation was continued by the Saxons. The proportion of Roman to Iron Age sherds, and of Saxon to Roman, in the surviving collection is quite large.

Colston Avenue. 278 648.
Five Roman and five pagan Saxon (?) sherds, found with much medieval pottery in building operations, in the catalogue at Carshalton U.D.C. The site is much more doubtful. The proportion of the sherds would be consistent with the discovery of a medieval farmstead built on land that had been cultivated in Roman and Saxon times.

Carshalton-on-the-Hill (Queen Mary's Hospital), centred 275 625.
An Iron Age Hillfort, excavated just before the war, *Sy.A.C.,* XLVI, xi; XLVII, xxiii; XLIX, 56–74.
The finds were deposited at the Grange Wood Museum, Thornton Heath, which was bombed in the war. The Museum Catalogue however survives in the possession of the Croydon Society; from the site it lists (p. 130) much early Iron Age and "late Celtic" (Belgic) material, a quantity of Roman pottery including "Gaulish or Samian ware," a brooch and spindle-whorls, and "four specimens Anglo-Saxon pottery."
The balance of this catalogue, in so far as it is reliable, differs from the record of Bunkers Field. The Roman pottery noted is of the early empire, and the proportion of Roman to pre-Roman, and of Roman to Saxon much less. This appears to be an Iron Age site which continued in use through the Belgic period into the early Roman empire. It may or may not have been re-occupied in late Roman times, and the Saxon use of the site seems, as far as the record, slighter than at Bunkers Field.

Carshalton Road, near the south end of Ringstead Road, 2704 6425.
Found during the widening of Carshalton road in November 1906. *Sy.A.C.,* XXIII, 213.
Several skeletons found at a depth of about 2 ft. 6 in.
Two skulls and a *spear* from the site were seen in a box in the Council Offices at the time. The site is within the ramparts of a large Iron Age fort, which also held Roman and Bronze Age material. *Sy.A.C.,* XXXVI, 104.
Undated.

CHEAM. 2312 6519. In 1941 at No. 3 Shrubland Grove, North Cheam, just west of Stane Street, two miles north-east of Ewell, *Sy.A.C.,* LI, 151, (Fig. p. 152), a *spearhead,* type E.
Undated.

CHOBHAM. 97 61. Perhaps the meeting place of Godley Hundred, *E.P.-N.S.,* XI, 103.

COBHAM. 114 602. South-west of Esher; Leigh Hill.
A *spearhead,* found near Bronze Age, Iron Age and Roman site, *Sy.A.C.,* XXXVII, 93 (Fig.) cf. XXI, 192; XXII, 137.
Undated.
Eaton Farm perhaps preserves the name of the Getingas. *E.P.-N.S.,* XI, 88.

COULSDON, *Cane Hill.* 291 587, approximately. Four miles south-west of Croydon.

Several skeletons facing east, a *knife* with each, found "in a field near my residence," by J. M. Moodie, together with hippopotamus and mammoth tusks, *Sy.A.C.*, XXVI, 139. The finds were made in 1912, "on the opposite side of the valley" from Farthingdown (*q.v.*). Cf. *Sy.A.C.*, XXVII, xiii.

The approximate area is fixed by the accession book of the Horniman Museum, which possesses a skull, registered in 1918, given by Sir John Moodie, described as found "in a Saxon grave at Cane Hill. The land concerned was owned by the L.C.C. The only L.C.C. land on Cane Hill is that belonging to the Hospital." (Letter from the Horniman Museum to Dr. Dance of Guildford Museum, 1 September, 1952.)

"A spearhead and some beads" were found at Cane Hill Asylum (built 1873) about 1881-2, *Croydon Advertiser*, 7 March 1885. The building of the Asylum may well have destroyed graves unrecorded, and the site may have been a large one.

An entry printed on the Ordnance Survey 6 in. sheet, at 2912 5798, reads "Human remains found A.D. 1910." This discovery may be part of the same cemetery. Measurements of two skeletons are given in *Biometrika*, XXVIII, 1936, 290.

According to Mr. F. G. Parsons, (letters to the Ordnance Survey, dated 14 October and 9 November 1933), the cemetery has been found scrappily at various times, but seems to have been a regular burial ground, with bodies in rows, some with spears, and a sprinkling of swords.

Undated.

Farthingdown. Between 2995 5835 and 3008 5743. Five miles south of Croydon.

Over 30 graves, 3 ft. to 3 ft. 6 in. deep, under and between low barrows, 18–30 ft. in diameter, two of them 40 ft. across, between 12 in. and 18 in. high, excavated about 1760 (*M.&B.*, II, 448); in 1871, *Sy.A.C.*, VI, 109, *V.C.H.*, I, 264; in 1939, *Sy.A.C.*, XLVII, 119; XLIX, 114; and in 1948–9, *Sy.A.C.*, LI, xi; LIII, x, cf. 21. Cf. *Archæological News Letter* II, (10), p. 170.

Half the graves were without grave goods. In the others were 1 *sword*, 6 *spears*, 4 *knives*, 1 *scramasax*, 1 remarkable conical *boss* (now in the Ashmolean Museum, *Sy.A.C.*, VI, pl. ii, Baldwin Brown III, 199, pl. xxiii, 3), 2 silver *pins*, 1 bone *pin*, (*Sy.A.C.*, VI, pl. i), 2 *buckets*, 1 *stoup*, (*Sy.A.C.*, VI, pl. iii; *V.C.H.*, I, 257, pl. Fig. 6), 4 *buckles* (one Frankish), a small string of *beads* (*Sy.A.C.*, VI, pl. i), a piece of *amber* and a *purse mount*, 1 *gold bracteate* with cruciform design (*Sy.A.C.*, VI, pl. 1), a small decorated *pot*, a pair of *shears* and a *comb* and *cowrie shell* in a bag, and a burial with the *wing* of a *goose*. A sword, boss, and "drinking cup" (perhaps a bucket) were placed in the "Museum of the Society lately established at Croydon," but cannot now be found. A knife and spear are in Guildford Museum (S6991-2). The stoup, the bracteate, the

Frankish buckle and probably the conical boss are of the late sixth or early seventh century; though many of the objects are of uncertain date, none suggests an earlier date. All the graves found in 1948–9 were orientated north and south.
Late sixth and seventh centuries.
The best survey of the barrows is by Grinsell, in *Sy.A.C.*, XLII, 45–47.

CROWHURST or LIMPSFIELD. A rough, plain urn, Guildford Museum S.7003, found 1881, is so labelled. It might possibly be from the same site as the Limpsfield urn, *q.v.*

CROYDON. 3117 6505. *Waddon Caves.* 41 Alton Road, Waddon.
Through the slope a hill, a long V-shaped flat-bottomed trench, some 8 ft. or 10 ft. deep, was cut into sandy soil, leading downward towards a spring, now a pond in the municipal park. The trench acted as street, and off it opened a number of wholly underground houses, entered by doorways with worked lintels. One of these was wholly excavated, others partially. They contained Iron Age and Belgic pottery, with a quantity of Roman pottery of the first three centuries A.D., including two minute scraps of Samian, and a few late Roman sherds. The finds also include a single Anglo-Saxon rim *sherd*, of dark grey ware, with parallel lines round the neck, and the impression of a banana-shaped stamp, probably half a rosette circle, similar to those common on late Roman rosetted wares, and very like the stamp used on a very late Roman bulging bowl, half of which is preserved in the London Museum. The rubble lying over the Iron Age, Roman and Saxon material was full of mesolithic flints, and, during an earlier excavation in 1902, caused the site to be listed as neolithic. *Proceedings of the Croydon Natural History and Scientific Society*, XII, 1951–2, 145.
The site is quite unique. Like the Carshalton-on-the-Hill fort, it is clearly an Iron Age and Belgic site that continued into the early Roman period, and has some slight trace of casual late Roman and Saxon reoccupation.

Edridge Road, Elms Estate, 325 650, immediately south of the Town Hall.
There is a sufficiently widespread scatter of Roman material to suggest that Croydon may have been the site of a Roman roadside village or posting-station. Numerous skeletons, etc., have been found at, and south of, the junction of George Street and High Street (400 yards to the north) from the foundation of Archbishop Whitgift's Hospital in 1596 onward, J. C. Anderson, *Saxon Croydon*, p. 91. In 1856, Mr. C. Lashman exhibited to the Surrey Society "a skull, found with a number of other human remains, iron weapons, sword blades, etc., at the bottom of St. George's Street," *Sy.A.C.*, II, xii. Many objects were recovered from builders in 1893–4, with no account of the graves,

Sy.A.C., XIII, 18 (=P.S.A., XV, 328)., V.C.H., I, 258. The objects recorded are 4 *swords*, 26 *spears*, 1 *angon* (a long spear of continental origin, used in Britain by the Franks), 12 *shield-bosses*, 3 *franciscas* (Frankish throwing axes); 9 *knifes*, 9 *brooches*, 2 *openwork triskele discs*, 1 *buckle*, 1 *bronze bowl*, 2 *buckets*, 1 whetstone or *sceptre*, several *coins*, 1 *belt-tab;* 1 faceted *disc*, 2 *rings*, 1 *"prickspur,"* 2 *needles*, 2 *pins*, 1 *pair of tweezers*, 1 *armlet*, 1 *bronze pendant object*, 1 *cow's horn*, 2 *glass vessels*, 4 *Romano-British pots* and 17 *Anglo-Saxon urns*. The quantity of objects recovered is comparable with that from the 200 odd graves recorded at Mitcham.

The bulk of the objects are in the British Museum (1895–3–13, 1–48), which has 2 swords, 13 spears, the angon, 9 bosses, 3 knives, 2 franciscas, 3 brooches, the buckle, 1 ring, the pendant object, the cow's horn, 1 glass vessel, and 9 of the Anglo-Saxon urns. Other objects were lodged in the Grange Wood Museum at Thornton Heath (Baldwin Brown IV, 631) which was bombed in the 1939 war. The catalogue survives.

Three of the British Museum urns are plain, six decorated; they include a large Bückelurn, heavily stamped with two separate stamps, the features in low relief, early, but not of the earliest period, perhaps of the late fifth century; one urn stamped with a running S and chevron pattern, and one vessel with a dotted chevron pattern on the lower part of the vessel, probably not earlier than the mid-sixth century.

The brooches include the cast saucer brooch[1] of Fig. 7A, perhaps of the first half of the sixth century, 1·2 in. diameter, the base of an applied saucer brooch, (B.M. 44), diameter 1·6 in., a disc brooch with four stamped circles (B.M. 42), a pair of flat ring brooches, and four small-long brooches (V.C.H., I, 257, plate 2–5) two of them closely matched at Mitcham (107 and 112). The belt-tab and faceted disc (Baldwin Brown, IV, 558, pl. clii, 1, 5 and 8), possibly the fitting of a sporran, are closely paralleled at Dorchester Dyke Hills,[2] a burial closely dated to the closing years of the fourth century, at Vermand at a date not later than c. A.D. 410, and also at Kempston (A.A.S.R., VII. 1864, 285), at Croxton, near Thetford in Norfolk (Baldwin Brown, IV, 558, pl. clii, 4, Norwich Castle Museum) and in the Elbe region. The bronze pendant object (B.M. 40, Baldwin Brown, IV, 419, pl. xcix 4) is decorated with ornamentation that also recalls Vermand, and has a simpler parallel at Droxford in Hampshire (Baldwin Brown, pl. xcix 5). One of the glass vessels Harden (D.A.B., 158 cf. 139 and Fig. 25 I a 1) dates to the fifth century. Four whole Roman vessels, including one of Castor ware and one of "Upchurch" ware, are also unusual survivals in Anglo-Saxon graves. Baldwin Brown also illustrates the bronze bowl (IV, 473, pl. cxvii, 3) and several of the weapons (III, 209,

---

[1] *Oxoniensia*, XVII/XVIII, 63.

pl. xxv 3 and III, 221, pl. xxvii 9 (swords); III, 199, pl. xxiii 2 (boss); III, 231, pl. xxix 6 (francisca); III, 237 pl. xxxii 15 (angon). One of the bosses was of conical shape cf. Mitcham 73; all such bosses found with dateable objects belong to the late sixth century or later.

The cemetery contained several objects that properly belong to the last decades of the Roman period, and might have survived into the Anglo-Saxon period; there are several Anglo-Saxon objects of the fifth century, and a number of objects of both the first and the second half of the sixth century, with several specifically Frankish items, and nothing that need be of the seventh century.

Fifth and Sixth cent.

CUDDINGTON. 233 618. A mile east of Ewell.
Anglo-Saxon *spearhead*, found by Mr. M. Flint, and identified at the British Museum in 1956-7, O.S. 19, N.W. 30.

DORKING, West of. 160 492. West Dorking Sandpit, Vincent Lane, about 200 yards from the probable site of the Roman posting station.
Two *spears*, a small *urn*, and a *glass bottle* in Guildford Museum, S6979 (rough small plain urn), *Sy.A.C.*, XL, 133.
Undated. .
An -ingas name, *E.P.-N.S.*, XI, 269.

EASHING. 94 44. An -ingas name, *E.P.-N.S.*, XI, 196.

ESHER. 139 650. The Warren, Sandown Park, 100 yards south-west of the grandstand.
Three graves, facing east, two with a *spear* and a *shield-boss* (hemispherical) each, the third empty, a *spear* loose in the surrounding soil; the graves were dug into an Iron Age site, with some Roman material, *Ant. J.*, XXVII, 24, cf. *Sy.A.C.*, L, ix.
Undated.
The hundred of Elmbridge is named from the bridge over the Mole at Esher 130 645, *E.P.-N.S.*, XI, 86.

EWELL. 2192 6239 to 2198 6227. Ewell House, The Grove, adjoining the site of a Roman posting station.
Quantities of human bones were dug up in the late seventeenth century in Mr. Fendall's grounds near the Epsom road, *Aubrey* II (1718), 219; cf. V, 363. Mr. Fendall owned Ewell House, *Sy.A.C.*, XLVIII, 13.
At least 10 inhumations and 2 cremations, found 1930-1932.
7 *spears*, 1 *shield-boss*, 1 *knife*; 1 cast *saucer brooch*, with leg-and-stroke pattern, probably about or just before the middle of the sixth century and the bases of a pair of *applied saucer brooches*. 1 pair of *disc-brooches* incised with hexafoil pattern. 1 *disc-brooch* with dot-and-circle pattern. 1 *bead*, 1 silver *ring*, 1 *spindle whorl*, 1 *buckle*, 1 *armlet*. 2 *cremation urns* and 1 plain red *urn*

from an inhumation. The finds in Guildford Museum (S6967-77) include a well-made shouldered urn.

The cemetery was dug into a Roman site with first- to fourth-century and Iron Age pottery. *Ant. J.*, XII, 442; XIII, 302; also cf. *Sy.A.C.*, XXXVIII, 227; XL, 13; XLI, 122; XLII, 113; XLIII, 16. The finds are in Guildford and London Museums (*London and the Saxons*, 131-6).

Two earlier discoveries, "skull and bones with a rusty iron bar," found at the junction of Meadow Mill and High Street in 1897 (2192 6284), (O.S. 13 S.W. 18), and "Human remains found 1912," a hundred yards to the southwest at 2185 6273, printed on the O.S. 6 in. map (13 S.W.), all on the edge of the Roman village, may belong to the same cemetery. If so, the few recorded relics of the Ewell burials may be the debris of a cemetery as large as those of Croydon and Mitcham; the undiscovered burials may have contained fifth-century material, but those which have survived do not.

Sixth cent.

FARNHAM, *Firgrove Pit.* 8422 4667. On rising ground, 100 yards south of the Wey, just east of the road to Bourne, Frensham and Hindhead, 100 yards west of a Roman cemetery.

Sy.A.S., 1939, *Survey of the Prehistory of the Farnham District*, p. 255, cf. *Sy.A.C.*, XXXVI, 123; XLIV, 138.

Anglo-Saxon village with huts 12 ft. to 15 ft. wide, sunk 2 ft. into the soil, with *clay loomweights* (Guildford Museum S7035), a bronze *clasp*, roughly paralleled at Herpes, in south-western France (British Museum Guide, 1923, p. 148, Fig. 196) a glass *bead*, a *knife*, sherds of *coarse pots*, including one heavily stamped sherd, probably of the mid-sixth century.

Sixth cent.

Castle Street, 839 471. Anglo-Saxon *stamps* on a Roman tile, cf. Titsey, Sy.A.S. Survey, pl. xxiii, p. 253, cf. 259.

Farnham. Anglo-Saxon *sherd* with basketry incisions and clay loomweights, find-spot unknown, found "about 30 years ago," Sy.A.S. *Survey*, pl. xxv, p. 258, cf. 259. *Ant. J.*, XIII, 324, fig. 2, cf. 325.

The Crondall Hoard of IXth century Anglo-Saxon coins was found about two miles to the west, across the county boundary.

Farnham Hundred met at Lawday House, 814 494, *E.P.-N.S.*, XI, 165.

FARTHINGDOWN—see Coulsdon.

FETCHAM, Hawkshill. From 1564 5539 to 1596 5617. Immediately south-west of Leatherhead, from the crest of Hawkshill near the junction of A2012 and A246 to the mill pond on the left bank of the Mole, ¼ mile south of Leatherhead station.

Between 60 and 100 inhumations, excavated at various times between 1758 and 1933.

A small proportion of the grave-goods were recorded and preserved. These are 3 *swords*, 3 *shield-bosses*, 7 *spearheads*, 1 *scramasax*, 3 *knives*, 2 *glass beads*, one or two *coins* of Constantine, a few *pots*, a Frankish *girdle-hanger*, apparently from the same mould as one from Maidstone, there found with a garnet-studded brooch of the mid-sixth century, *bucket* plaques with human face in punched outline, similar to the late sixth-century saucer brooch "Maltese Cross" designs (p. 84, Fig. 6 above), and a decorated *bronze disc* (British Museum 1934-5-7). In Guildford Museum are the girdle-hanger and a sword-knot bead (S7007-8). *Sy.A.C.*, XVI, 251; cf. XX, 119; XXXVII, 93; XL, xvii; XLII, 136; *P.S.A.*,[2] XVIII, 253, *V.C.H.*, I, 267, cf. III, 284; IV, 362, 365; *Ant. J.*, XIII, 48; *M.&B.*, I, 482.

The scramasax, bucket, bronze disc, and girdle-hanger are probably of the late sixth or early seventh century. Nothing recorded suggests an earlier date.

Late sixth and seventh cent.

The main group of graves lies 50 to 100 yards from a large Iron Age and Roman occupation site, which also had some Bronze Age material. The material is in Guildford Museum, S7006-13.

GODALMING. 96 44. An -ingas name, *E.P.-N.S.*, XI, 195.

GODSTONE. 351 514, between Godstone and Stratton.
Urns, bones, "*glass bottle*," *spears*, *tiles*, *armlet*, *P.S.A.*,[2] IX, 101. The armlet and a small plain urn are in Guildford Museum, S.7005.
Undated.

GUILDOWN. 9883 4884. In the garden of "Chalk Hill," Guildown Avenue, immediately south of the Old Road, on the Ridgeway, just before it dips down the hill to cross the Wey. *Sy.A.C.*, XXXIX, 1, cf. xii; XLI, 119; cf. LIII, pl. xxv-xxviii.

35 burials of the pagan Saxon period, together with 189 skeletons interred with a coin of A.D. 1043; attributed to a massacre of A.D. 1046.

The grave goods were 5 *spearheads* (one with a closed socket) and 6 *knives*, but no swords or shield-bosses. There were 20 *brooches*, including 9 *saucer* brooches, three cast and six applied, eight of them closely matched at Mitcham, 2 pairs of *disc* brooches, 1 great *square-headed* brooch (Leeds, *Corpus* 70, from grave 116, not 46), 3 small Kentish *square-headed* brooches (two of them, grave 206, Leeds, *Corpus* 7) and 3 *small-long* brooches, one of them very like Mitcham 107. The other objects were two *glass vessels* (Harden, III a i, 6-7), 9 *strings of beads* and 9 loose *beads*, 2 *spindle-whorl beads*, 1 iron *key*, 2 bronze and 1 silver *ring*, 2 bronze *pins*, 1 *ear-ring*, 2 *rock crystals*, 1 *bucket*, 14 *buckles*, 1 *hone*, whetstone or sceptre, 2 small *bronze objects*, 1 fragment of *samian* ware, and a large bossed and rosetted *urn*, heavily stamped, with three other decorated and four plain urns. The finds are in Guildford Museum. Cf. *Biometrika*, XXVIII, 1936, 290 for measurements of a skeleton.

The saucer brooches do not include any of the certainly earliest or latest types; they, and the square-headed brooches, large and small, belong within the sixth century, and so probably do the urn and the glass; the burials recorded probably began some time after 500 and ended before 600.
Sixth cent.

GUILDFORD, Mareschal Road, Mount Street. 9921 4925.
Twelve skeletons, found September 1930, with a fluted *urn*, some *sherds*, and two *whetstones* or hones, Guildford Museum G6993-4, 2410, *Sy.A.C.*, XXXIX, 4, cf. 163; XL, xi.
The site is about 400 yards from the Guildown cemetery.

GUILDFORD, St. Martha's. 028 483.
Small plain black Anglo-Saxon *urn*, Guildford Museum S6999, *P.S.A.*,[2] XXVIII, 230; *Sy.A.C.*, XXIX, 152, plate, cf. LIV, 42, fig. 9.

St. Martha's is a Saxon church (much rebuilt in the nineteenth century), standing in isolation on the summit of a sharp conical sandy hill nearly 500 ft. above the valley, two miles south-east of Guildford. The church lies in the centre of a semicircle of round earthworks, some 100 ft. in diameter, for which an analogy with Bronze Age sacred sites is claimed, though excavation found no Bronze Age objects (*Sy.A.C.*, LIV, 10, ff.). From the summit of the hill come Mesolithic and Neolithic flakes and an axe, some Iron Age sherds found by Pitt-Rivers in 1874 (*ibid.*, p. 39), a Roman pot found recently, in private possession in Guildford (O.S. 32 N.W. 4, S. S. Frere), tiles which may have been Roman, and the Saxon urn, found within one of the "Bronze Age" circles (*ibid.*, p. 41). There is a considerable scatter of Bronze Age, Iron Age and Roman sites in the immediate neighbourhood, an Iron Age pottery-making site at the foot of the hill 400 yards to the east of the church, and half a mile to the north-east a small Roman cremation cemetery of the first century A.D., just outside the gates of Tyting Farm (023 487), which is an -INGAS name (*E.P.-N.S.*, XI, 245). The earth circles are ignored by the copious writers of the seventeenth and eighteenth centuries, and are first mentioned in 1850; from 1876 onward, but not earlier, there is record of an allegedly ancient procession with folk-dancing to the site.

The urn is of the sixth century. The site has certainly been sacred since the Christian Saxon period; it is a pre-eminently awe-inspiring position, still inaccessible to wheeled vehicles, and may possibly have been sacred from the Neolithic or Bronze Age onwards. The occasional presence on the hill of peoples of all ages is proven; but the purpose of their presence is not established.

No other church in England is dedicated to St. Martha. An alternative name, Martyr Hill, persists from 1273 onward,

E.P.-N.S., XI, 244; cf. *Sy.A.C.*, XLIV, 62. There is no association with St. Thomas the Martyr, though the site is on the Pilgrim's Way to Canterbury, and no tradition of Martyrs on the site. The dedication is a puzzle.

It might conceivably be a solitary lowland instance of "Martyrium," Welsh "Merthyr," a term bestowed on a variety of sacred sites in the sixth century by British- and Latin-speaking peoples. The precise significance of the term in Wales is not clearly understood; it certainly does not necessarily imply the martyrdom of saints, but carries the vaguer significance that there some saint "bore witness" to Christ, occasionally by the forcible dedication of pagan holy sites to Christianity. The names Walworth, Walton and Wallington show that British was still spoken in Surrey in the sixth century; it is possible that a name so given was preserved in ecclesiastical Latin as Martyrium, and later corrupted to Martha.

HACKBRIDGE—see Beddington.

HAM. 1693 7159.
Anglo-Saxon village, one hut excavated, Hope-Taylor and S. S. Frere, February 1950, 170 yards from an Iron Age site. Pottery, loomweights and animal bones were found, *Sy.A.C.*, LII, 101.

HAWKSHILL—see Fetcham.

EAST HORSLEY. 09 52.
A Saxon youth, with *knife*, *Sy.A.C.*, LIV, 136, discovered during building operations.
Undated.

KINGSTON-ON-THAMES—see Ham.

LEATHERHEAD—see Fetcham.

LIMPSFIELD. 425 534. Two miles east of Oxted on the Redhill-Sevenoaks road, near a Roman cremation-cemetery, on the line of the London-Lewes Roman road.
Anglo-Saxon *urn*, probably mid to late sixth century, Guildford Museum, S7002, *P.S.A.*,[2] XIII, 249–250, (Fig.). See also Crowhurst.
Sixth cent.

MERTON. 25 69. On Stane Street, one mile north-west of Mitcham and 5 miles north-west of Croydon.
Cast *saucer brooch*, with central cross, of the late fifth or early sixth century, British Museum 1923–5–7. It is possible that the brooch is a stray from the cemetery at Mitcham, a mile to the south-east.
Late fifth or early sixth cent.

MICKLEHAM. 1725 5270. On Stane Street, two miles north of Dorking.

In 1780, when Juniper Hall was being built, two skeletons and a spearhead were found. Brayley, (*B.&B.*), IV, 457; *V.C.H.*, III, 302.
Undated.

MITCHAM. 270 682. 4 Miles north-west of Croydon.
Several hundred burials recorded over more than a century, pp. 51-131 above.
Fifth and sixth cent.

PEPER HARROW. 942 445. Two miles west of Godalming, four miles south-west of Guildford.
Heathen place-name. *E.P.-N.S.*, XI, 207, cf. xii.

PURLEY. 3232 6075. Junction of *Mitchley Avenue* and Riddlesdown Road, eight or more skeletons, heads to the east, with a *knife* of type A, 6 in. long, *Proc. Croydon Nat. Hist. & Scientific Soc.*, X, 1931-3, 199.
Four of the skeletons were presented to the Croydon Natural History and Scientific Society Museum, *Sy.A.C.*, XLI, 137.
Undated.
Russell Hill. 3118 6225. 18 or more gigantic skeletons, found 1865, buried 18 in. deep in the chalk, parallel to the road, which might be the Roman road. *Croydon Advertiser*, 17 March 1877.
A further skeleton was found in the garden of No. 3, Overhill Road, 3120 6247, and was the subject of a coroner's inquest reported in the *Croydon Advertiser* between 1924 and 1929 (information from Mr. A. F. L. Rivet).
There are Bronze Age pots and implements from the site in the British and Guildford Museums, *Sy.A.C.*, XXI, 208-9.

RICHMOND PARK, centred 18 72. Bun-shaped loomweight, diameter $4\frac{1}{2}$ in., in Guildford Museum, S7037.

RIPLEY. 0370 5641. Seven miles south-west of Esher. *Papercourt Farm.*
Anglo-Saxon *spear*, type D (and Bronze Age Mace). Guildford Museum G6399. *Sy.A.C.*, LII, 81.
Undated: cf. Woking.

SANDERSTEAD. 3313 6247. Two miles south of Croydon, direct on the alignment of the London-Brighton Roman road. 300 yards south of Sanderstead railway station east of the Croydon road. 11 or 12 skeletons all facing east, 18 in. to 2 ft. deep, with a handmade *urn* and two *knives*.
Finds in Guildford Museum, 921, and S6983-8, *Sy.A.C.*, XLI, 136. *Croydon Advertiser*, 7 March 1885; *P.S.A.*,[2] XXVIII, 233; *V.C.H.*, I, 267.
There was an Iron Age site with storage pits very near, and a Roman site 500 yards to the east, at Crohamhurst Farm, *Sy.A.C.*, L, xxiii.
Undated.

SANDOWN PARK—see Esher.

SEALE. 883 474. Three miles east of Farnham.
Binton Farm perhaps is an -ingas name, *E.P.-N.S.*, XI, 181.

SEND—see Ripley, Woking.

THUNDERFIELD CASTLE, Horley. 300 426. Five miles south of Redhill, *E.P.-N.S.*, XI, 295, cf. xii. Heathen place-name.

THURSLEY. 9021 3953. Eight miles south-west of Guildford. Small plain Anglo-Saxon *urn*, with impressions of barley, *Sy. A.C.*, LI, 152, pl. xviii, b.
Heathen place-name, *E.P.-N.S.*, XI, 211, cf. xii.
"Thor's Stone" is said to be at 9073 4160, *Sy.A.C.*, LIV, 138–41. Undated.

TITSEY. 406 544. "Anglo-Saxon" stamps on a Roman tile. Sy.A.S., *Farham Survey*, 1939, pl. xxiii, p. 253, cf. 259.

TOOTING. 27 72. An -ingas name, *E.P.-N.S.*, XI, 35.

TUESLEY. 96 41. Two miles south of Godalming. Heathen place-name. *E.P.-N.S.*, XI, 200, cf. xii.

TYTING—see Guildford, St. Martha's.

WALTON-ON-THAMES. 094 665. Three miles east of Chertsey.
A "range of barrows" formerly existed near Walton Bridge at "Windmill Hill." In 1793, "when the stone bridge was building, the foreman of the work was in possession of a *boss* of a *shield*, some *spearheads*, and *earthen vessels*, taken from these barrows, which I made drawings of; and which were similar to those I have heretofore described in other tumuli." Douglas, *Nenia Britannica*, 94; *M. & B.* III, clx. Douglas does not say whether the tumuli lay on the Surrey bank or the Middlesex bank where there are also Saxon cemeteries at Shepperton and at Walton Bridge Green (*P.S.A.*,[2] IV, 118; Vulliamy, *The Archæology of Middlesex*, 227–30). E. Gardner, *Sy.A.C.*, XXV, 1912, 134, cites Douglas, adding "on the left-hand side of the approach to Walton Bridge, on the Surrey side of the Thames." This may be a guess, since Douglas' note is embedded in an account of Wimbledon; or the name Windmill Hill may have survived in 1912. If so, the site is presumably the same as "Anzac Mount" below.

A cinerary *urn* was exhibited to the Archæological Institute in 1867, *Arch. J.*, XXV, 178 (cf. *V.C.H.*, I, 268) together with "calcined bones," a bead and a bronze ornament.
Sy.A.C., XLII, 38, cf. 29.

Decorated pot, Ant. J., XIX, 323. British Museum, 1928–2–11, "found in 1927 on high ground overlooking Cowey and Walton Bridge, west of the bridge approach, now called Anzac Mount, formerly part of Mount Felix Estate," perhaps the same site as Douglas' discoveries.

The barrows were perhaps grave-mounds as at Farthingdown. Undated.

WHITMOOR COMMON—see Worplesdon.

WILLEY HO. 813 454. Two miles south-west of Farnham, on the Wey.
Heathen place-name. *E.P.-N.S.*, XI, 175.

WOKING. About 029 571. Two miles south-east of Woking.
A *spearhead*, 4 in. long, type D, found "in the moat around the wood in Woking Park Farm in 1904." *Sy.A.C.*, XXV, 140, pl. Fig. 2.
Undated.
Cf. also Send and Ripley.
Woking is an -ingas name. In the middle ages the Hundred met at Harmes Hatch, (02 55?), Send. *E.P.-N.S.*, XI, 135, cf. 148.

WORPLESDON, Whitmoor Common. About 992 537. Two miles north of Guildford.
Six grave-mounds with "Burnt bones, an iron Saxon *knife*, and other remains." *British Association Report*, 1877, 117 (Anthropological Section, Maj.-Gen. Pitt-Rivers); *Sy.A.C.*, XLII, 49, cf. 30; cf. XIV, 219.
Undated.

WOTTON. 117 484. Three miles west of Dorking, north of Deerleap Wood.
Anglo-Saxon *pot-sherd*, *Ant. J.*, XIX, 325, *Sy.A.C.*, XXXVII, 222. British Museum, 1927, 1–4, 2. Found in a Roman cremation cemetery of the first century A.D.

DOUBTFUL SITES

ADDINGTON PARK. 37 66. Three miles east of Croydon.
"About twenty-five tumuli . . . one in diameter nearly 40 ft., two about half that size . . . the remainder very small . . . Salmon says that some broken pieces of urns taken out of them . . . were . . . in the possession of an apothecary at Croydon." Lysons, *Environs of London*, I, 1. *Sy.A.C.*, XLII, 30, cf. 39.
A heathen place-name, *Thunderfield Common*, was apparently still in use in the area in the early years of this century, *P. Croydon N.H. & S.S.*, VIII, 1916–17, 162–3, (map p. 164), cf. cix.

ASHTEAD. 1821 5670. One mile north-east of Leatherhead.
"In the grounds of the Goblin Factory, by the pre-Roman track called Green Lane, south of the Leatherhead-Ashtead road, near Stane Street," 1927.
A pit, with several bodies thrown in, whose condition suggests Dark Age or mid to late Saxon. A. W. G. Lowther in *Sy.A.C.*, LI, 151, note 1.

CUDDINGTON, Court Farm. 2418 6172. East of Ewell.
"Between Sandy Lane and the road to Banstead and Ewell railway stations," skeletons of men and women with late Roman pots, roof and flue tiles, perhaps used to frame a tomb. *Sy.A.C.*, XXXVII, 242. Possibly post-Roman.

EASHING. 9434 4334. Five miles south-west of Guildford.
On the Godalming By-pass ¼ mile above the east bridge, October 1931.
Seven skeletons, one with a Roman pin, some buried long after death. Rough apparently hand-made "Romano-British" potsherds were found in the surrounding soil.
Possibly post-Roman. *Sy.A.C.*, XL, 118, cf. xxi; XLIV, 151.

EFFINGHAM. 111 529. Four miles west of Leatherhead.
In 1758 four or five skeletons were found in making the turnpike road near the barrow "still called Standard Hill," *M. & B.*, II, 688, cf. 708; I, 482, *Sy.A.C.*, XLII, 51.
Effingham gives its name to a Hundred. Barrows were sometimes chosen as hundred centres, and such hundred-centre barrows were sometimes pagan Saxon burial grounds, as at Lovedon Hill, a large pagan cemetery, that gives its name to Lovedon Hundred in Lincolnshire. At Redbourne, in Redbournestoke Hundred in Hertfordshire, ten Anglo-Saxon burials were found in 1178 in a barrow called Standard Hill, "where the folk used to meet by ancient tradition" (Roger of Wendover and related Chronicles, sub. anno 1178). In the middle ages, Effingham Hundred met at "Lethe Croyce" or Leithepitt," *E.P.-N.S.*, XI, 99, (142 553, two miles north-east of the barrow, *Sy.A.C.*, L, 157). Effingham barrow may have been a pagan Saxon cemetery, and the original meeting place of the hundred, as at Loveden and Redbourne, and known as Standard Hill for that reason.

EPSOM. 2168 6072. Allotments near the north end of College Row.
Six skeletons found in 1929, *Sy.A.C.*, LI, 151, note 1, and several more found at 2179 6062, 120 yards to the south-east in Copse Edge Avenue, in 1934 (O.S. 19 N.W. 26).
The burials may be of the Anglo-Saxon period, either pagan, or perhaps later.

EWELL. 23 60. Some barrows with bones and weapons opened in the North Looe area in 1803 may possibly have been Saxon. *M. & B.*, II, 581; *Sy.A.C.*, XLII, 43.

GODSTONE. 355 504. Tilburstow Hill Common.
A burial urn found in a gravel pit, a few years before 1874, with spiral markings on the outside and a black band round the neck, which A. W. Franks thought resembled "what is found on Gallo-Roman and early Merovingian pottery." From the same pit came a bronze spear and a "saucer and bottle." *P.S.A.*,[2] VI, 155-6.

HORSLEY DOWN. About 07 51.
"Rings and many ancient copper coins and medals, both Roman and English . . . and . . . skeletons of several human bodies . . . found near some buildings belonging to George Shepley, Esq.," in 1800. MS Minutes of the Society of Antiquaries, XXVIII, 236; *V.C.H.*, IV, 364.

In 1800, saucer brooches were sometimes regarded as Roman medals; Anglo-Saxon cemeteries were still comonly described as Roman, unless swords and spears were plentiful, when they became battlefields. The burials might have been Roman, though Roman coins are at least as common in Saxon as in Roman graves. The "English" (not, as V.C.H., "Saxon") coins may well have been lost in medieval or later centuries, unconnected with the burials.

WALLINGTON. 288 646. At the junction of Alcester Road and Manor Road, 25 yards north of Holy Trinity Church.

Seven or more skeletons, facing east, at a depth of 3 ft., with a *bronze spearhead*, found in February 1869, *J.B.A.A.*, XXV, 517, with "Roman fragments" near. If the spear was really of bronze, it is unlikely that it was Anglo-Saxon. "Some glass beads, found with a skeleton, with the head westward, at Wallington" in 1896 may have been Saxon, *V.C.H.*, I, 268.

WIMBLEDON COMMON. 22 71. North of Wimbledon.

About 23 barrows were visible in the late eighteenth century. Douglas, *Nenia Britannica* 93; *Sy.A.C.*, XLII, 30, cf. 34.

These barrows may or may not have been Saxon. From one of them Douglas excavated, on 29 September 1786, what seems to be a Roman beaker, (his plate XXIII, 4).

B. THE ANGLO-SAXONS IN SURREY

In the year A.D. 410, the Imperial Roman Government, which had administered the province of Britain for nearly 400 years, announced that it was no longer able to defend the island; it told the authorities to organize their own defence, which they did successfully for a while. Somewhere in the second quarter of the fifth century,[1] the Romano-British leaders invited Anglo-Saxon mercenaries to defend them against the Picts. The Anglo-Saxons drove back the Picts, but then rebelled against their British employers. In half a century of bitter war, the towns, the villas, and the economy of the lowlands were destroyed. The Britons, however, alone among the western peoples of the Roman Empire, defeated the barbarians. The decisive victory was won by King Arthur at Mount Badon not far from the year 500. For half a century, the British remained on top; forty years after, one contemporary blames the degeneracy of his fellows who "had never experienced the troubles, and know only our present security ... now that our foreign wars are over." But between 550 and 600 the Anglo-Saxons rebelled again, and made themselves masters of the greater part of England, the land that bears their name.

In the south the decisive campaigns were those of Ceawlin (Colin) of Wessex; in 568 "Ceawlin and Cutha fought against King Ethelbert and drove him into Kent, and slew two aldermen at Wibban-

---

[1] Two separate traditions name alternative dates, of about 430 or about 450. Modern opinion, rightly in my view, is tending to prefer the earlier date.

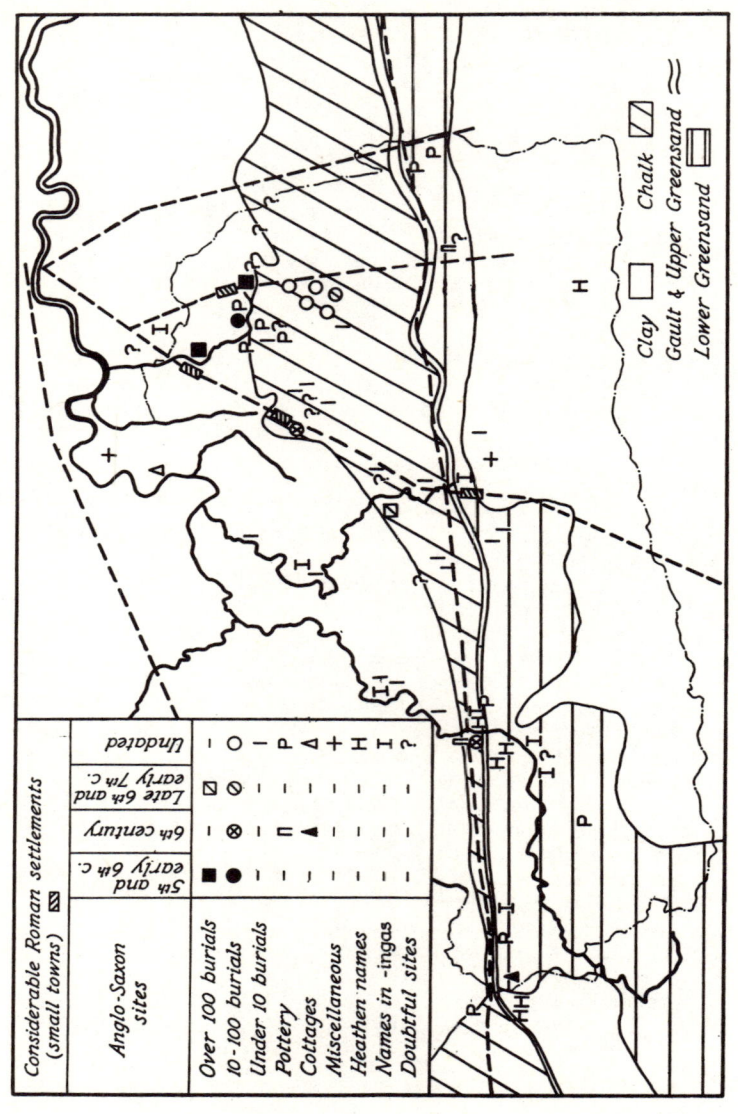

Fig. 1. Pagan Saxon Surrey.

dune." In 571 they mastered Bedfordshire, Buckinghamshire and the middle Thames, and in 577 Gloucester, Bath and Cirencester. But in 591 Ceawlin was "driven out" and died in 593. A few years later Ethelbert was master of all England south of the Humber, and was converted to Christianity by St. Augustine.

The bald account in the written sources can only be filled out by inferences from archæology. Fortunately for us, the Anglo-Saxons buried a rich variety of grave-goods with their dead, and almost all that we know about the pagan Saxons before their conversion to Christianity comes from a study of these grave-goods.

The study of Anglo-Saxon grave-goods is not easy, but anyone who would make sense of Anglo-Saxon England or Surrey must be familiar with the rules of the game. Those scholars deserve sympathy who sometimes wonder if there is anything in it at all, if it is any more than a series of subjective guesses for specialists to quarrel about and wiser men to leave alone. There is just enough in it to make the study worthwhile. Two things must be done. A relative typology must be worked out, and it must be given fixed dates. The first is not so hard as the second. We may say that this is a copy of that, and demonstrate the connection in a way that any man with two eyes and common sense will accept. But no typology will ever tell us how long the evolution took, whether it developed evenly or unevenly, at different rates in different places, or whether A went on making his old-fashioned traditional brooches long after B had begun experimenting with his fancy derivative copies. Therefore the typology is without meaning, unless it is anchored by a certain number of fixed dates.

In Anglo-Saxon archæology there is a bare minimum of fixed points, just enough to outline the limits of typology. There are three main anchors; at the beginning, a number of cemeteries in north-eastern France contain a mixture of Roman and Teutonic objects, buried together in the same grave, often with dated coins, in the late fourth and early fifth centuries. At the end, from the mid-sixth century on the Rhine, and from about 600 in England, dated Byzantine and Frankish coins are found in graves. In between, the Anglo-Saxon settlement in England is itself a fixed point. The grave goods found in Saxon cemeteries in Germany evolve steadily from about A.D. 200 to about A.D. 500, and there they stop short.[1] Throughout this period there is a continuing and fairly even

---

[1] Why the date 500 is commonly agreed, no one has clearly argued. But it makes sense. In England, France and the Rhineland, Frankish and Saxon objects begin to be found together in some numbers at about the stage when Saxon objects cease in Hannover. These objects are also found in the cemetery of Herpes in Aquitaine, which did not become Frankish till A.D. 507. In Frisia, Saxon objects cease at about the same stage as in Hannover, to be followed by a few late Frankish objects. The Frisian king seems to have been a subject ally of the Franks before A.D. 515; in or about that year Hygelac the Great raided King Theudebert's coast (Gregory of Tours, *History of the Franks*, III, 3) and was killed. He was killed in Frisia fighting against Franks and Frisians (*Beowulf*, 1202 ff., cf. 2354 ff., 2501 ff., 2910 ff.). Theudebert subsequently

evolution of pots and brooches, and there are very many of them. Thereafter the great numbers of cremations cease, and only a few inhumations in a few cemeteries continue. For the last two or three generations of this evolution, during the fifth century, the pots and brooches are matched piece for piece in Germany and in England, and in Scandinavia. In eastern England and on the middle Thames, numerous Saxon objects appear all at once in many cemeteries, at the same stage in their evolution, roughly early fifth century. It is to be assumed that these are the burial grounds of the settlements of the second quarter of the century, of which Gildas, Nennius, Bede, etc., speak. The date of this settlement in England controls and corrects dates calculated in Germany, on the basis of long typological evolution; it is not itself determined by that typology. In the sixth century, the same pots and brooches continue to evolve in England and the brooches in Scandinavia. But these later developments are not found at all in Germany, and the English and Scandinavian brooches evolve on diverging lines, growing more and more different from each other. At the same time, the English cemeteries begin to contain Frankish material, paralleled in cemeteries in south-western France, in regions the Franks did not conquer till A.D. 507. The date "A.D. 500 or a little before" is therefore a watershed. Most of the objects common to England and the main German cemeteries are fifth-century: most of those not found in Germany are sixth-century or later.

This is the framework of the dating. Upon it has grown a very complicated and forbidding body of knowledge, built upon the principle of association: object A was found with B, B with C, C with D, and D is typologically earlier than E which is dated by coins and the like. Though modern scholars sometimes forget the framework, and are content to talk pure typology, or to rely too trustfully on the opinions of their colleagues, all that is known or inferred of the dating of Anglo-Saxon objects rests on these few fixed dates. Perhaps the most important single element in the typology derived from it is the history of the motives known as "animal ornament," for whose evolution Mitcham offers a representative selection of objects. Animal ornament begins with the more or less naturalistic representation of animals in late Roman art; the Roman buckle from grave 38 is made up of two fishes, whole and entire, with tails, and no argument about what they are. The barbaric imitations lead to making a pattern of separate limbs of animals, in which the theme of a dog chasing a hare is most popular; the outer border of the head-plate of the brooch of Fig. 8c is a good example. These Scandinavian brooches are generally regarded as

---

boasted to Justinian that he ruled all the peoples from the Danube to the "shores of Ocean" (Migne, *Patrologia Latina*, LXXI, 1165A). Since burials peter out at the same typological stage in Hannover and Frisia, the date is presumably much the same. The date of "about 500" seems valid, though with an ample margin of approximation. Some scholars, including the late E. T. Leeds (*e.g. Arch.*, XCI, 6) incline to a date a little before rather than after 500.

mid or late fifth-century, on quite good evidence. This stage, where the individual animal limbs are quite clearly to be distinguished, is still there in the cast saucer brooch of grave 208, where, however, abstract patterns already dominate recognizable limbs. The date of its origin abroad is a matter of dispute; but in England the date is quite clear; such ornament is not normally found during the overlap period, when German and English grave goods are identical, in the fifth century; it is found with the earliest Frankish objects of the early sixth century. In a third stage, recognizable limbs almost disappear, and the broken-down shapes of Mitcham 208 become patterns in their own right, with an emphasis on lines that cross under and over each other, and on a pattern that recalls the human eye. This stage is very well instanced by the great square-headed brooch of grave 205. In a fourth stage, the eye pattern is forgotten, and the crossed lines are tidied up to a regular interlacing that suggests the coils of a snake. This stage is contemporary with coins of the very late sixth and early seventh century. Much more can of course be said of animal ornament; but it is valid for England only if it takes meticulous account of the evidence of deposits in England.

There is a good deal in the Surrey cemeteries that can be dated by these criteria. There are only three cemeteries so far known which have contained objects of the fifth century; the Croydon "sporran" disc and tab are quite rare objects, dated by association in France and England to the very beginning of the century. The Croydon pendant object and the buckle of Mitcham 38 are almost as early. At least one urn and some other objects from Croydon, and the five-scroll saucer brooches of Mitcham 66 and Beddington are of the fifth century. While any or all of these objects might in theory have been generations old when buried, or archaic survivals made by an old-fashioned craftsman, it would be irresponsible speculation to suggest that they are in Surrey out of their normal and proper context. Croydon and Mitcham have several grave-goods as early as the earliest Saxon settlers. The probability is that they, and perhaps Beddington, were settled when the British first invited Saxons to help them against their enemies, in or before the middle of the fifth century.

These three cemeteries of the Wandle were placed on the nearest inhabited land to London. It was not the easiest agricultural land, and the chalk downs show no sign of settlement before the sixth century. The motive which inspired the exact place of the early settlement must remain a matter of guesswork. But the strategic effect of the settlements needs no argument. Placed on the Wandle between Merton and Croydon, these garrisons blocked all access to London from the south. They covered the London-Chichester and London-Brighton roads at the two Roman roadside villages nearest to London. Moreover, they centred round a remarkable concentrated group of Iron Age fortified sites, whose ramparts were certainly still standing, and serviceable, all probably reoccupied in late

Roman times, and all of which show some slight trace of Saxon use. The position enabled the Saxons to defend London from the south; all the authorities that we have aver that the original settlers were invited by the Romano-British authorities and settled where those authorities chose to establish them. It is therefore not surprising that the earliest settlements are found in places advantageous to the defence of Roman Britain, rather than on the easiest agricultural land.

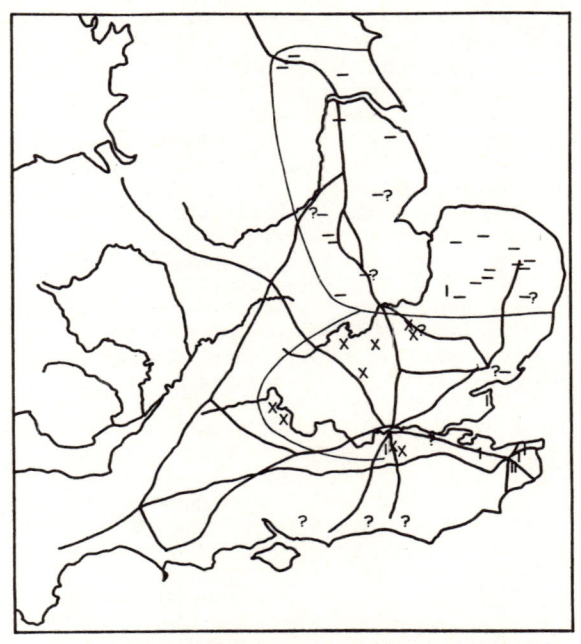

Fig. 2. Cemeteries of the Earliest Period.

Cremation —
Inhumation |
Mixed ×

Fig. 2 shows these Surrey cemeteries in the context of fifth-century England. The map distinguishes those cemeteries in which the earliest objects of the fifth-century migration, or overlap, period have been discovered, principally pedestalled bückelurns and a few other types of vessel (which many German scholars would be happy to regard as fourth century), cruciform brooches[1] of Åberg's Group

---

[1] See footnote on p. 103.

1a, and a few other of the earliest brooches and other objects (equal-armed brooches series 2 (but not 7), sporran discs, etc.).

It is as near as we can get to a map of the earliest Anglo-Saxon settlements. The map shows striking contrasts between the modes of burial in different parts of the country. All along the east-coast counties, from East Anglia to Yorkshire, all the earliest cemeteries use cremation only. They retain the custom of cremation into the seventh century, apart from a few very late inhumations without grave goods added at the close of the cemetery's life at Caistor-by-Norwich and occasionally elsewhere. Along the Icknield Way and for twenty miles or so north of it, from Cambridge to the Oxford region, cremations and inhumations of the earliest period were made side by side in the same cemeteries of mixed burial custom. In Kent and in Sussex, and later in Hampshire, there is no cremation apart from two exceptional sites of uncertain date, Northfleet in Kent and Hassocks in Sussex, and a few burials beside the great inhumation-cemetery at Highdown, Sussex. Inhumation is otherwise universal. These three sharply differentiated areas are those which Bede and the continuing county names assign to the Angles, Saxons and Jutes; but the pattern is not so simple as that; for, though continental Anglian urns are virtually limited to Anglian England, the Anglian or Anglo-Frisian cruciform brooch and Saxon saucer brooch mingle in the fifth century in the area of mixed cemeteries, and typically continental Saxon urns are common in the Anglian regions. Though there is a mainly Saxon and a mainly Anglian area, the two are not rigidly exclusive. These three groups have effective contacts only at two points; a few miles north-east of Cambridge lies the frontier between East Anglian cremation and the mixed cemeteries of the interior; and in Surrey, Croydon and Beddington are mixed cemeteries, while at Mitcham there were no cremations among more than 200 interments. From the beginning, Surrey was a meeting point of two major groupings within the Anglo-Saxons.

During the fifth century, new sites spread to parts of the midlands, notably beside the Fosse Way between Lincoln and the Watling Street. The earliest dateable objects in Sussex are the five-scroll saucer brooches; they are certainly fifth-century, but may or may not be as early as the first settlements. Since the Anglo-Saxon Chronicle

---

[1] The cruciform brooches, characteristic of the Anglian regions, form the spinal column of Anglo-Saxon typology. Thirty years ago, Nils Åberg (*The Anglo-Saxons in England*, Cambridge and Uppsala, 1926, pp. 28–56), classified them in five chronological and typological groups, and thirty years' further work has amply confirmed the outline of his classification by newly discovered associations. The series begins from the brooches dated at Vermand and Dorchester to the very early fifth century, and groups I and II are equally prolific in Germany and England; groups III and IV are not found in Germany at all, and group V just reaches into the age of late sixth-century coins. There are no cruciforms south of the Thames, except for a few early ones in Kent, but the ornament of Mitcham 210 is like enough to some cruciforms of the turn of groups IV–V to suggest that its maker had seen them.

and the British historian preserved by Nennius agree to date the settlement of Sussex a generation later than the main settlements, it would be unwise to contradict them on so doubtful evidence; certainly none of the undoubtedly earliest objects signalled on Fig. 2 have yet been found in Sussex. In most of the older areas, the number of cemeteries in use increases; or, more accurately, there are a number of fifth-century cemeteries which have not shown evidence of the earliest period. But there are no new sites in Surrey. The three small poor settlements on the Wandle are all that are known for the period of the British-Saxon wars of the fifth century.

In the early sixth century there is even less evidence of territorial expansion, except in west Wessex, and that may well not be earlier than about 530–550. In a few parts of the midlands, notably at Kempston, in Bedfordshire, the dated grave-goods of the period, common elsewhere, are altogether unrecorded, though of course undated brooches, especially "small-longs", may be early sixth century; but in most of the older settled areas, the number of burials and the number of cemeteries increases. There are unmistakable signs of new influences, the Frankish jewellery in Kent and the coming of the Gippingas bringing the great square-headed brooch with strong Scandinavian associations to Ipswich; and there is clear evidence, documentary and archæological, of a reverse migration of Anglo-Saxons to Europe. English Saxons were held in the ninth century to have played a considerable part in the growth of modern, inland, Saxony; they received land in modern Belgium as mercenary allies of the Frankish kings, and they fought wars upon the Rhine. There is plenty of Saxon pottery in a great Frankish cemetery at Anderlecht (Brussels) and plenty of Kentish jewellery at Herpes in southwestern France; in north-eastern France, there is a scatter of purely Saxon place-names, with a number of cruciform brooches of the first half of the sixth century (Åberg's groups III and IV) to accompany them, but none earlier or later. It would appear that the effect of the British victory was to contain the Anglo-Saxon settlers within their previous limits, if not to reduce those limits, and to coerce their increasing population either to emigrate overseas or to expand within existing territories. Surrey shares in that expansion. The Wandle cemeteries are reinforced by Ewell, the next substantial Roman site down the Stane Street, and Guildown, where the ridge of the North Downs is cut through by the passage of the river Wey.

It is in this period that the Wandle Saxons lived most to themselves. They may have made their own brooches, and made them well, trading them up and down Stane Street, and setting new fashions which the men of Wessex copied to advantage in the next generation, when Surrey made no more brooches. They gave something to Wessex, but received nothing, and they had nothing to do with the fashions of Kent or of the Anglian areas. Their influence did however reach eastward as far as the valley of the Darenth and the flats beyond Gravesend, and, at least in this period, the effective frontier with Kent probably lay between the Darenth and the Medway.[1] The effective centre of this community, covering rather more than the modern county, clearly lay at Mitcham or Croydon, or between them, in the area of original settlement.

In the second half of the century came the second rising and the final victory of the Anglo-Saxons. Again, the emphasis lies on the Saxon and not on the Kentish connections. There are a few brooches, weapons, and buckles that are Kentish, or imitate the fashions of Kent. But they are few and poor, and of the kind that spreads widely over southern England; it is quite safe to assert that the proportion of Kentish grave-goods is no more than in Cambridgeshire or Bedfordshire, less than in Berkshire, and very much less than in Hampshire or Sussex. Within Surrey, Guildown on the Ridge Way has more share in Kentish wealth than the Wandle. This heavy bias in the grave-goods underlies the Anglo-Saxon Chronicle's note of the battle of *Wibbandune* in 568. Where the place is, we do not know; Wimbledon is a somewhat similar name, but no more; it is better to leave the name as that of a place unidentified. But wherever it was, Surrey was before the battle, and had long been, a part of the culture of Wessex; when the young king Ethelbert emerged from Kent, whither Ceawlin "drove him back," it can only have been Surrey that he entered. If the battle was not fought in Surrey, it was certainly fought for the possession of Surrey; its result was to bring Surrey within the orbit of Wessex for another 25 years, though the Wandle was perhaps no longer its natural centre. On Ceawlin's fall, in 591 or so, Surrey cannot but have come under the control of Ethelbert, who commanded the obedience of all England south of the Humber. But it was too late to affect the character of the cemeteries; the custom of interring grave-goods had already ceased.[2]

During Ceawlin's time, the number of Surrey settlements increased. By the middle of the century the village of Farnham was in being; and new sites of considerable size at Farthingdown, perhaps also at Sanderstead south of Croydon, and at Fetcham by Leatherhead have grave-goods of the second half of the sixth century, but not earlier. Many of the miscellaneous undated sites must have come

---

[1] It is scarcely correct, in a period of such relatively sparse habitation, to speak of frontiers as lying "on" rivers. Normally rivers united rather than sundered the people who lived on opposite banks. What separated them was the empty country between the rivers. The Medway is so large a river that it may have been exceptional.

[2] The disappearance of grave-goods has no rigid and automatic connection with the coming of Christianity, though it happened at roughly the same time. In Kent, grave-goods certainly continued to be interred half a century after the conversion; on the Rhine they were buried in a churchyard beneath a Christian inscribed head-stone (cf. p. 107 above, note 3). At the other extreme, grave-goods ceased to be interred in the cemeteries of Mercia half a century before Christianity was first preached there, though in Mercia as elsewhere kings and chiefs were commonly richly buried in isolated barrows throughout the first half of the seventh century. The social structure and the beliefs of society were changing.

into existence by this time, but almost all of them are, as far as our record goes, small individual burials, not the grave-yards of considerable communities. Other evidence besides archæology points to the existence of communities whose burial grounds have not been discovered. It has long been thought that place-names terminating in *-ingas* probably belong to the pagan period, for they are normally prefixed by a personal name; Tootingas are the "men of Tuda." Such names are most likely to arise in the days of easy settlement and mobility. There is however nothing in the name-form to suggest whether such names came into being in the fifth century, in the sixth, or in the early seventh; a number of them were already in being in the seventh century, when Bede relates incidents that happened at them, and kings begin to name them in charters. In Surrey, they are not found in the areas of earliest settlement, but around its edges; the nearest is Tooting, a few miles north of Mitcham; elsewhere is Dorking, the third major Roman site along Stane Street, the Getingas of Esher and a few more at either end of the Hog's Back in the extreme south-west of the county. The same relationship between names in *-ingas* and pagan cemeteries has been noted in other counties; in Surrey, as elsewhere, they are better connected with the sixth century, perhaps even the middle or late sixth-century expansion, than with the initial fifth-century settlements.

The surviving pagan place-names are similarly located; five of the six lie at the two ends of the Hog's Back, close to sixth-century settlements and to place names in *-ingas*; the sixth, Thundersfield Castle, is stuck way out in the wealden clay, far south of the Downs and of any other trace of pagan Saxon life. If it is a really ancient name, it has nothing to do with the main community of the *Suthrige*.

This name, the "southern district," was perhaps already in existence. It implies that the territory belongs to some unit located to the north. Nothing is known of the fate of London until after Ethelbert's conquests, when he and his son-in-law, the king of Essex, controlled the city. It was then English and pagan. Its sixth-century history is surmise, and can really only be judged in the light of Saxon Surrey. If Mitcham, Beddington, Croydon, Ewell and Guildown were able to trade or intermarry with the people of Luton, Cambridge and the Oxford region, and perhaps belonged to the same political unit, then it is extremely probable that their contacts crossed by London bridge, and that London fell within the same unit, until Ethelbert's victory transferred its control to Kent and Essex.

Beyond A.D. 600, the Anglo-Saxon burials have nothing to say of the history of Surrey. The latest objects are a glass vessel from Mitcham, perhaps the cist-burials, if they are genuine, and a few miscellaneous ornaments of uncertain late date from Farthingdown and Fetcham. Some of them might have been buried just after the beginning of the seventh century; but none of them need have been, as far as our present knowledge goes. The small communities of early Surrey remained as they had begun, small groups of heavily-armed poor farmers, limited to the banks of the rivers and the chalk downs, tending to concentrate along the lines of the major Roman roads (including the Ridge Way), especially preferring the same sites as their Roman predecessors, located where the roads crossed the rivers. What mattered for the future was that London had again become an inhabited town of great moment; and Surrey, the nearest workable agricultural land to the city, again became a suburb, its history wholly dependent on London's.

The Anglo-Saxons in Bedfordshire*

IN 410 A.D. Britain had been a Roman province for nearly four hundred years. In the midlands and the south, an integrated agricultural economy rested on a dozen cities, several scores of smaller towns and villages, and a large number of substantial farms and country mansions; politically, a dozen self-governing states, whose members felt themselves to be both British and Roman, as Roman as their descendants are today English, were run by established local aristocracies, co-ordinated by a central government appointed by the imperial authorities in Italy.

In 410 the Goths took Rome, and the imperial administration declared itself unable any longer to appoint that central government, thereby legalising whatever central British government the separate states might succeed in establishing. For a generation, Roman civilisation continued unaffected in town and villa; then, the national government, beset by foreign and internal enemies, invited in Saxon mercenaries to defeat the Picts, from beyond the Forth and Clyde. The Saxons were settled in eastern Britain, and did their job; but by bluff, intrigue and force they much increased their original numbers, and rebelled against the British, probably in the 440's, destroying the material basis of Roman civilisation in Britain. The greater part of the aristocracy emigrated across the channel, but some remained to organise a resistance movement, initiated by Ambrosius Aurelianus. It relied principally on fairly small 'commando' units of heavy cavalry, effective against Saxons who fought exclusively on foot, and ended with the decisive victory of the British, captained by Arthur, not far from the year 500. For two generations, the British remained in effective control of the island; but the mounted war bands formed the effective government of post-Roman states, and fought each other, until, in the years between 570 and 600, a second Saxon revolt swept them away and mastered a leaderless Britain, whose political fabric was totally destroyed.

In these two centuries there was no such thing as a county of Bedford.[1] The area formed part of the state of the Catuvellauni, whose capital was Verulamium (St. Albans). No document records more than a faint tradition of its history; all that can be known derives from the archaeological record of the Saxon settlers. Unlike the Romano-British, the Saxons were customarily buried with a wide range of objects, ornament, weapon and clothing. The bare skeleton of a Briton of the period cannot be distinguished from a medieval burial made 1000 years

---

* Reprinted from *Bedfordshire Archaeological Journal* 1 (1962) 58–76, by kind permission of Bedford Archaeology Society.

[1] See Gazetteer p. 63 ff. and Map fig 1, p. 64.

later; but the articles interred with the Saxon dead not only signal their race, but often give rough indications of their date. Some objects, notably brooches and decorated urns, follow an evolutionary pattern, wherein early, middle and late styles may be plainly seen; several other kinds of object, for example wrist clasps, workboxes, gold ornaments and elaborate jewellery, the Frankish throwing axe or the evil looking dagger called the scramasax are found only in later graves, while some of these are found buried with 7th century coins. It is therefore possible to make certain rough inferences about the extent and character of the Saxon settlement and its spread at different times. Little reliance can be placed on a single object; one early brooch at Bishopstone near Aylesbury or at Dunstable does not establish early settlement; but quantities of early, middle, and late objects at cemeteries like Luton and Kempston do argue the duration and origin of the settlements they served; and the distribution in space and time of a large number of cemeteries warrants certain general conclusions about the evolution of the earliest English.

Several thousand Anglo-Saxon burial grounds have been recorded in England; a limited number of them contain several diverse objects of the earliest period, and suggest the limits of the first settlers at the time of the first revolt in the middle of the fifth century. Nearly all these earliest cemeteries lie on or east of the road from Colchester by Cambridge to York; a few lined the south of the Thames estuary in Kent, and three guarded the southern approaches to London by Croydon and Mitcham. The only others known reach down southwestward, on or parallel to the Icknield Way, at Sandy and Kempston, Luton and perhaps Toddington, and at Abingdon and Long Wittenham on the middle Thames. The majority of these early cemeteries lie within a mile or two of Roman towns and cities; if, as we are told, they were designed to protect the British against a Pictish invasion, then it is evident that the government anticipated a sea-born invasion whose goal was to penetrate by the Icknield Way towards Oxfordshire and the Cotswolds, the richest areas of late Roman Britain.

These earliest cemeteries lie in three main groups. Those in Norfolk, Lincolnshire, and Yorkshire all practised cremation, were known as Angles, and used as their characteristic ornament the long brooch known as 'cruciform'. Those in Kent practised inhumation, were known as Jutes, and, after the first generation or so, abandoned the cruciform brooch for an elaborate and beautiful jewellery derived from the Franks; but the Icknield Way cemeteries, from the Cambridge to the Oxford region, practising both burial rites simultaneously from the beginning, were styled Saxon, and wore the round brooch known as 'saucer'. The Bedfordshire cemeteries lie in the middle of this Saxon area, their main centre in the Dunstable-Luton region, though at first they were clearly small isolated groups of Germans in a British countryside.

During the course of the wars, the original settlement areas were reinforced, and several new areas occupied, most of them by people who practised inhumation alone. There are many cemeteries which certainly began in the fifth century, though present evidence does not suggest that they are quite as early as the earliest. The most important of these areas are East Sussex; and Leicestershire. In Bedfordshire and the surrounding counties, there are few new sites. The cemeteries of the Aylesbury area were certainly in being by 500, while the Middle Thames sites were flanked by a line of cemeteries running up into Northamptonshire, with others down river at Reading and Shepperton. An important group of cemeteries came into existence south-west of Cambridge, at Barrington and Haslingfield, with many saucer brooches and almost all the dead inhumed; while newcomers with strong Scandinavian affinities appear at Ipswich, not far from the year 500, and bring with them a new type of brooch known as the great squarehead, which soon spread to almost all areas. It is however, noticeable that throughout the pagan Saxon period there are virtually no burials between the Icknield Way and the Thames; it is especially remarkable that the extensive excavations in and around Verulamium over a long period have not yet produced a single certain Saxon object. The explanation can only be a guess; it need be no more significant than the refusal of the local authorities to accept billetted Saxons earlier in the fifth century, and the tendency of later settlers to nucleate around their original settlements.

In the early sixth century, a contemporary British writer condemned an age of 'security' after the defeat of the Saxons, while Saxon record claims no new advance. What the victorious British did about the surviving Saxons is not recorded; the graves offer a little comment. The demarcation between the different brooch fashions, not quite absolute in the fifth century, now became entirely rigid. The Luton, Aylesbury, Thames-side and Surrey peoples used only saucer brooches; the Cambridge cemeteries alone used both saucer and cruciform, while the Anglian areas have not yet produced a single saucer brooch of the early sixth century. These harsh frontiers imply that there was little movement between one area and another; and some areas have an absolute shortage of objects of the period. The cemeteries of the Ouse, Nene and Welland, from Kempston northwards, have produced scarcely any ornament that can be positively dated to the first half of the century, while numerous such ornaments come from the Icknield Way sites. Inferences from these odd variants are far from secure; but it may be that the Icknield Way reservations enjoyed some greater autonomy than those further north. Nothing whatever is known of the political organisation of the area, save that a hazy British tradition remembers a great state called 'Calchvynydd', the land of the limestone hills, between Trent and Thames, whose prince Catraut was lord 'of Dunstable and Hamtoun (Northampton)'.

The first movements of the second Saxon revolt are recorded in the year 552, when a prince named Ceawlin (Colin) seized Salisbury. Five years earlier, the British record that the great plague of Egypt, Gaul and Italy hit western Britain; it did not affect the Saxons; for the trade of western Britain came exclusively by way of Biscay and Brittany, where imported mediterranean pottery of the period is found. Presumably the ships that brought pottery and wine also brought the plague. Sixteen years later, in 568, Ceawlin and another ruler called Cutha combined to drive the young king Ethelbert back into Kent; and in 571 Cutha fought against the Brit-Welsh at Bedcanford, and took four towns, Limbury, Aylesbury, Benson and Eynsham; and the same year he died. The entry in the Anglo-Saxon Chronicle names the enemy as British, presumably the same power whom British tradition remembered as 'Calchvynydd', but credits Cutha with the capture from the enemy of four towns with Saxon names. These towns are all in the centre of the pre-existing Anglo-Saxon settlements, and the Chronicle implies that they had previously obeyed a native British authority. The earlier texts of the Chronicle do not say who Cutha was; some later manuscripts add a footnote, evidently a wild guess, to the effect that he was Ceawlin's brother. The distribution of brooches however offers a more convincing suggestion; the most striking saucer brooch of the late sixth century is the type known as 'Maltese Cross' (figured in *V.C.H. Beds*. I., p. 180, bottom row), and its derivatives. A dozen of the Maltese Cross type brooches have been found near Cambridge, and eight at Kempston; they and their derivatives spread westwards to Warwickshire and south-westward down the Icknield Way to the Thames, where, however, the commonest type (Aylesbury and Dunstable, Puddlehill) is native to the Oxford region. The origin of the brooch seems fairly clear, for at the Barringtons it emerges from a long ancestry of saucer brooches, while at Kempston it appears out of the blue, with no earlier antecedents. It seems that this brooch was fashionable among the Barrington women, and that Cutha was their chief. His name is also preserved in Cuddington and Cuddesdon along the line of the Icknield Way, and at Cuttleslowe, Cutha's burial mound, in north Oxford, where he presumably died. The decisive event would seem to be that Saxons from south-west Cambridgeshire destroyed the last remnant of British authority in Bedfordshire, liberated the Saxon settlements in the area, and marched down to meet Ceawlin, on his way up from the south, in the Oxford region. Though 'Bedcanford', in the form in which the name is preserved, cannot be Bedford, the site of the battle should none the less lie in the area roughly between Bedford and Hitchin or Dunstable.

In the next few years, Ceawlin continued his conquests westwards, while the Angles overran northern Britain. But in 584 Ceawlin fell and died. Then or soon after, king Ethelbert of Kent became master of all southern Britain, his frontier marching with Northumbria on the Humber. Bede reports only the bare fact; its archaeological counterpart is a considerable spread of late sixth and early seventh century Kentish objects over southern Britain. It is probable that the two cemeteries of Leighton Buzzard and Dunstable (Marina Drive), whose ornament is characteristically Kentish, were the burial grounds of Kentish colonies or garrisons, planted down on the edges of the largest single concentration of Saxon settlement in the area. Ethelbert was converted to Christianity by St Augustine; but when he died, in 616, his children reverted to paganism, and his empire collapsed. Its collapse may well have occasioned the apparently speedy end of the Marina Drive settlement.

During the sixth century, the settlement around Dunstable grew greatly; that around Kempston and Bedford did not. Even on the banks of the Ouse, sites are few, and elsewhere ten or twelve individual burials about Hitchin are the only infiltration into new areas. Men still spoke Welsh by the river Beane in the early seventh century, and in the wide areas between the deserted Chilterns and the Thames there is still no English settlement; that was not to come until the monasteries of the late seventh and eighth century set about the clearance of the land. Two stray finds near High Wycombe are all that are earlier.

The graves have a little to say of the social evolution of the communities that used them; as elsewhere in England, most of the earlier burials are simple, one much like another; during the sixth century, an increasing proportion of rich women and girls are buried with ample grave goods, while beside them lie more and more bare skeletons, wholly unadorned. The swords and spears of their husbands cannot unfortunately be dated; but the increasing difference must surely reflect a difference in society. After several generations of farming and fighting, the primitive egalitarian communities were dividing into rich and poor. The political sequel finds its memorial in the chieftain's barrow of the early seventh century; no really rich barrow survives nearer than Taplow, though the fame of Goldenlow at Dunstable argues that it may have been of comparable splendour; and the densely populated area near Dunstable could surely have supported a chief no less magnificent than the ruler of the Maidenhead region.

Such princes made the underkings, occasionally named in Bede, who obeyed with greater or less willingness the authority of great kings. In Wessex for nearly two centuries, the underkings prevailed, and no powerful dynasty emerged. But the bulk of Bedfordshire, including Dunstable, fell to the authority of Mercia, whose kings firmly eliminated smaller local rulers. Their great king Offa (died 797) is held to have refounded St. Albans and had a palace at Offley; and it was probably under Mercian rule that the strong place of Bedford on the Ouse replaced the ill-defended Dunstable area as the main centre of the region, to give its name to the later shire.

GAZETTEER OF PAGAN ANGLO-SAXON DISCOVERIES IN BEDFORDSHIRE

THE Anglo-Saxon remains of Marina Drive and Puddlehill have their own antiquarian interest; by themselves, individual cemeteries have little historical significance. They matter because we lack any coherent record of our national history for the Roman and pagan Saxon periods; in default of such record, our history is reconstructed from a multitude of these small individual fragments of local history, each significant only when it is put into context with adjacent sites.

The Gazetteer includes all sites known to the author and to the Manshead Archaeological Society. The Society welcomes additions to the list and corrections thereto.

After the modern name, the national grid reference is given as closely as it is known.

Then follows a list of what was found, with a note of where the objects are now preserved, when known, and a reference to the source of our information. In the references, the following abbreviations are used:
(The names of periodicals are followed by a figure denoting the volume and page where the reference is to be found).

A.A.S.R.	Associated Architectural Societies Report.
A.C.R.	Cyril Fox, Archaeology of the Cambridge Region.
Ant. Jl.	Antiquaries Journal.
Arch.	Archaeologia.
Arch. Jl.	Archaeological Journal.
B.B.	Baldwin Brown The Arts in Early England, Vols. III and IV. 1915 followed by page and plate reference.
B.B.A.A.	Bulletin of British Archaeological Association.
B.M.	British Museum (followed by numbers denoting the appropriate entry in the Museum Accession Book, British and Medieval Department).
B.M.G.	British Museum Guide to Anglo-Saxon Antiquities 1923.
C.A.S.P.	Cambridge Antiquarian Society, Proceedings.
C.A.S. 4to	Cambridge Antiquarian Society, Quarto Series.
Col. Ant.	C. Roach Smith, Collectanea Antiqua.
Horley MS	Manuscript by W. Horley of Toddington, now in the possession of Mr K. Horley, 4 Park Street, Toddington.
Leeds Corpus	E. T. Leeds, Corpus of Early Anglo-Saxon Great Squareheaded Brooches 1949.
J.B.A.A.	Journal of the British Archaeological Association.
O.S.	Ordnance Survey Archaeological Branch, 6 in record sheet.
P.S.A.	Proceedings of the Society of Antiquaries of London, 2nd series.
V.C.H.	Victoria County History, Bedfordshire, Volume 1.
E.P.N.S.	English Place Name Society, Vol. III, The Place Names of Bedfordshire and Huntingdonshire. 1926.

CHALTON. *Probably about TL 02 26.* "A great battle was fought in Chalgrave Field"[1].
"I was informed by a person of Toddington that some years ago human skeletons, with pieces of armour, etc., were found in the valley of Chalgrave towards Charlton . . . also in the fields and gravel pits near Charlton, skeletons have been found . . . Likewise in this Charlton field, gold rings of ancient and curious workmanship have been ploughed up at different times, with other ancient articles, coins, etc."[2] "In a field at Chalton now (i.e. *c* 1875) in the occupation of

[1]*Gentleman's Magazine*, Nov. 1803, 1005.
[2]*Dunno's Originals*, IV, 1822, 15.

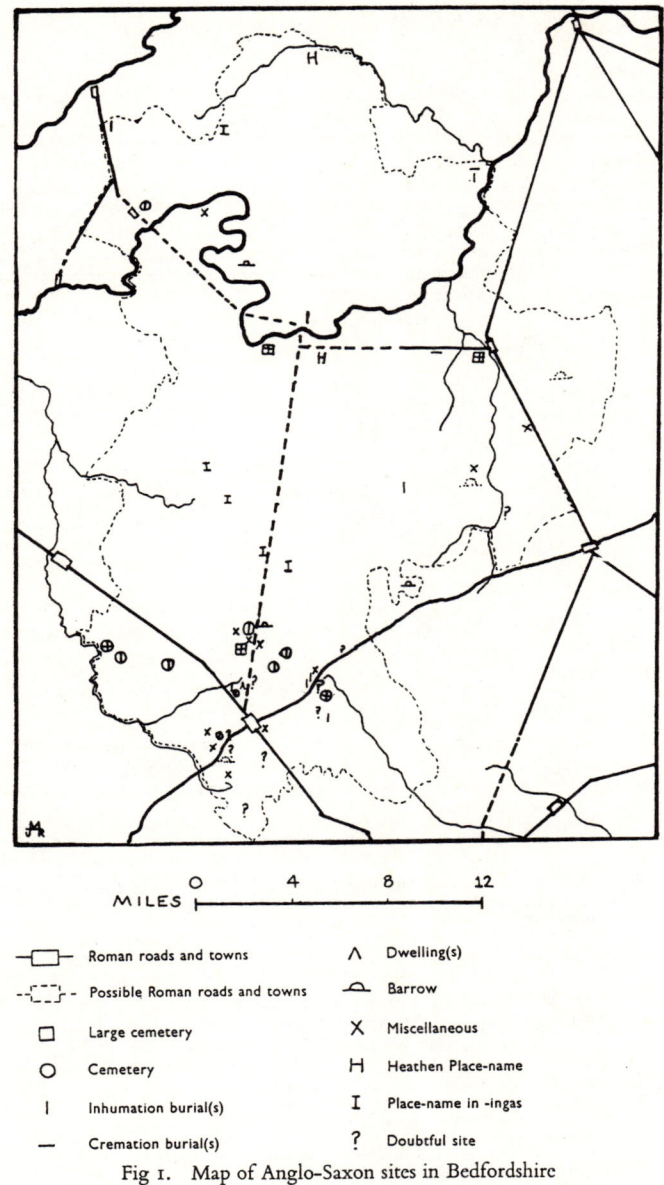

THE ANGLO-SAXONS IN BEDFORDSHIRE

Fig 1. Map of Anglo-Saxon sites in Bedfordshire

Mr Anstey ... some years since, whilst digging for gravel, many skeletons, weapons and gold rings were found"[1]; "large numbers of Saxon graves have been found at Chalton, the bodies facing north and south, each with a knife at the waist"[2]; two skeletons, with a shield boss and two knives survive[3].

The original account distinguishes between the 'gold rings' and coins, found without skeletons, in a different field from the skeletons with armour, ploughed up, whereas at least part of the cemetery was found in a gravel pit. The 'gold rings' may have been torques, commonly regarded in the early nineteenth century by local, as national, antiquaries, as 'gold-ring money' (cf., e.g., *Arch.* 27, 1838, 96); with the coins, they suggest a Belgic hoard, as, for example, at Snettisham in Norfolk (*Proceedings of the Prehistoric Society*, 20, 1954, 59; Norwich Museum). The cemetery clearly lay in the 'valley', presumably the low ground between Chalgrave Manor Farm and Chalton Manor Farm, and was found in the late 18th century. Later writers, except Worthington Smith, have confused the two sites. Weapons and knives without brooches are probably sixth century rather than fifth.

Sixth century?

CLIFTON. *TL 168 388*, between Shefford and Henlow. A small Saxon pot, found 1930, in Bedford Museum. The site might be the same as that called Henlow, see below.
Sixth century?

DEAN. *TL 058 683*, on the Northamptonshire boundary, between Rushden and Kimbolton. Harrowick, surviving as a farm name, is probably a heathen place-name, *E.P.N.S.* 14.
Fifth to seventh century.

DUNSTABLE. *TL 01 21*. A heavily stamped whole urn, with chevrons and four or five separate stamps, of the middle or late sixth century. Roach-Smith, *Col. Ant. II*, 233, pl liv. 2. Cambridge Museum
Mid to late sixth century.

DUNSTABLE. *TL 000 213*, Marina Drive. Forty-nine skeletons, found in 1957 with one small-long brooch, two workboxes, girdle-hanger, hanging bowl escutcheon, two scramasax, one spear, beads, pins, cowrie shells, amulets, etc., cf. pp 25 above.
Late sixth to early seventh centuries.

EASTCOTTS. *TL 067 472*, two miles south-east of Bedford, Harrowden Hill is a heathen place name, *E.P.N.S.* 91.
Fifth to seventh century.

[1] *Horley MS* (cf. Toddington B, below).
[2] Worthington Smith, *Dunstable, Its History and Surroundings*, 62.
[3] Luton Museum 1/28/373/4, excavated and presented by Worthington Smith in 1891. Hence Davis, *History of Luton*, 1874, 4; Blundell, *History of Toddington*, 1924, 5; *P.S.A*^{2}., 21, 1906, 59; Baldwin Brown IV, 636.

EATON SOCON. *TL 173 612* Crosshall, between Hail Weston and St Neots. A cremation urn and beads, found 1932. OS TL 16 SE.
Undated.
TL 1721 60, 37, north of Duloe Hill Crossroads, about half a mile south of the site above. Two Anglo-Saxon inhumations with an elaborately worked scramasax *C.A.S. 4 to. 5, 32.*
Seventh century.

EGGINGTON. *SP 958 254*, near Eggington House. Spears, knives, etc., with a bronze tube-like object, similar to that from Luton, Biscot Mill, grave 27, found in a gravel pit whence also came Iron Age and Roman occupation material.
Ant. Jl. 20, 1940, 230.
Fifth or sixth century.

FARNDISH. *SP 92 67*, south of Irchester, 'in a bank which forms the parish and county boundary, near the Roman road', a skeleton found early in the nineteenth century, with tweezers, knife, buckle, combe, three necklaces, mostly of amber beads, and a horned small-long brooch with lappets, as Leeds, *Arch.* 91, 35, fig 22 g.h. (Holywell Row). The type is confined to the Suffolk-Cambridgeshire borders, apart from this brooch and another at Sleaford, Lincolnshire.
B.M. 1828 11, hence *B.M. Guide* 84, fig 98; *V.C.H.* 190.
Late sixth century.

FELMERSHAM. *SP 990 578*, 80 yards W.S.W. of the church, two handmade pots, not earlier than the sixth century. *Ant. Jl.* 31, 1951, 46.
Sixth (or ? seventh) century.

FLITWICK. *TL 038 339*, Worthy End is a place name in-ingas, *E.P.N.S.* 150.
Fifth to seventh century.

HARROLD. *SP 9534 5725*, seven miles NW of Bedford, in a gravel pit north east of the village, seven or eight skeletons with part of scramasax, knives, beads, metal fragments and potsherds, and a sword possibly Saxon, found together with ditches and hearths, with pagan Saxon bone pins, potsherds, and beads; and with Iron Age querns, sword and spear. *B.B.A.A.* 49. Oct. 1952, 1. Bedford Museum.
Late sixth or seventh century.

HENLOW. *TL 17 38*, a small plain pot, probably from an inhumation, B.M. 1915 – 12 – 8. (Ransom collection), (hence *B.M. Guide* 23, *A.C.R.* 267) of the sixth or seventh century. Other pots B.M. 1915-12-2 and 7 (Ransom collection). The site might be the same as Clifton (p. 65 above), the adjoining parish. cf. Doubtful Sites. p. 74 below.
Sixth or seventh century.

HOUGHTON REGIS. *TL 004 234*, Puddlehill, a mile NW of Dunstable.
  1. Inhumation with shield boss, broken spear and smashed skull.
  2. Inhumation cemetery, with saucer brooches, etc.
  3. Cottage, perhaps part of village.
     (cf. p. 48 above, and doubtful sites, p. 75 below.)
(1) Fifth or sixth centuries: (2) and (3) Late sixth or seventh century.

KEMPSTON. *TL 0310 4764*, two miles SW of Bedford. A very large cemetery, excavated 1863, with over 100 inhumations and many cremations of which twelve are recorded in detail. From the graves came four swords, many spears, knives and shield bosses (one conical) and over 100 brooches. The brooches include five fifth century 'cruciform' and one fifth century 'saucer' brooch, with one very late sixth century 'cruciform' and twenty late 'saucer' brooches, eight of them of the 'Maltese Cross' type (cf. *Surrey Archaeological Collections* 56, 1959, 89, cf. 84, fig 6 e), found in quantity elsewhere only near Cambridge, and in scattered burials westward to Warwick and south-westward down the Icknield Way to the Thames. The urns (figured *VCH* 178–183; *Baldwin Brown*, 499, pl cxxxiv) include an early 'Bückelurn' (grave of Dec. 9–10, 1863); other early objects include an 'equal-armed' brooch (series 2), paralleled in England only at Luton (p. 68 below), but common in Germany (cf. J. Werner, *Bonner Jahrbuch* 150, 1950, 337, cf. 381 and 408) which is among the earliest brooches found in any Anglo-Saxon cemetery in England; an early fifth century sporran attachment (*Baldwin Brown*, 599, etc.); and an 'equal-armed' series 7) brooch of the fifth century. Late objects include a great squareheaded brooch (*Leeds, Corpus* III, B 8), several wrist clasps and three bronze workboxes, as at Marina Drive, Dunstable, (p. 39 above) a fish shaped badge (*Baldwin Brown* 202). There were many bead necklaces, but only one buckle, and none of the girdle hangers common in sixth century Anglian graves. Notable graves include that of 20 Oct. 1863, with 120 beads (including seven large crystal beads, a gold mounted carbuncle, a glass cone cup (Harden, *Dark Age Britain*, 159, III ai 1) probably of the sixth century, and a bronze earpick; 25 Jan. 1864, with a silver bead and ring, five amethyst pendants, and a crystal ball in slings; and 16 Nov. 1863, a half burnt body, with the bones of a rat and a leaf shaped spear, as Bekesbourne A, Breach Down, Kingston Down, etc., in Kent.

The fifth century ornament of Kempston is most closely matched in the Cambridge region, and in the cremation areas of Norfolk and northward; its late sixth century ornament is altogether without the common Anglian brooches, and is closer to the Saxon traditions of the south midlands, especially linked with the cemeteries south-west of Cambridge (Haslingfield and the Barringtons), with considerable Kentish influence in some graves. There are no objects dateable to the first half of the sixth century, though some of the many undateable objects might belong to this period. *A.A.S.R.* 1864, 269 ff; Roach Smith, *Col. Ant.*, 6, 201, ff, cf. 166 summarised in *V.C.H.* 1, 176 cf. 2, 8 and *Baldwin Brown* 784, cf. 192. Most of the objects are in the British Museum (1891 6–24, 1–340; 1875, 6–2, 1; 1876, 2–12, 17–25; 1884, 3–22, 19; 1896, 5–9, 1–4) and in the Bedford Museum; Luton Museum has reproductions of two brooches (217–218/35), and Letchworth Museum 8042 is an urn probably from Kempston; *PSA*[2], 13, 1889–91, 240 records another urn. Fifth century and late sixth to early seventh century.

KNOTTING. *TL 003 635*, on the county boundary, three miles SE of Rushden, is a place name in -ingas, *E.P.N.S.* 15.
Fifth to seventh century.

LANGFORD. *TL 18 40*, two miles south of Biggleswade, a 'francisca' (Frankish throwing axe), common from the middle of the sixth century onward. *A.C.R.* 267, 'in the Ransom collection".
Late sixth or seventh century.

LEAGRAVE. *TL 060 243*, Wauluds Bank. Two contracted inhumations, found in 1905, with a 'Klapperschmuck' pin (*Baldwin Brown* 369, pl lxxxv, 2), a gilt bucket disc (*Baldwin Brown* 463, pl cxii, 2; *BM Guide* 67, fig 75), a stylus, two pairs of 'disc' brooches, and an ivory armlet. (casts in Luton Museum).

B.M. 1096 2-12, 1-8. *P.S.A.*² 21, 1905-7, 59; *Baldwin Brown* IV 636; hence *VCH.*
Mid to late sixth century.

LEAGRAVE. *TL 065 238*, Sarum Road. Skeletons found when laying a gas main in 1953, with a bone comb and iron knife. Luton Museum 264/53.
Undated.

LEAGRAVE. Uncertain location. Potsherd, found 1898. Luton Museum 143/33.
Undated.

LEIGHTON BUZZARD. 'A' *SP 9215 2652*, Brickhill Road sandpit (Deadman's Slade). Many cremations, in urns with 'warts', and 'chevrons, dots and rings' were recorded about 1850; a sherd from a sixth century stamped urn, and two brooches, probably from inhumations, were found in 1880 and are now in the British Museum. The name Deadman's Slade (cf. R. Richmond, *Notes on the History of Leighton Buzzard=Extracts from the Leighton Buzzard Observer*, 22 Feb. - 30 Aug. 1910, p. 24 cf. p. 1) suggests that numerous burials had been unearthed in the distant past. The brooches are a 'saucer' brooch with curved, sharp star pattern, of the mid sixth century, and a triangular 'small-long' brooch with a shovel foot (*Aberg*, p. 60; *Arch.* 91. 1945 98), of the sixth century. Two tumuli existed a mile to the north (OS SP 92 N.W.) *PSA²* 9, 1881-3, 29; *Baldwin Brown*, 636, 784, hence *VCH* 187; B.M. 1882, 8-24, 1-4.
Sixth century.

LEIGHTON BUZZARD 'B'. *SP 9270 2642* Chamberlayne's Barn Pit. Seventy inhumations (with 22 more from an adjacent site) and three cremations, excavated by F. G. Gurney in 1932. The skeletons and grave goods were heavily corroded by the acid sandy soil. The finds include two spears and one conical shield boss; three brooches; two pendants, with punched dot and chased decoration, as at Bifrons (Kent); several buckles, including one of the Boars Head type (site 1, 8a), common on Kentish and Frankish sites; several bead necklaces with wire rings, and several large beads; one Frankish bottle vase, with several stamped and plain; one small urn with three rough lugs, and a spearhead 17 in long. Some sherds (site 1 grave 9) seem seventh century. The brooches consist of one disc or quoit brooch, 4·8 cm in diameter, the surface entirely covered with dots and triangles, and a fragmentary, much corroded version of the great Sarre I Brooch from Kent (cf. *Antiquity* 7, 1933, 427); the Sarre brooch was found with coins of the emperors Mauricius (592-602), Heraclius (610-641) and King Clothair II (613-628).
Luton Museum 14/57; B.M. 1935, 10-11, 1 (the lugged urn).
A brief report of the first few graves, written before most of the grave goods had been excavated or identified, appeared in the *Leighton Buzzard Observer* in August and September 1935, and is reproduced in the *Bedfordshire Archaeologist*, 1, 3, August 1956, p. 120.
Late sixth and seventh centuries.

LIDLINGTON. *SP 991 388*, three miles west of Ampthill, is a place name in -ingas, *E.P.N.S.* 77.
Fifth to seventh century.

LUTON. *TL 0815 2292*, Biscot Mill, Argyll Avenue and Montrose Avenue. Over forty inhumations and at least three cremations, with many burials destroyed without record.

The finds include one sword, sixteen spears, two of them with closed sockets, eight shield bosses, several urns and thirty-two brooches, with numerous small finds. The brooches consist of one 'Equal armed' (series 2), as at Kempston, among the earliest in England, eighteen saucer brooches ranging from early to mid-sixth century, one Great Squarehead (*Leeds, Corpus*, 95, b 6), seven disc and three small-long, one small Kentish squareheaded, and one late equal arm. The urns included one fine early "Bückelurn". In contrast to Kempston, there were no cruciform brooches or wrist clasps, and the great majority of the saucer brooches are of types common in the first half of the sixth century in Wessex and Sussex.

Luton Museum 411 (41/27) 127 (the main collection): 61-621 37; 5-6/45; 106/50. *Ant. Jl.* 6, 184; 8, 172; 11, 282. *Dunstable Museum Report* No. 2, 1926-27, 1924 contains a full list of finds. Early to mid-fifth century to late sixth or early seventh century.

LUTON.   *TL 028 215*, Dallow Road Gas Works, by the main gate. Skeleton of a woman, with a pair of iron shears and a cowrie shell. Luton Museum 91/30; *Ant. Jl.* 11, 1931, 282-4. Late sixth century.

MOGGERHANGER.   *TL 1385 4905*, five miles east of Bedford. An Anglo-Saxon cremation found in 1934. Bedford Museum.
Sixth century,

OAKLEY.   *TL 01 54*, three miles NW of Bedford. Bucklow, *Bucca's Hlaw*, means the barrow of an Anglo-Saxon named Bucca. *E.P.N.S.* 25. The place was somewhere near Oakley; the crown of Oakley Hill, *TL 017 543*, is a possible site.
Late sixth or early seventh century.

PEGSDON.   *TL 127 340*, four miles WNW of Hitchin. 'A skeleton with a knife in a barrow' excavated by Ransom in April 1870. Hitchin Museum has two Anglo-Saxon spearheads (one barbed) and boss, with leg bones, from 'Pegsdon Common', together with a Saxon bead necklace, while a box of sherds 'from the tumulus on Pegsdon Downs' includes two sherds from small Anglo-Saxon vessels. 'A few feet' from the tumulus Ransom found 'broken urns of brown pottery of the usual type' and 'underneath' them 'ruder urns...handformed...containing human bones mixed with pieces of wood and charcoal and iron nails'. The Ransom collection in the British Museum contains four Romano-Belgic urns from 'Shillington' and one from 'near Pegsdon'. A painting by Samuel Lucas, in Hitchin Museum, of William Ransom excavating the tumulus on Pegsdon Common locates what is probably the site.

These records may relate to several adjacent sites or to a single site; the barrow might be Anglo-Saxon, but it is equally possible that a small Anglo-Saxon cemetery was located in and around a Belgic-Roman barrow and surrounding cemetery. The absence of ornaments suggests a late date. *Herts. Nat. Hist. Soc. Trans.*, 4, 1886, 39; Hitchin Museum 854-6, 858; British Museum 1915. 12-8, 13; 16-19.
Sixth century?

PULLOXHILL.   *TL 074 332*, 2 miles east of Flitwick. Kitchen End is probably a place name in -ingas, *E.P.N.S.* 161.
Fifth to seventh century.

SANDY. *TL 18 48.* Inhumations and urns[1] found at various times in the eighteenth and nineteenth centuries, in and around the Roman cemetery outside the Roman town. Five urns survive; two[2], formerly kept at Ickwell Bury, are among the earliest found in any Anglo-Saxon cemetery in England; another[3], is a fine large early stamped 'Buckelurn', and another [4], stamped with chevrons, is of the type common at Lackford in Suffolk, and perhaps made there, of the late sixth century. A lead chalice, found in 1850 with wooden coffins, and published as Anglo-Saxon, is of the thirteenth century.
Early to mid fifth to late sixth century.

SHEFFORD. *TL 1350 3874.* A pair of mid-sixth century saucer brooches found in 1839, in or near a Roman cemetery. Cambridge Museum; *Arch.* 7, 1785, 71, fig. p. 79. A.C.R. 267.
Mid sixth century.

SHILLINGTON. See Pegsdon.

SUNDON. *TL 03 27*, five miles NW of Luton, Cement Works. Skeletons with an Anglo-Saxon spear, 10 in long. Luton Museum 137/32.
Undated.

TODDINGTON 'A' *TL 013 293* Sheepwalk Hill. At least seventeen bodies discovered in 1844, 1861, 1868. 1873, 1884-5, with one shield boss, one sword*, three knives (1*), one buckle, two disc and one applied* brooch (1½ in diameter), seventeen beads (12*), one bronze pin*, six rings (two of wire, with a knot*, three of bronze, one of silver), a piece of folded bronze with rivet holes, possibly a wrist clasp, an earscoop* and tweezers*, a girdlehanger (?), a purse mount, four urns (one Frankish), and two stamped sherds (1*).

The objects marked with an * are preserved in St. Albans City Museum, 153-2, R 241-5. Cf., Doubtful Sites, Harlington (Wickhern and Dyers Hall Farm), and Toddington, Wadlow, below, *P.S.A.*[2] 1, 1861, 399; 10, 1883-5, 35 and 173; 25, 1913, 183, hence *V.C.H.* 1, 185. Luton Museum, 71 and 73/49 (urns, found 1884 and 1868).
Sixth century.

TODDINGTON. 'B' *TL 002 283* Warmark. "In the year 1819 in a field in the parish of Toddington . . . they discovered, for the length of a furlong or upwards of 200 yards and breadth of twelve yards or more, considerable quantities of human bones, pieces of armour, numbers of spearheads, with sockets and rivets . . . an ancient helmet of singular form."[5] They 'were dug up from several fields . . . near the road . . . called Frenchman's Highway . . . in digging gravel. Since writing my former account . . . a person who was daily on the spot informs me that the extend of ground was of far greater dimensions that I have set down before; for those things were found all over that field belonging to Mr Hicks of Toddington; he considers that there were some thousands of bodies buried there . . . spears, daggers, etc . . . pieces of swords or daggers with two or three edges, and others like spits, were found, with numbers of buckles, rings, and other brass pieces of circular form . . . embossed with ornaments . . . a . . . small urn, containing

[1]*Arch.* 7, 1785, 412; *A.A.S.R.* 2, 422, 427; 8, 117; *PSA*[1] 2, 1849-53, 109; [2]23, 1909-11, 378. *Ant. JL.* 37, 1957 224, hence V.C.H. 1, 184 cf. 2, 10; *Baldwin Brown* 636; *ACR* 267.
[2]B.M. 1937, 11-11, 8-9. 1866, 10-28. *Ant. JL* 34, 1954, 201.
[3]*ACR* 260, pl. xxxi, 4, *Baldwin Brown* 497, pl. cxxxiii, 5; *V.C.H.* 1, 184.
[4]B.M., W.G. 2281
[5] W. Nicholls, *Dunno's Originals*, "containing a sort of real, traditional and conjectural History of the Antiquities of Dunstable and its Vicinity, Dunstable, by a Totternhoe shepherd", part II, 1821, p. 13 cf. p. 8.

beads ... Some ancient coins were found, but not many. Considerable quantities of spearheads, pieces of sword blades, parts of daggers etc., were dug out of both fields. A person of Toddington asserts that many of the pieces of swords etc., were worked up by the smiths of the town ... Among other things were found a piece of copper, overlaid with a thin plate of gold; it is part embossed, other parts engraved or chased, and highly ornamented ... the length is near five inches and the breadth three in the widest part. This ornament was also dug out in that field in the year 1819 ... (The) beads ... generally were composed of stone, though some were of a composition of glass, of many colours; the smallest were black or dark brown; others appeared to be made of agate or very hard white stone. Several of the ollae (pots) were filled with small bones, apparently the bones of human fingers, toes, etc. ... A labourer ... employed in digging gravel in these fields ... found four of those circular sorts of plates before mentioned ... of superior workmanship ... composed of gold ... of the shape and size of saucers, of 5 or 6 inches diameter, marked with flowers and figured work ... Beads ... of all sorts of colours ... were found in masses in various masses in various parts of the field ... The small pots ... filled with little bones, were very numerous in one part of the field."[1]

The account is accompanied by a plate; fig 1, the 'helmet of singular form', 'dug out with the gravel from a field belonging to Mr Hicks near the Frenchman's Way', is a shield boss; fig 2 is an Anglo-Saxon spearhead; fig 3 and 4, the embossed piece of copper 5 in by 3 in is a Great Square-headed brooch, identified by the late E.T. Leeds from the plate as nearest to his *Corpus* 103, B 6, from Coleshill in Berkshire, ( ) 'not, I think, early'. Fig 5 is a string of Anglo-Saxon beads, fig 6 a plain wide mouthed full bellied urn, ill engraved, that might be Saxon. Figs 7 and 8 are Bronze Age spearheads, found in the east of the parish, near Cowbridge and Wadelows, by the mill stream (about *TL 023 287*). The 'brass pieces of circular form', and the four similar saucer shaped ornaments, 'five or six inches in diameter', are clearly large late saucer brooches with incised medley ornament, perhaps of the Aylesbury region type, like that from Puddlehill p. 53 above).

An eye-witness account written down over 50 years later records 'numbers of spearheads, swords, etc. ... The urns, of which great numbers were found, were all of coarse material and very plain. Some few had the zig-zag ornament on them and were found in shallow parallel trenches filled with a fine black mould mixed with bones etc. I saw several perfect human skulls, and in many instances the plough had taken the lip off many of them (presumably the urns), which in every instance contained bones apparently as of the extremities.'[2]

Mr Hicks' field was a strip (*TL 002 283*) east of the Toddington-Tebworth road (Frenchmans Way, 1581 estate map in Luton Museum; Blundell, *Toddington*, ch. XV), just opposite the lands of Warmark farm. 'Several human skeletons have been dug out near the farmhouse of Mr John Osborne', on 'a tract of land called Warmark, west of the Leighton road' (Frenchman's Highway)[2]. The present owner of Warmark Farm reports skeletons discovered many years ago on his land and taken away for sale to London Medical Schools, together with the recent discovery of a coin of Claudius. His children found 'pieces of tin with writing on them' in making a pond in the front garden of the farmhouse in 1954. The name Warmark occurs in the Dunstable Annals in the thirteenth century, *E.P.N.S.* 139; the editors suggest that the name means *wearg(a)-mearc*, 'outlaws

---

[1]Dunno, Part IV, 1822, p. 3 ff. plate p. 8. Nicholls' text is reproduced, with a few omissions, by Sir Henry Brandreth, in *Arch.* 27, 1838, 96, and his plate was reprinted, with a short careless summary of his text, by Charles Lamborn, *The Dunstapelogia*, Dunstable, 1859.

[2]*Horley MS*; the text of a lecture delivered by Mr W. Horley of Toddington on the Early History of Toddington, undated, but citing Davis' *History of Luton*, (published 1874), transcribed by kind permission of Mr K. Horley of 4 Park Street, Toddington.

mark, referring perhaps to a place where such were to be found, or where bodies might be thrown after execution'. If so, some burials had clearly been ploughed out well before the thirteenth century. Local tradition records a great' battle fought all the way from Chalton (cf. p. 63) to Warmark'; evidently based on a recollection of the distinct Anglo-Saxon cemeteries; the early nineteenth century writers imagined the battle as between Aulus Plautius and Tododumnus in 43 A.D., Congerhill becoming a corruption of 'Tongerhill', the burial mount of 'Tongodumnus' (sic) (Nicholls), or as between Cutha and the British in 571 A.D. (Brandreth and Horley), the 'fingers and toes' found in cremation urns being 'the different members of the combatants lopped off during the fight and collected on the battlefield' (Horley).

The site is clearly a large cremation and inhumation cemetery on the scale of Kempston, the principal finds being weapons, beads, buckles and large late saucer brooches; a cruciform and a disc brooch in Northampton Museum (cf. Toddington, Doubtful sites, below), might be from this burial ground. The few recognisable objects are sixth century, but nearly all such large mixed cemeteries elsewhere in England began in the fifth century.
Fifth (?) to late sixth century.

TODDINGTON. *TL 019 284.* Fancot. "The writer has in his possession several fine specimens of Saxon earthenware obtained from the same (Sheepwalk) Hill and at Dyers Hill Farm, and at the old brickworks at Fancot" (Blundell). Of three Saxon urns presented by Blundell to Luton Museum, two came from Fancot. Two urns from Fancot, owned by Cooper-Cooper, may or may not have been Saxon. Luton Museum 70.75.77/49; Blundell, *History of Toddington*, p. 4. *Beds. Notes and Queries* 3, 63, cited by Blundell (urns).
Undated.

TODDINGTON. *About TL 022 306*, Wadlow, Redhill Farm, is *Wada's Hlaw*, the burial mound of an Anglo-Saxon named Wada, *E.P.N.S.* 138. The site adjoins Toddington 'A' above.
Late sixth or early seventh century.

TODDINGTON. *Probably about SP 99 29*, Herne Farm. Saxon potsherd, found by W. G. Smith in 1889. Luton Museum 75/38/28.
Undated.

TODDINGTON. Uncertain location. Finger ring; blue glass bead; fragment of 'small-long' brooch. Luton Museum 361/40.
Sixth century.

TOTTERNHOE. *SP 988 288* Well Head, Shirrell Springs. Late equal armed brooch, found by F. G. Gurney in 1915. Luton Museum, 284/52. *Dunstable Museum Report*, 1, 1925–6, 7.
Seventh or eighth century.

TOTTERNHOE. *SP 989 207*, Roman Villa site across the road from the Church. Decorated potsherd, ascribed by J. N. L. Myres to the late fifth or early sixth century. Manshead Archaeological Society Collection, Dunstable.
Late fifth or early sixth century.

WHIPSNADE. *About TL 01 17*, Sherd of a heavily stamped urn of the middle or late sixth century. St. Albans City Museum.
Mid to late sixth century.

WOOTTON. *TL 009 405*, NW of Ampthill, Wootton Pillinge is a place name in -ingas, *E.P.N.S.* 87.
Fifth to seventh century.

Doubtful Sites

ARLESEY (?). On railway line, probably between *TL 188 325 and 189 355*. "I hear that in carrying on the excavation and cuttings of the Great Northern Railway, some other sepulchral relics have since (i.e. about 1848/9) been discovered on the opposite side of the Wilbury Hills (i.e. opposite to Wymondley in Hertfordshire), but of this I have not yet learned any particulars except that among the bones, spearheads and other weapons have been found".
W. Newton, describing the Romano-British cremation cemetery at Little Wymondley, in *J.B.A.A.* IV, 1849, 73.

The inhumation cemetery 'with spearheads and other weapons' was almost certainly Anglo-Saxon; the vague siting presumably refers to the stretch of the main north-eastern line between Ickleford (Cadwell) and Arlesey, then under construction.

BEDFORD. *TL 0611 4960* Russell Park, Newnham, three-quarters of a mile east of Bedford, about fifty yards north of the Ouse. Three inhumations with a sword and three spearheads, found in 1896. *PSA*[2] 16, 1895-7, 114, hence *V.C.H.* 1,186. Bedford Museum. A Viking sword was found nearby and the Saxon burials may or may not belong within the Pagan period. Bedford Museum.

DUNSTABLE. Rifleman Inn (Rifle Volunteer) *TL 007 214*. Skeleton found in 1906, Luton Museum 142/33, 'Rifleman Inn'. 'Four Saxon skeletons' found in 1924, 'Rifle Volunteer Inn', West Street, *Dunstable Museum Report*, 1, 1925-6, 7. The Inn, which changed its name between 1906 and 1924, is near the Marina Drive cemetery, but the evidence for calling these skeletons Saxon is not clear.

DUNSTABLE. Five Knolls *TL 006 211*. In 1929 G. C. Dunning and R. E. M. Wheeler excavated nearly 100 skeletons inserted into one of the Bronze Age barrows that name the hill-top; one skeleton (B 22) had a pierced Roman coin at the neck, and another (B 21) was buried with a bronze tube and a buckle, that might be either Roman or Saxon; elsewhere in the surface soil, but not in graves, were a variety of objects ranging from a pre-Roman brooch to a Roman goblet and Saxon potsherds and a buckle. Six of the ten groups of bodies, all young adults, three quarters of them men, nearly half of them with their wrists crossed behind the back, as though tied, lay in ordered rows, one group often displacing the skulls and limbs of burials beneath them.

The excavators somewhat surprisingly concluded that 'it is evident that most of the burials were carried out at one time', and suggested Saxon raiders executed by Romano-British captors[1]; the anthropologists who examined the skulls, however, made the counter suggestion that they were Britons executed by Saxons, since the average cephalic index differs from the Anglo-Saxon

[1] *Arch. Jl.* 88, 1931, 193.

group examined elsewhere, and is 'such as would characterise any collection of modern English skulls' and 'does not differ sensibly from the average given for Cambridge undergraduates or for convicts'. Since, however, it was 'distinctly more divergent' from the 'Iron Age group', they were led to postulate either a 'Bronze Age survival' or a colony of 'mediterranean Romans' in the Dunstable area[2]. The number of pre-Saxon skulls so far examined seems, however, rather too small to warrant such deductions, in few of the considerable racial mixture of the population in the 2000 years between the beginning of the Bronze Age and the coming of the Saxons; but pagan Saxon skulls, more plentiful, and markedly divergent from both earlier and later norms, appear to be a more reliably distinguishable group, though their peculiarities seem later to have been absorbed into the prevailing type of the pre-Saxon population. Mr Don Brothwell of the Duckworth Laboratory, Cambridge, has kindly re-examined the Five Knolls skulls and reports that they differ significantly from the 263 Anglo-Saxon skeletons, including those from Marina Drive (p. 45 above) which he has examined; it is therefore unlikely that they were the skulls of pagan Saxons of the first few generations of settlement.

The 'battle-massacre' suggestion is, however, a doubtful interpretation of small groups of orderly manacled burials that cut each other out; Wheeler noted that the Five Knolls, on the northernmost lip of the Downs above the high road, was an ideal site for a gallows, which seems a much more likely explanation. Hanging was a Germanic, not a Roman penalty, and the pierced Roman coin and the buckle argue a date not many centuries after the Roman period, while the few Saxon objects in the top soil of the barrow suggest no more than that the soil was turned over in or after the sixth century. The Knolls might have been the site of a periodical assembly before the later Manshead Hundred centre at Tingrith (*E.P.N.S.* 112) was established, perhaps at some time in the seventh or eighth centuries.

HARLINGTON. *TL 033 298* Wickhern. "Some fine specimens of Anglo-Saxon urns were found, many years ago, in a field called Wickhern, belonging to the late Mr Pearse; they were given to the late Mr James Wyatt. I do not know what has become of them . . . Wickhern adjoins Sheepwalk Hill (Toddington, cf. p. 70 above)." From the same field, the Horley MS records a Roman burial with Samian dishes and deer antlers, apparently the same site as that cited by Blundell, 5.

The Anglo-Saxon urns might be part of the Sheepwalk Hill cemetery; or might be a confusion with the Roman burial. *P.S.A.*[2] 11, 1885–7, 311.

HARLINGTON. *TL 043 295* Dyers' Hall Farm. "The writer has in his possession several fine specimens of Saxon earthenware from the same (Sheepwalk) Hill and at Dyers Hall Farm and at . . . Fancot". The Fancot (cf. p. 72 above) urns survive. Dyers Hall Farm fields adjoin Sheepwalk Hill, and, if they were Saxon, may have formed part of that cemetery.

HENLOW. *About TL 17 38. Haenna Hlaw*, the Hens' Burial mound, an exceptional form. *E.P.N.S.* 170. If the derivation is correct, the barrow may have been Saxon or earlier; there were Saxon burials nearby, cf. Henlow, Clifton, pp. 66 above.

HOUGHTON REGIS. *About TL 023 043*, East Hill and Chantry Farms. Cobbled paving with late Saxon, St. Neots' and medieval pottery, with an Anglo-Saxon coin, and a pair of shears, which might possibly belong to the pagan period. Luton Museum 65/52; 206–7/53.

---

[2]*Arch. Jl.* 88, 1931, 210. and *Biometrika* 25 May, 1933, 15.

HOUGHTON REGIS. *TL 000 247* Thorngreen Farm. Two Saxon knives which might have come from a pagan burial. Luton Museum L/7/338.

KENSWORTH. *TL 036 184.* Pottery vessel 'found in making the new parsonage cellar'. Luton Museum 76/49.

LUTON. *TL 072 245* Watery Lane, Biscot. Under the foundations of a new bridge, 1913. A slender spearhead, later than types normally found in pagan Saxon graves, perhaps sixth to eighth century. Luton Museum 113/46.

LUTON. *TL 065 230.* 149 Beechwood Road. A skeleton with an iron knife is probably Saxon. Luton Museum 48/40.

POTTON. *Somewhere about TL 22 48.* The half hundred of Wenslow took its name from a lost barrow. *Woden's Hlaw,* probably somewhere in the Potton-Sutton area; *E.P.N.S.* 100. Galley Hill and John o'Gaunt's Hill are possible sites. The name suggests that the original settlers who bestowed it did not know who was buried there, and the barrow may therefore have been pre-Saxon.

STREATLEY. *Centred about TL 087 265*, Dray's Ditches, Galley Hill, Bramingham.
"When the old road was being made from Luton to Barton . . . in 1832 . . . from the old road which leads to Bramingham and Stockenbridge . . . earthenware pots were discovered, and a few British and Saxon coins. Antiquaries say that the Saxon soldiers were fed on oysters, which may account for so many shells being found there . . . At . . . Dray's Ditches, when the road was being made, a number of earthenware pots . . . some pieces of iron of singular shapes, etc. and a few Roman coins were found. Nearly at every rising ground between Luton and Barton, pitchers, pieces of iron armour, coins, etc., have been dug up"[1]. The 'armour' and 'iron of singular shapes' might be echoes of the swords, spearheads and shield-bosses common in pagan Saxon graves. Four skeletons without grave goods buried in No. 3 tumulus on Galley Hill, excavated in 1951, might or might not be Saxon[2].

STUDHAM. *About TL 01 15*, Deadmansey. In a list of Anglo-Saxon burial places, in W. G. Smith, *Dunstable, its History and Surroundings*, 62, Studham is the only one not otherwise attested. Smith probably had evidence; but it is just possible that he was making an inference from the field name.

TODDINGTON. Uncertain location. A cruciform and a disc brooch in Northampton Museum, bought at the sale of the Cooper-Cooper collection in 1911, are entered in the accession book as 'Toddington, Beds.' This is probably where they were found, but might possibly refer only to where they were bought; since no such brooches are listed among the Sheepwalk Hill finds, they may have come from Warmark. The cruciform brooch, published by Aberg, 171, as from Finedon, Northants, presumably because it is exhibited with a comb from Finedon, without separate label, is an unusually well made group IV brooch, with double quatrefoil decoration, as on A3 Great Squarehead brooches, paralleled at Haslingfield, St John's, Cambridge, etc., and should date to about 550 A.D. or a little later. If it comes from Toddington, it lies well south and west

[1] Davis, *History of Luton*, 1874, 33–34.
[2] Luton Museum L/12/52; *Bedfordshire Archaeologist*. 1, 2, 1955, 39

of any other mid-sixth century cruciform brooch in England. Northampton Museum catalogue entry 359 (formerly 355).

WHIPSNADE (?). *About TL oo 18.* Goldenlow. King Edward I's seneschal and marshal came to Dunstable to enquire after treasure found at 'Goldenclowe' in the reign of Henry III; the finder's son-in-law Adam Russ of Dunstable had 'become rich'; he and his effects valued at £30, fell to the king, and he compounded the fine for £10. The barrow had evidently contained an exceptionally rich gold treasure; it may well have been Anglo-Saxon of the seventh century. *Annals of Dunstable Priory* (Rolls Series) 1290 (1286); *Calendar of Fine Rolls*, 1292; *E.P.N.S.* 120. The site might be Golden Row in Whipsnade.

Rejected Sites

BIGGLESWADE. *TL 214 403* Edworth, Topler's Hill. A jewelled brooch with human remains is medieval. *Publications of the Cambridge Antiquarian Society*, 1, 1840-6, 1845, p. 20 and pl iv., hence *Arch. Jl.* 12 1855, 96, *V.C.H.* 2, 7.

TODDINGTON. *TL 045 288* Foxburrow. The finds reported are Iron Age, Belgic and Roman. 'Clay lumps', 'used in cremation by the Anglo-Saxons' are probably kiln bars, and the speculations on the place name do not command support. *P.S.A.*[2] 6, 1873-6, 184, hence all later references.